Robot Technology
Volume 6: Decision and Intelligence

Robot Technology Series

Series Editor and Consultant: Philippe Coiffet

English Language Series Consultant:
I. Aleksander, Imperial College of Science
and Technology, London, England

Series Translator: Meg Tombs

Editorial Supervision: Jenny Willison

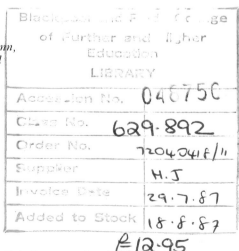

Robot Technology

A Series in Nine Volumes

Series Editor and Consultant: Philippe Coiffet
English Language Series Consultant:
I. Aleksander, Imperial College of Science and Technology,
London, England

Volume 6

DECISION AND INTELLIGENCE

Igor Aleksander, Henri Farreny and Malik Ghallab

Kogan Page
London

First published 1986 by Hermes Publishing (France)
51 rue Rennequin, 75017 Paris, France

Copyright Chapters 3-8 © Hermes Publishing (France) 1986

English language edition first published 1986
by Kogan Page Ltd, 120 Pentonville Road, London N1 9JN
Reissued in paperback 1987

Copyright Chapters 1, 2 and 9 © Igor Aleksander 1986

English language translation copyright Chapters 3-8
© Kogan Page Ltd 1986

British Library Cataloguing in Publication Data
Aleksander, Igor
　　Decision and intelligence. — (Robot
　　technology; v.6)
　　1. Robots, Industrial　　2. Artificial intelligence
　　I. Title　　II. Farreny, Henri　　III. Ghallab,
　　Malik　　IV. Series　　V. Fonction décision et
　　intelligence. *English*
　　629.8'92　　TS191.8

　　ISBN 0 85038 651 9 Hbk
　　ISBN 1 85091 407 9 Pbk

Printed in Great Britain by Biddles Ltd
and bound by Kadocourt Ltd

Contents

Chapter 1

Prospects for knowledge-based robots

1.1 Introduction

This volume describes the principles of the advanced programming techniques involved in decision making. Such principles are founded in mathematical logic and are an example of the way in which robotics demands a knowledge of a wide variety of disciplines. Automated decision making in the context of robotics can adopt many aspects. At the most obvious level, a robot may have to plan a sequence of actions on the basis of signals obtained from changing conditions in its environment. These signals may be quite complex, for example, the input of visual information from a television camera.

At another level, automated planning may be required to schedule the entire work cycle of a plant that includes many robots as well as other types of automated machinery. The often-quoted dark factory is an example of this, where not only some of the operations (such as welding) are done by robots, but also the transport of part-completed assemblies is automatically scheduled as a set of actions for autonomic transporters and cranes. It is common practice for this activity to be pre-programmed to the greatest detail. Automated decision-making is aimed at adding flexibility to the process so that it can absolve the system designer from having to foresee every eventuality at the design stage.

Frequent reference is made in subsequent chapters to *artificial intelligence* (AI), *knowledge-based* and *expert systems*. Although these topics are more readily associated with computer science than with robotics, it is the automated factory, in general, and the robot, in particular, that will benefit from success in these fields. In this chapter we try to sharpen up this perspective, while in Chapter 2 we aim to discuss the history of AI.

Chapter 3 deals with expert systems and knowledge-based languages which are the areas of current practical achievement in the field. Chapters 4 to 8 discuss the detailed principles associated with logical programming, with particular reference to those techniques that accelerate the computation. This is of vital importance if real-time decision-making is to be achieved. In Chapter 9 we return to discuss the industrial prospects for the field.

1.2 Three levels of robot 'intelligence'

1.2.1 FIRST GENERATION

Ever since the installation of the first industrial robot for die casting in
1961, it has been customary to compare human ability with the prowess
of the robot. Most such comparisons are based on the mechanical power
of the robot which, as one might expect, exceeds that of man in its capacity
for handling heavy weights and its high accuracy at reasonable speeds.
Such was the concern to develop these properties that less time was spent
on the development of the brain, or the computer of the robot.

In his scene-setting book *Robotics in Practice*, Joseph Engelberger (1980),
among 13 areas of activity, makes the man-machine comparison in the
following way:

'Human operative:
  uses any one or all of his five senses to follow the operation of the
  machine and to activate the controls as necessary. Has a memory
  with which he can learn the sequence and timing of the operations.

Robot operative:
  a robot must be pre-programmed to carry out its operations according to a timed sequence. A man has to do the teaching, and the
  robot has to have an internal memory to store the information.
  Computer technology has made this possible.'

This is a characteristic of what are now called *first generation* robots: the
presence of a computer memory is seen as the sum total of the required
'intelligence' of the machine. This, indeed, is an improvement on some
of the earliest robots whose actions were controlled by a 'pinboard' of
meticulously worked out connections scanned mechanically in sequence.
That could be truly said to represent the 'zeroth' level of intelligence.

The ability to teach a robot a sequence of actions that could then be
repeated in perpetuity with a considerable degree of accuracy was all that
was necessary. Probably, 80% of the robots in use up to the late 1980s
are likely to rely on this open-loop type of intelligence. But while this is
adequate for work such as spot welding or pick-and-place labouring, it
cannot be applied to even simple seam welding or depalletizing tasks. The
reason for the deficiency is simple; the actions of the robot must be based
on measured contingencies in the work place. No two seam welds are
likely to be the same, and without sensory feedback the welding robot
might apply its gun to fresh air, or ram it into the work piece with costly
consequences.

This book is not about robot sensors; Volume 2 of this series entitled
Interaction with the Environment: Robot Sensors and Sensing, covers this area
copiously (Coiffet, 1983). This book is concerned with what the computer
'brain' of the robot can do in response to a changing environment. In

programming terms, this means being weaned from a sequence of pre-programmed instructions to being capable of modifying the instruction path according to environmental occurrences. Programmers call this *branching*.

1.2.2 SECOND GENERATION

Robot designers in the mid 1970s found themselves in the same position as those dreaming about computers before the Von Neumann report of 1946; the stored program revolution was still to come (Burks *et al.*, 1946). Branching is often complex and it is the crux of general programming. So the implication is that robots should become fully programmable in the same way as a general-purpose computer, rather than being just pro-grammable sequencers. But the robot designers of the 1970s were more fortunate than the computer pioneers of the pre 1950s, they could buy microprocessors as components out of which they could structure robot 'brains'. In other words, the evolution of the general-purpose computer into a component that barely occupies a cubic inch (fully packaged) combined with the considerable dexterity of robot manipulators led to the appearance of *second generation* robots.

The vexing question was whether these systems should be programmed in a conventional high-level language, or whether special languages directly aimed at robots needed to be developed and marketed. The needs of the robot were not only those of decisions to be made on environmental contingencies, but also those of having to control the trajectories of six or so limbs in real time.

Ideally, the robot programmer would like to write block-structured programs where the blocks were procedures such as:

MOVE GRIPPER   FROM X1 Y1 Z1 TO X2 Y2 Z3
                             WITH END ORIENTATION X3 Y3 Z3

or

SLOW FORWARD   IN X1 Y1 Z1 UNTIL ENDSTOP
                             THEN GRIPPING PROCEDURE P

Within these procedures the system programmer will wish to perform standard computing functions. This may mean that he would be well served by pre-declared data types such as speed, torque force, velocity etc. This clearly spells out the need for special-purpose robot languages, written in some efficient run-time way so that reactions in real time may be obtained.

Thus the second generation robot era was characterized by the develop-ment of such languages. They are well documented in Volume 5 of this series entitled *Logic and Programming* (Parent and Laurgeau, 1984),which describes how languages such as VAL are being adopted in Unimation robots while PLAW is being developed in Japan specifically for welding robots. The latter allows welding sensor input so that the weld head can be prevented from leaving the task.

Of the dozen or more robot control languages the following facilities (with % of coverage across the languages) were provided:

PROGRAMMING FACILITIES
Structured programming (50%)
Parallel limb drive (50%)
Move interrupt (67%)
Handshaking with robot signals (85%)
Real time clocking (25%)
Substantial program memory: mainly floppy disk (75%)

ROBOT CONTROL FACILITIES
Coordinate transformations (50%)
Trajectory control: linear or circular (100%)
Maximum effort drive (50%)
Compliance feedback (8%)

ENVIRONMENTAL FEEDBACK
Differential feedback (100%)
Manual training (90%)
Network facilities (67%)
Vision:low resolution and embryonic (75%)
Strain gauges (67%)

In summary, it is the ability of robotic programs to branch, that is to obey 'if...then' statements, which is characteristic of second generation robots. The main feature that distinguishes second from *third generation* robots is the complexity and interaction of the 'if...then' statements.

1.2.3 THIRD GENERATION

Consider the robot in Figure 1.1. It has stored in its memory the target of the task to be achieved. The 'if...then' ability needs to be applied to the planning of the task. For example, the correct actions for the program are to go through a reasoning process that includes:

> IF I remove C THEN B and D will fall down (avoid)
> IF I remove B THEN ...

This process goes under several fashionable titles, for example *automated reasoning, knowledge-based processing, problem solving, automatic planning*. In computer science this activity used to fall under the heading of AI, and the clear characteristic of third generation robots is the coming together of robot programming and AI. Without wishing to pre-empt subsequent chapters of this book (particularly Chapter 2 where the parallel develop-

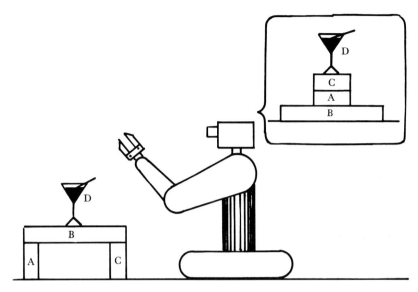

Figure 1.1 *A problem solving robot*

ment of AI and robotics is discussed), a few introductory points should be mentioned at this stage.

In theoretical terms, the step between second and third generation robots is much more significant than the increased degree of complexity of 'if. . .then' statements implied above. Interestingly, the complexity can be unravelled by the use of mathematical logic. For example, a statement such as:

'It is true that A and B are true or that A is true and B is false'

may be simplified to 'A is true'. It is this type of simplification that forms the theoretical basis of running programs as described in Chapters 7 and 8 of this book. The significance of this in terms of robot programming lies in the applicability of a totally novel style of programming: the *declarative* style.

As will be seen in subsequent chapters, new languages such as LISP and PROLOG emerged from AI research. Their objective is to allow their user to state directly or *declare* the nature of a logical problem and the rules that may be applied to its manipulation and then sit back while the machine solves the problem. In conventional programming, the programmer is under obligation to include explicitly in his problem the *method* of solution. In declarative programming, the machine searches for a solution using implicit methods that are well founded in mathematical logic.

Clearly this may not improve on-line dynamic control of robot limbs; that will always reside as an *imperative* (ie not declarative) program in a competent machine. However, such imperative programs are subordinate to the declarative ones. It is also the declarative program, particularly if PROLOG is the medium, that acts as an efficient man-machine interface. The style of such programs is based on a series of logical statements of the 'if...then' type. These may be written directly and executed as such by the machine. This is in contrast with the need to write structures of procedures as was indicated in the case of second generation declarative programs.

1.3 The 'fifth generation' of computers in relation to robots

There is bound to be confusion over generation numbers. Above we have written of third generation robots, whereas most readers will have heard of *fifth generation* computers. This does not mean that the development of robots is behind by a couple of generations. On the contrary, fifth generation computers are being used to provide the 'brainpower' for third generation robots. But why is the term 'fifth generation' used? And why has the development of fifth generation computing become the mainstay of political involvement in high technology in most Western nations?

1.3.1 TECHNOLOGICAL ADVANCES

The technological escalation over five stages is quite simple. The first four generations refer largely to the hardware that constitutes computing machines. The *first generation* describes the first commercially available computing machines. Their circuits used thermionic valves which not only required vast storage space but also created a heat removal problem. A first generation computer not only required a large hall, but also required another hall of equal size to house the heat extracting plant. This era had more or less come to an end by the time the first industrial robot had been installed in 1961.

In the *second generation* machines, the transistor replaced the valve and ferrite rings of one millimetre in diameter replaced pairs of valves for storing individual bits of information. The heat dissipation problem was solved, and the digital computer began to be seen not only as a tool for scientific research but as a vehicle for making businesses more effective. This was the age of the mainframe and the creation of large number-crunching systems which distributed their computing power mainly through a 'hand-it-in-then-come-and-get-it' shop. Towards the end of the 1960s, the concept of multi-entry machines and multi-user terminals began to be seen as a better way of distributing computer power. But for the roboticist, second generation computer philosophy held little joy, since should he need to control his machine, he would need an umbilical connection to an expensive mainframe that would almost certainly not react at sufficient speed.

The appearance of the minicomputer in the late 1960s heralded the *third generation* of computing machinery. The development of early silicon-integrated circuitry, particularly memory chips as opposed to magnetic devices, was responsible for the design of machines that could be afforded by small university and research departments and were not much larger than a desk and a few filing cabinets. Robotics research laboratories began to think of the possibilities of positioning the smaller versions of such machines on board experimental mobile robots. Also, as mini-computers developed further, sensible control boxes were being fitted to commercial, stationary manipulator arms confirming the introduction of second generation robots.

In synchronism with these developments, there was increased activity among language designers, particularly block-structured languages such as ALGOL and interactive languages such as BASIC. Despite the fact that BASIC is hardly ever used by computer scientists (due to its unstructured nature), it did make programming available to a large number of people. It also became an early standard in minicomputers. Indeed, in robotics, ROL (RObot Language) and VAL (Vic Arm Language) are BASIC-like languages. The first is still available for IBM PC machines, while the second was originally designed for PDP 11 minicomputers and it now runs on LSI 11 microcomputers.

Of course, it is the microcomputer that is the trademark of the *fourth generation* machines. Silicon technology in the mid 1970s was pushed to such an extent of miniaturization that it came up with a complete computer on a chip which occupies less than a cubic inch when fully packaged (where, for roughly the same computing power, a first generation machine would typically cover 3,000 cubic feet), weighs a fraction of an ounce (where the other was 30 tons) and uses about 2.5 watts (as against 140,000 watts). For the robot designer, the computer on a chip offered opportunities of deploying computing power where it was most needed, possibly both to control the individual arms of a manipulator and to coordinate the work of these distributed processors from an additional processor.

In terms of robot generations, this development in computing simply boosted the second generation. For example, the Unimation Pumas built since 1979, in addition to the use of an LSI 11 for program execution, use seven 6502 processor chips that are set off independently to ensure optimal trajectory control. These machines have also been designed to be programmed in VAL II, a nicely structured language in the style of Pascal.

1.3.2 FIFTH GENERATION STRATEGY

But this book is about *fifth generation* computing techniques for robots. Why has this generation merited so much more attention than any of the others? A good account of the historical factors associated with the fifth generation phenomenon is found in Feigenbaum (1983). Here we extract some of the features that are of relevance to a study of robotics.

Where the first four computer generations were defined by technological advances, the fifth generation is based on strategy with respect to potential for technological advance. The thrust of this effort, as is well known, came from Japan. In October 1981 the Japanese government announced its $1,000 million programme in collaboration with industry aimed at a new computer concept with some machines planned for production by 1990. The concept centres on computers that can converse with humans in natural language and be capable of seeing and hearing. They would be capable of using input data to reason and make inferences in human-like ways.

It is interesting that this decision was made at a time when Japan was well established as a leader in consumer electronics, and was beginning to make major advances in heavy industry: automotive production and shipping. It was the USA that led the world in fourth generation computers. The announcement pointed to the fact that the effort was not only intended to foster creative computer design but also to provide Japan with bargaining power. Feigenbaum describes the fifth generation as 'an exquisite piece of economic strategy'.

When the news of this announcement reached the USA, there was much debate and agitation particularly among those academics who were involved in AI research. Several calls for an effort of national priority went largely unheeded. There may well have been a very good reason for this, since the leading intellectual effort in the field was securely lodged in the major universities, with a few notable exceptions in industry. However, the Japanese event gave researchers more political power in obtaining funding for AI, and encouraged the private sector to strengthen its investment. So, due to the good base of funding that already existed, plus this strengthening, the total investment in what may best be called *knowledge systems* equalled, if not exceeded, that in Japan.

It was in Europe that more directed programmes were announced in response to the Japanese fifth generation plans. It was soon after the Japanese announcement that the Department of Trade and Industry in London rushed through the formation of a committee chaired by John Alvey of British Telecommunications. It contained representatives from government, industry and academic institutions. The target was a broad one and dubbed *advanced information technology*. This was further subdivided into four fields: *very large-scale integrated systems* (the furthering of the fabrication of advanced silicon chips), *intelligent knowledge-based systems* (the AI heart of the operation), *software engineering* (the production of advanced software) and *man-machine interfaces* (the improvement of computer usability). When announced in 1982, the programme was to be given £450 million over five years, of which the government would provide

£200 million. All the work was to be done collaboratively among at least two industrial partners with or without the presence of an academic group.

It is noticeable that no *explicit* direction towards robot development was planned in this programme. This was no accident since there already existed in the UK a specially promoted programme on robotics. But that which concerns this book is largely encompassed in the areas of intelligent knowledge-based systems and the man-machine interfaces. We return to these areas in Chapter 9, where some of the practical prospects for the development of this work are discussed.

As far as the rest of Europe is concerned, the European community took the Japanese challenge seriously. In 1983 the European Strategic Programme for Research in Information Technology (cunningly leading to the acronym ESPRIT or 'mind') was announced. This was financially of the order of the Japanese effort standing at $1,500 million. This programme includes automated manufacture and hence, applications to robots.

1.4 Conclusion

This introductory chapter has attempted to put a historical framework on the task of decision and control of a robot as based on the logical principles that will be discussed in the rest of the book. Sadly, concepts of AI, knowledge-based systems, logical programs and so on appear to run into one another. This is sometimes true even for those who have lived through this traumatic period of history. The main thread for the reader to bear in mind is that all these topics are concerned with endowing computers, and in the case of this book, computers that control robots, with programs that can find their way through stored data that represents human knowledge. The following chapter is written with the intention of stressing this line of reasoning by tracing its development under the heading of artificial intelligence.

Chapter 2

Robots and artificial intelligence: parallel developments

2.1 Introduction

Despite the curious historical fact that computers and robots have undergone a totally separate development until the late 1970s, writers on the future of computers foresaw the completely automated factory as being merely a matter of advancing the calculating performance of computational machinery. The potential for such progress was clearly foreseen as an improvement in the 'intelligence' of the task carried out by the computer. But in which way can a computer be said to be intelligent? This question comes into focus when the logical power of a computer is made to mesh with the mechanical power of a robot.

This combination creates an image of the uncomplaining slave who will inspect, manipulate with an acuity greater than that of man and venture into areas too dangerous for humans. Production areas exposed to paint fumes or tasks under the sea have often been quoted as examples. But, traditionally, the digital computer is renowned for its calculational power. Taking the example of a production line worker who is trying to assemble an electrical appliance, it becomes clear that this is not necessarily a question of carrying out sequences of calculations. In fact, the task is one of solving problems such as what has to be picked up first, where it has to go, and so on. In mathematical terms this is a *logical* problem. In broader terms the task may be described as one of solving problems which if done by man would undoubtedly require 'intelligence'.

In fact, this is precisely the definition given by Marvin Minsky (1975) to what, in the mid 1970s was a controversial area of computing: artificial intelligence (AI). The phrase was coined some years earlier by John McCarthy (1968) whose intention it was to demonstrate that computers could find their way through logical arguments with the same speed and agility that hitherto had only been exploited in calculations. He argued that searching through 'trees' of potential decisions to find decisions that lead to a desired conclusion gives computers a semblance of 'common sense'. It is against this background that the next section of this chapter considers the historical development of the AI paradigm.

Clearly an uncomplaining robot endowed with common sense would be of considerable use on the production floor. But, as the historical account will show, the enthusiasm of the early 1960s was a little ahead of its time largely because the precise nature of logical (as opposed to numerical) programming was not properly understood. As is evident from the contents of the major part of this book, logical programming is a vast subject that needs to be understood before any planning with 'smart' robots in mind can take place.

2.2 Early hopes for 'intelligent' automation

In the late 1960s the persuasion of those working in AI that this was the ultimate answer to most problems in automation was at its peak. Typical is the October 1968 issue of the British *Science Journal* which devoted its entire issue to *Machines Like Men*. Several research laboratories in the world had undertaken to investigate the possibility of building AI 'brains' for robots. The work of the Applied Physics Laboratory at the Stanford Research Institute in California where a mobile, 'intelligent' robot was being designed, was typical of this period. Charles Rosen, manager of this laboratory wrote in the *Science Journal*:

> 'Exciting possibilities exist for the use of both man-controlled and auton-omous robots which can operate in manmade environments where it is either difficult or impossible to maintain humans for protracted periods of time. Fabrication processes exist which require either very high or very low temperatures or an oxygen-free atmosphere or high vacuum . . .'

Although this kind of statement appears to be better directed at space exploration than the factory floor, it was somewhat misleading since it also blatantly stated that robots already existed which:

> '. . . can manipulate objects, move around laboratory environments autonomously, explore, learn and plan.'

Perhaps the scientists themselves were misled, not because the above statement was not true, but because the laboratory environments in which these successes were achieved were far too simplified. All objects had to be simple geometrical shapes that the computer could 'under-stand and describe': blocks, pyramids, spheres etc. It was believed that extending successes from such simplified worlds to a factory environment was merely a matter of bigger and faster computers. Now it is known that complex worlds may require vast logical data bases (known as *knowledge stores*) before a robot could be expected to function with any degree of competence.

A similar lesson was being learned in the UK at Edinburgh University where Donald Michie's group was developing a robot called FREDDY. This contained a television camera to assess a visual scene and was intended to assemble a simple toy cart (Ambler, 1975). Even this simple task exhausted the computational power of a sophisticated computer without giving clear guidelines as to how a problem in the real world might be tackled.

This credibility gap was documented by Sir James Lighthill in his highly controversial, but influential report to the UK Science Research Council (Lighthill, 1973). He coined the phrase 'the combinatorial explosion'. This described the effect whereby computational overheads grow exponentially with the complexity of the problem. This meant that unless much more efficient computing algorithms could be found, with the amount of research funding available, computer technology would not be capable of growing fast enough to produce usable robots.

Lighthill's criticisms went even further. First, he argued that an intelligent robot would have to be cost-effective. Even in dangerous environments it was inconceivable that vast computing resources could be deployed in the resolution of simple tasks such as, for example, the assembly of radioactive materials. Alternative solutions such as the use of remote manipulators controlled by a human operator would immediately eliminate the need for AI. Second, he took to task researchers in this field who claimed that through their efforts, they were shedding light on human intelligent processes. This seems well justified as there is no evidence of a combinatorial explosion in human problem-solving activity. Third, he questioned the intrinsic value of the vast programming effort that was going into the creation of programs flawed by the combinatorial explosion itself.

Despite the protestations of those working in AI, either as a result of the influence of Lighthill or not, the mid 1970s saw an upsurge of the concern to endow AI systems with some of the efficiency with which man uses logic. There was a greater concentration on studying natural language interaction with computers and the development of efficient data bases that store human knowledge, with a concern to focus programs on specific packages in narrowly defined, but none the less useful areas of human knowledge. This led to what are now known as *expert systems*. Although these systems have had their greatest successes in areas such as medicine and oil prospecting, they are likely to be the nucleus of the intelligent interactive robot, the need for which has been discussed in Chapter 1.

2.3 Motivating notions in artificial intelligence

There are two major notions that excite AI researchers. Both of these are relevant to robotics. The first is mainly held by psychologists and philosophers for whom AI has provided a more rigorous framework

within which to describe the behaviour of man than was hitherto available
to them. Margaret Boden (1977) puts this point of view with some
clarity:

> '...(AI is) the use of computer programs and programming tech-
> niques to cast light on the principles of intelligence in general and
> human thought in particular.'

To those interested in factory automation this has significance not only
through its implications for replacing man by machines (which is usually
a poor alternative), but mainly to provide an understanding of systems
in which human and machine efforts are mixed. If good automation
implies the extension of human faculties, human decision making and
problem solving has undeniably to be understood. For example, as fewer
human operatives are used on a factory floor, and the use of robots and
flexible manufacturing systems increases, scheduling has to be done with
increasing speed and has to cope with increasing complexity. At low
speeds a human scheduler can cope, but at higher speeds he needs a
machine to assist him. If his own scheduling activities are not understood in programming terms, there is no hope for the design of such
systems.

The controversy over views such as Boden's centres on whether
or not AI has achieved its aims of being a theory of intelligence. Certainly, in 1980 Nils Nilsson felt that this was not so and drew attention
to the fact that AI had a further, engineering significance:

> 'If... a *science of intelligence* could be developed, it could guide the
> design of intelligent machines as well as explicate intelligent
> behaviour as it occurs in humans and other animals. Since the
> development of such a theory is still very much a goal rather than
> an accomplishment of AI, we limit our attention here to those
> principles that are relevant to the engineering goal of building
> intelligent machines.'

As can be seen in much of this book, it is clear that the engineering
problems involved in introducing 'intelligence' into computers so that
they can be helpful in robotics are not only formidable, but also present
a fascinating challenge to the enlightened engineer. Probably, the aim of
providing a theory of human intelligence will remain a target rather than
an achievement for some time to come, but this too is a significant
challenge.

In summary therefore, the engineering challenge to AI programmers
is based on the following two simple points:

1. How can human knowledge be stored in a computer?
2. How can this knowledge be retrieved by a human interlocutor, or
   retrieved on-line, to perform a production control operation?

Now we review the answers to these questions from a historical perspective, and then we present the substance of the contemporary techniques in this quest based on formal logic, leading to expert systems.

2.4 Game playing

There is no doubt that the ability to play games such as chess or draughts (checkers) is seen to require some sort of intelligence. Even without a close definition of the meaning of the word, playing games of this kind is very much a human activity and, were it to be done by a machine, it would be a feat of AI, at least according to Minsky's definition given in Section 2.1. This clarity has made game playing an early target for those interested in program writing. Even during the infancy of computer development Claude Shannon (1950) of the Bell Telephone Laboratories in the USA was developing techniques for playing chess on these slow and inefficient machines.

But why should one have to discuss game playing in the context of robotics? Donald Michie (1968) was ready with an answer:

> 'Machine intelligence is about what can be generalized. Into this category fall various tree-searching techniques initially developed in mechanized game playing. Although the first explorations of these designs were made in attempts to program computers to play games, the nascent playing abilities of intelligent machines will increasingly be devoted to playing the game against nature.'

Although the control of robots can, in some distant sense, be seen as 'playing the game against nature', this now seems an unnecessarily flamboyant statement. More pertinent is the reference to tree searching which is a technical statement for a process of decision taking and prediction of the results of such decisions so that further decisions may be taken and so on. This is a rough model of what may go on in a player's head when playing a board game. It may therefore be safely predicted that if robots are to solve problems in factories they will need to be programmed in a manner similar to that of a game-playing machine.

Much of this book is about tree-searching techniques. Here we shall mention those invented by Shannon for playing games, but their formal representation will be discussed in Chapter 6.

The immediate problem with a game such as chess is that at each point of a playing strategy there is a large number of possible successive moves. Therefore if a program has to look several steps ahead, the number of moves that needs to be evaluated becomes very large. For this reason Shannon saw it was necessary to suggest ways of cutting down the amount of computation. He presented two algorithms. The first is called MINIMAXING and the second ALPHA-BETA processing.

2.4.1 MINIMAXING

MINIMAXING is intended to require the game-playing machine to evaluate only the moves found at the most advanced level of lookahead and from this to calculate the optimal next move. To do this, a rule is required to evaluate the states of the game, that is, the board states in the case of chess. It is at this point that human knowledge needs to be programmed into the machine. In chess this is done by the discovery of features, that is, grouping the pieces and basing a value (in terms of winning potential) on these identifications. For example, the discovery of a grouping that 'checkmates' (ie wins the game) has the very highest value. Other groupings such as those leading to the capture of important pieces may be given intermediate values by the program designer.

Assume that the machine is about to take a move. It has the current state of the board stored in its memory, as well as a list of rules for taking a move. It can therefore compute all the next possible board states. This could be called the set of moves at 'level 1'. By the same procedure and given enough computing time, all the moves at level 2 and subsequent levels can be calculated, bearing in mind that the number grows alarmingly as one progresses through the levels. Therefore the number of levels ahead that the machine computes is determined by the size and power of the computer. Say that level N is this upper limit.

Shannon's simple realization is that the machine does not need to bother with evaluating moves at level numbers less than N, since they are only routes to whatever advantage (or disaster) may lurk at that level. If N is 1, it is clear that the machine must select the most valuable move. If N is 2, this is the opponent's turn and it is safe to assume that he will generate the board state that has the least value to the machine. It thus becomes possible to 'back up' the values of the moves calculated at the Nth level to the (N-1)th level and so on until the first level is reached, bearing in mind that values at odd levels are MAXimized while those at even values are MINimized. Although this gives us the origin of the name of this algorithm, it requires a little more illustration to clarify its operation.

Say that the Nth level is odd and contains a total of X moves. Say that the (N-1)th level contains Y moves. This means that the set of X moves is partitioned into Y groups, each group representing the moves that follow from one of the moves at level (N-1). Assume that all the moves at level N have been evaluated, but at this stage it is not known which move will be taken at level N-1. As N is a MAX level the machine has to select the most valuable move in each of the Y groups, since this is to its greatest advantage. This leaves a list of Y values. The 'backing up' procedure consists of assigning these Y values to the related moves at the (N-1)th level as they form a prediction of what the opponent ought to imagine the machine will do.

Now the process may be repeated, only this time given, say, Z groups at level N-1, the minimum value of each group is taken and backed off to the previous level. Eventually one is left with a list of values for level 1, one for each available immediate move. The machine takes the move with the maximum value. At this point, a numerical example might help.

Say that at level 1 there are three, possible moves A, B and C. Then at level 2, from each of these moves there follow three other moves, the total being labelled as:

AA AB AC   BA BB BC   CA CB CC

The code is such as to make AA, AB and AC be the three moves that follow A and so on. (Of course, move B at level 2 is not the same as move B at level 1: it is simply a convenient label.) Continuing to level 3 we have:

AAA AAB AAC ABA ABB ABC ACA ACB ACC

BAA BAB BAC BBA BBB BBC BCA BCB BCC

CAA CAB CAC CBA CBB CBC CCA CCB CCC

Again the coding implies that, say, CBA is the first move that follows the route: move C then move B. Say that level 3 is fully evaluated on a scale 0 to 9 giving a set of values corresponding to the above set as follows:

4 1 6 8 4 3 9 2 0

2 3 3 6 8 0 1 7 2

0 5 5 6 7 2 4 1 9

As this is a MAX level, each group such as AAA, AAB and AAC relate to a move at level 2 and assume the maximum value for the group. This is 6 for the named group (that is, move AA). Hence the backed-up values for level 2 are:

level 2 move:	AA	AB	AC	BA	BB	BC	CA	CB	CC
backed-up value:	6	8	9	3	8	7	5	7	9

As level 2 is a MIN level, the lowest value in each group related to a level 1 move is taken. For example AA, AB and AC being the group related to move A at level 1 provide a backed-up value of 6 for this move. The complete set of backed-up values for level 1 is:

level 1 move:	A	B	C
backed-up value:	6	3	5

The computation may now be completed with the machine taking the maximum move which happens to be A. At this point the opponent takes a move (which may or may not be the predicted one) and the machine starts the computation all over again.

If, on average, there are M possible moves following each board state, there is a total of M to the power of N states at the Nth level and this (as opposed to the sum of this expression for all the levels below N) is that which needs to be evaluated. However this number is still very large, and this is where Shannon's ALPHA-BETA algorithm is helpful.

2.4.2 ALPHA-BETA PROCESSING

Without going into great detail, this algorithm relies on searching the tree in depth but only partially and discontinuing the search where the partial back-up cannot be changed by further search. For example, if a MIN level feeds a 9 in the above example to a MAX node, other groups feeding the same MAX node need not be searched as the value can only increase and the maximum is already achieved. This algorithm reduces the amount of work that needs to be done in backing up values by about 40% in most games.

The fundamental nature of these algorithms is underlined by the fact that most chess-playing machines that can be bought in high-street shops use them to provide up to 10 or 12 levels of lookahead in a reasonable time. This too is sufficient to give a human chess player a reasonably interesting game. The point must be made, however, that despite the engineering excellence of these algorithms, they are most unlikely to be accurate models of what goes on in a chess master's head. In terms of robotics this does not matter, as engineering excellence is paramount. In that case, the central significance of Shannon's work is that it initiated a close study of the formal properties of tree searching and its engineering implications, as reported in later sections of this book.

2.5 Learning

One crucial point that was skimmed over above was the question of where the methods of evaluation of board positions came from. It was said that this was part of the programmer's task. But clearly, the success or otherwise of a chess program depends upon the way in which this evaluation is done. Therefore, inserting a fixed program into the machine for doing this condemns the machine to a specific and inflexible competence in playing the game and predicting the opponent's moves.

A human player *learns* to appreciate the value of board positions. Indeed, the difference between a good and a bad player may be that the winner spots board positions that are advantageous at an early stage and therefore does not rely so heavily on lookahead tree searches. It is with this thought in mind that A. L. Samuel (1959) developed a checkers-playing program in which the allocation of values to features was left flexible so that it could be adjusted according to successes and failures recorded during games. The scheme used by Samuel required that important features be extracted automatically from the board according to pre-programmed rules. Such features are the presence of a fork (where the player is in a position to take one of two pieces, where his opponent can only defend one of them), the creation of a King (by reaching the opponent's baseline) and so on.

This list of features is given the labels:

$$f1, f2, f3 \ldots$$

In any one board state, the features that are present are given the value 1 while the absent ones are assigned a 0. The evaluation of a board state is a number E which is computed as follows:

$$E = w1.f1 + w2.f2 + w3.f3 + \ldots$$

Coefficients such as $w1$ are called the weights of the evaluation equation, and the ability for the system to learn resides in the variability of these coefficients.

At this point it is necessary to identify where the information that leads to weight alteration comes from. There are several strategies for doing this, but a simple and obvious one is to assume that the opponent is not only trying to win but is also taking moves from which good playing may be learnt. This means that the program adjusts the weights after each move that the opponent takes. For example, say that three possible moves by the opponent are evaluated (on a scale of 0 to 99) as:

Move A: 45, Move B: 70, Move C: 22

For simplicity, assume that only one feature is present for each move, say $f1$ for A, $f2$ for B and $f3$ for C. Say that the opponent takes move A. This implies that $w1$ has to be increased so that it becomes greater than $w2$ which currently dominates. The amounts by which the weights are changed and the way that one ensures that weights converge to the correct values has become a science in its own right (see Rosenblatt, 1962).

Interestingly, Samuel's ideas for incorporating learning from experience into an AI system were not pursued by others for several years. It is only relatively recently that notions of learning have reappeared in the AI literature. A comprehensive review of this subject has been published by Robert Holte (1985).

From the point of view of smart robots, the issue of whether a control program is allowed to learn or not is of immense practical significance. In learning systems the training and choice of training examples is done by experts in factories, and continuous improvements may be implemented while the machinery is in use. When changes are required in systems with fixed evaluation strategies, the original manufacturers of the software need to be brought in on a consultative basis which could be very expensive. In a sense, expert systems, as described in Chapter 3 get around the learning problem, since some of them (written in declarative styles) may be reprogrammed without the need for software experts.

2.6 Problem solving

The central direction for AI in robotics has been stated to be the endowment of 'reasoning power' to robots or factory scheduling systems to solve strategic problems. In robots assembly planning is such a task while if the robot is mobile, finding its way around the factory floor may be seen as a problem-solving task. Job scheduling of either robots or other forms of automation in a factory is also a clear instance of the need for problem-solving programs.

In a sense, the game-playing techniques discussed in Section 2.4 are examples of problem-solving tasks. However, the issue has to be seen from a greater distance in order to appreciate the more general aim. This was first done by Newell, Simon and Shaw in 1960 in a program called the 'General Problem Solver' (GPS) (Newell, 1960). In this program the evaluation function is replaced by a 'distance' function. This is a measure of how far the program has gone towards a solution for the problem. In the case of a robot finding its way through a factory, this distance can actually be measured in metres. In a scheduling task, however, the distance may be a measure of what percentage of total production is the current work in progress. The states of a general problem are the sub-goals and, instead of rules as in game playing, one has *means* that are applicable to the states of the problem. Once the problem is expressed to the GPS in these terms, this defines a tree which the GPS proceeds to search, using short-cuts similar to those discussed in the case of game playing.

There is one major difference, however, and that is the possibility of working backwards from the solution as well as forwards from the initial state of the problem. In such a case it is clear that the concept of 'distance' is a useful one. For example, if I wish to go from my home in London to see my cousin in Pelham, Westchester County, USA, I can reduce the problem of distance by simultaneously finding ways of getting from New York to Pelham and getting from home to Heathrow Airport. If I achieve these sub-goals the problem is reduced merely to the finding of a suitable flight from London to New York. More will be said about formal algorithms for such graph searching in Chapter 5.

There is one kind of problem, however, which cannot be tackled by the methods proposed so far. This is the problem for which the 'distance' cannot be easily identified. This is a very common occurrence particularly in assembly tasks in production. One cannot build the top three floors of a four-storey house first, although this is materially as close to completion as building the bottom three floors. In such a case the search needs to be exhaustive and short-cuts different from those found in game playing need to be invented. Typical of such is the notion that several actions may be pursued in parallel, and this is the nature of AND/OR graphs as described in Chapter 7.

Here we shall present a classic example of a problem with no distance measure, in the context of a simple assembly task. Imagine that an intelligent system, attached to a robot, is capable of sensing the contents of a table before it, and the state of its hand. The contents of the table are simple square blocks, coloured differently. The problem consists of getting the robot to stack blocks in a given order called the *target*, after the blocks are delivered to the table in some other order, called the *initial state*.

For this example, imagine that the initial and target states for three given blocks A, B and C are:

A	C	
B	A	
C	B	
--------	--------	table
initial	target	

In addition to the ordering of the blocks on the table, the state of the hand completes the state of the problem at any point in time. This is denoted as:

H(0) means: hand is empty;
H(X) means: hand holds X where X is A, B or C.

Knowledge about each block is recorded in the computer using the code: S(X, Y) means: X is stacked on Y (Y too belongs to the set
{A, B, C});
  C(X)   means: X is Clear;
  T(X)   means: X is on the Table;

Putting this notation together, the initial state is described by the set of items: { T(C), S(B,C), S(A,B), C(A), H(0) }

So much for the mode of representation. It is now necessary to tell the program how a problem state may be changed. This is done by defining a set of rules:

The PICKUP rule: if C(X) and T(X) and H(0) then H(X)
          is possible;

The UNSTACK rule: if S(X,Y) and C(X) and H(0) then H(X)
          is possible;

The PUTDOWN rule: if H(X) then T(X) is possible;

The STACK rule: if H(X) and C(Y) then S(X,Y) is possible.

Note that the content of the rule between 'if' and 'then' forms a simply testable precondition for any state of the problem. This means that for every state, a simple test will reveal which rules are applicable, and for which values of X and Y this applicability is true. For example, given the starting state, only one rule is applicable, that is the UNSTACK rule with $X = A$ and $Y = B$.

This means that if the starting state is the node of a search tree, there is only one subsequent state that can be reached, and that is the state that results from applying the UNSTACK rule with $X = A$ and $Y = B$. So far, it is noted that the procedure is totally mechanical. This trend continues with the creation of a mechanism for changing state once a rule has been selected. Each rule has associated with it a 'change list' which, too, can be mechanically applied. For example, the UNSTACK rule has the following 'change list':

H(0) becomes H(X);
S(X,Y) becomes C(Y);
C(X) is deleted.

It may be a useful exercise for the reader to derive the change lists for the other three rules. The effect of applying the change list for the UNSTACK rule to the initial state is to produce the new state:

$$\{ \ T(C), \ S(B,C), \ C(B), \ H(A) \ \}$$

It may now be noted that after any state change has taken place, a rule that reverses that change is applicable. For example, in the last state above, STACK with $X = A$ and $Y = B$ is applicable, which returns the problem to the original state. The significance of this reversibility is that it is possible to work backwards from the target state and forwards from the starting state simultaneously. This reduces the tree-searching computation considerably.

Enough has been described now to enable the reader to derive the entire search tree for this problem and show that the solution consists of the following sequence of operations:

move no.	rule	X	Y
1	UNSTACK	A	B
2	PUTDOWN	A	
3	UNSTACK	B	C
4	PUTDOWN	B	
5	PICKUP	A	
6	STACK	A	B
7	PICKUP	C	
8	STACK	C	A

This type of approach to robot plan formation was first suggested by Fikes and Nilsson in 1971 for a planning program called STRIPS. It too has been responsible for the deployment of a great deal of research effort on studies of efficient tree searching as discussed in this book. Another phenomenon can be associated with the rise in importance of tree searching and that is the development of special languages for AI. The oldest of these is LISP (McCarthy *et al.*, 1965); a more recent one is PROLOG (Kowalski, 1979).

Although these languages (particularly LISP) were designed to facilitate the representation and searching of trees, they led to novel attitudes to programming. It is characteristic of these languages that they are declarative as opposed to being imperative. In a declarative language the desired function is stated directly, while in an imperative language (such as PASCAL or BASIC) the machine must be told how to achieve a function. In addition, PROLOG leads to a style of programming deeply based in formal logic, first order predicate calculus to be precise. This means that every program has the precision of a mathematical equation, making its verification for correctness far easier than for a non-logical language. The subject of logical programming is covered in detail in Chapter 8.

2.7 Blocks worlds

A major assumption made in Section 2.6 is that a robot would at all times be able to see the objects it is trying to manipulate. This assumption hides a set of major problems. In AI these problems can be categorized under the title of 'scene analysis'. In general this is the problem of pattern recognition and image processing which to the present day continues to challenge the ingenuity of computer engineers. Early workers in AI sought to simplify the problem by assuming that the field of view of a television camera contained simple geometric shapes such as blocks and wedges. It was further assumed that programs could be developed that would take the signals generated by the television camera and turn them into neat, accurate line-drawings of the blocks. Over the years those have turned out to be reasonable assumptions, and much has been published regarding image processing techniques that achieve this task (for example, see Aleksander, 1983). Further discussion of this processing aspect is beyond the scope of this book. In terms of decision and intelligence, it is the logical data that can be extracted from such scenes that merit further attention.

The earliest approach to the problem was taken by Roberts (1965) who stored all possible two-dimensional projections of line drawings of a very limited number of objects such as boxes and wedges (Roberts, 1965). The storage was executed by encoding the two-dimensional projections as topological graphs. This ensured retrieval of the correct information irrespective of its size or orientation. Retrieval was also arranged for partial occurrences of such graphs. This ensured that if an object was partially covered by another, it would still be retrieved. Indeed, by completing the missing parts, the program could infer which objects were in the foreground and which were not. That is, it could output statements such as: 'There is a wedge in front of a box' for a scene as shown in Figure 2.1.

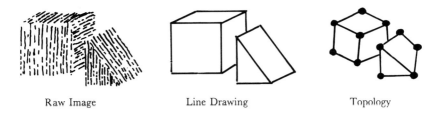

Raw Image   Line Drawing   Topology

Figure 2.1   *Roberts' Method*

The objection to this method centres on the fact that the models stored in the computer held no information about concepts such as an 'edge' or a 'surface' as a result of the topological representation. These are essential if a larger set of objects is to be acted upon. Adolfo Guzman (1969) at MIT advanced the field by suggesting that features of the scene should be extracted such as the forks, arrows and tees as shown in Figure 2.2. Surfaces in a scene of flat-sided objects (polyhedra) may then be identified as being enclosed by straight lines and these are represented as vertices in a stored graph as shown. The features act as the arcs between these vertices in a way that allows several features to confirm that two surfaces are linked. A complete graph then represents one object. Special features such as tees serve to separate different objects and consequently complete (connect) such graphs as shown.

Despite the fact that many others added their talents to the development of this field it became exceedingly clear that every time the problem was stepped up in complexity (eg through the addition of curves and

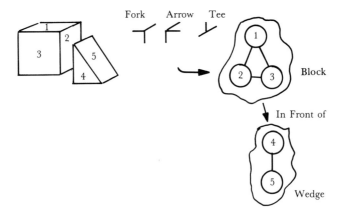

Figure 2.2   *Guzman's Method*

shadows) new methods of representation had to be invented. This simply made the task of representing real scenes for real robots in real factories somewhat remote.

Nevertheless, these historical areas of research are worth studying since they add weight to demonstrations of the power of logical programming. After all, the topological graphs illustrated above are a logical outcome of their input data (eg if feature x and feature y then . . .). Therefore more recent developments have sought to retain this logical way of operation but approach the question from a different, parallel point of view which is discussed in Section 2.8.

2.8 The Marr legacy

David Marr was a young Englishman when he left the MRC Neuro-physiology unit of Cambridge to work in the AI laboratories at the Massachusetts Institute of Technology (MIT) in the mid 1970s. There he vigorously advanced work on computer vision that took significant account of what was known of vision in living things. Sadly, he died of cancer in 1982, but left a framework in which exciting research can continue. Details of his work may be found in Marr (1982).

He believed that the process of making vision systems was wholly bound up with understanding how such systems work in man and animals. He laid down three 'commandments' that need to be observed if this understanding is to be rigorous. First, the task must be specified in an unambiguous way (that usually means a mathematical way). For example, whether one is studying a local task such as edge detection or a more general task such as inference of depth from stereoscopic inputs, the input-to-output transformation must be specified in a watertight way.

Second, an algorithm must exist to ensure that the transformation specified in this rigorous way, can be tested on a conventional computer. Third, and it is here that Marr departed from tradition in AI, there must be a plausible 'brain hardware' model which not only explains how the living visual apparatus might accomplish the feat, but also will provide design for a fast hardware implementation in man-made electronics.

Within this framework, Marr defined four levels of vision that are linked in terms of image understanding, but which might merit research in their own right. The first relates to the initial storage of the image. Here are the technological questions such as the number of bits associated with each picture point (pixel), the coding of this information and so on. This information has to be transformed to the second level which Marr called 'the primal sketch'. This level holds markers for important events in the original image: boundaries between different textures or intensity levels, the identification of blobs or spaces and the like. This mirrors what is known about the operation of cells in living vision systems in the sense that such cells have been shown to be sensitive to precisely the features just mentioned.

The third level has been called by Marr the two and a half-dimensional (2&1/2-D) description, because it labels local events in depth. For example, programs can be written which, given information about the position of the lights and some knowledge of the objects, can calculate the relative slants of the faces of the object by doing calculations on the shading as seen by the camera. This field too contains much useful work on stereoscopic images taken with two cameras and image understanding of motion from pairs of images taken at slightly different times.

At the fourth level, Marr proposed that a proper three-dimensional evaluation be attempted, describing objects and their relation to one another. For example a program might use the 2&1/2-D information, and through the application of stored knowledge of 2&1/2-D surfaces in such things as chairs and teddy-bears, infer that 'there is a teddy-bear sitting on a chair'.

The significance of Marr's work in the context of decision and control of robots is that the paradigm has been accepted as being central in current research on vision-based AI. Most of the world's major research programmes in this area (fifth generation in Japan, the US Knowledge-Based Systems programme, the Alvey programme in the UK and ESPRIT in Europe) are supporting work centred on this paradigm and aimed in part at robot control.

In the meantime work on a much lower scale is looking even further ahead.

2.9 The Barlow principle

As a central contributor to the understanding of living vision systems, Horace Barlow had a major influence on Marr when he was at Cambridge. His principle is to insist that an understanding of the most complex characteristics of vision in living creatures must develop from an understanding of the behaviour of complexes of cells with known, or inferred, characteristics. In contrast to digital computers, the brain does not have scheduling programs, well-defined housekeeping schemes or even anything that could be thought of as an executable instruction. The brain is structured in well-defined layers of neuron cells which perform all the miracles which we know as vision. Recognizing a school friend despite the passage of years, understanding the flight of a tennis ball in a split second, reacting to a dangerous situation while driving seem feats well beyond the capability of the cleverest computer vision program. And at the bottom of it all, Barlow reminds us that there is no program, just 100,000,000,000 neurons, much evolution and a massive capacity for adaptation (Barlow, 1982).

The engineering implications of this fact are formidable. A neuron is nothing more or less (in terms of its function) than a random-access memory. These are mass-produced in silicon and form the basis of the memory of conventional computers. But in conventional computers they are not wired in the somewhat hectic and layered way that is found in the brain. Nor are they allowed to be addressed by data and build up their own content by being 'taught' by example. On the contrary, they are connected so as to provide a blank slate which is brought into action only by the storage and perfect retrieval of programs and data generated by the programmer. It is quite possible, however, to wire these up in ways that better resemble the brain, particularly to allow learning by example.

Electronic models of neurons have been known for some time. They were first proposed in 1943 by a neurophysiologist called Warren McCulloch who was collaborating with a mathematical logician, Walter Pitts. But in 1969, perhaps as a result of the apparently unlimited powers of algorithms, or perhaps as a result of credibility cracks appearing in early AI programs, Marvin Minsky and Seymour Papert of MIT published a book which was to put an end to research into these artificial brain-like structures. It argued that any successes obtained with artificial neural networks could not be properly understood and controlled. They also pointed to the fact that simple networks have to have specific geometric properties of patterns and that scientists would be better employed in improving conventional approaches.

Now, with the astonishing downward trend in the cost of silicon memories, the building of learning networks for pattern analysis is not only a possibility, but has been achieved and proven to be effective. The WISARD system first built at Brunel University in the UK, and now marketed as a properly engineered instrument by a UK manufacturer is unashamedly based on neural network principles. The drawbacks stressed by Minsky and Papert have turned out to be only of academic interest, not preventing such machines from being capable of learning to recognize and distinguish the most complex of patterns under the control of users who do not need to know how to write programs (Aleksander, 1983).

In the USA too, interest in cellular learning automata has increased. A major research team at Carnegie-Mellon University is being led by Geoffrey Hinton, who was previously at the MRC Neurophysiology Unit in Cambridge. Calling his networks 'Boltzmann Machines' because they use noise as a way of finding stable solutions to pattern analysis problems, he has shown that these devices can not only recognize patterns, but can store and access most efficiently knowledge of the kind that is normally associated with expert systems (Hinton, 1985).

Thus, looking beyond the logical programming methods that are central to this book, massively parallel systems with properties emerging along the lines of those sought by Barlow are appearing. But this does not cancel the value of the logical principles in logical programming; it merely means that they need to be applied simultaneously in a way in which they interact. It is this constraint effect that will remain a challenge to researchers in smart robotics for some time to come.

2.10 Near-natural language communication with robots

As in the case of vision systems, there are pressures on the makers of robot control software to allow the line operator to interact with the machinery directly. This means that the instructions to the robot must be given in some way that does not rely on knowledge of a formal programming language. Since the early 1970s AI laboratories have addressed this problem. Best known is the contribution made by Terry Winograd (1972) at MIT which was based on the facilities made available by the early LISP-based AI development languages, CONNIVER and PLANNER.

The starting point of near-natural language interaction is the almost natural ability that computers have to check the syntax of language-like statements. This comes from the fact that software compilers and interpreters parse formal language input as a fundamental step of the business of computing. Therefore the syntactic side of natural language does not present too great a problem, provided that the syntax of such a language is properly stated and used both by the users and the program designers. The problem arises from the need to extract meaning (or, in technical words, do the semantic as opposed to the syntactic processing) from such statements, which in the context of robot control, say, is different from the process of extracting machine language instructions from programming language statements.

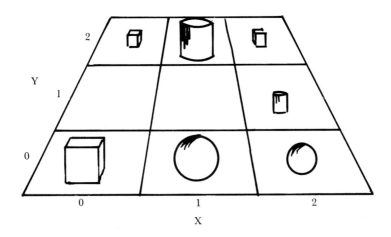

Figure 2.3 *A blocks world to 'talk' about*

Winograd's proposal centres on the idea that in the same way as one needs to curtail the grammatical rules so as to make the syntax processing tractable, one needs to curtail the 'meaning world' so as to make the semantic processing tractable. Indeed, Winograd's work was done in the context of the 'blocks world' discussed earlier.

To illustrate the process, consider the view that a robot might have of a highly simplified world (say, processed through a vision system) as shown in Figure 2.3.

As indicated, the first step is to develop a grammar that expresses statements about this world and actions within it. The usual way of describing syntax is used: : = reads 'becomes'; / reads 'or'; ⟨⟩ includes non-terminal symbols that are used to generate the grammar but do not appear in the language itself.

⟨sentence⟩	: = ⟨question⟩
	/⟨assertion⟩
	/⟨command⟩
⟨question⟩	: = Is ⟨nounphrase⟩⟨relation⟩⟨nounphrase⟩ ?
⟨assertion⟩	: = ⟨nounphrase⟩ is ⟨relation⟩ ⟨nounphrase⟩.
⟨command⟩	: = Pick ⟨nounphrase⟩.
	/Pick ⟨nounphrase⟩⟨relation⟩⟨nounphrase⟩.
	/Place ⟨nounphrase⟩⟨relation⟩⟨nounphrase⟩.
⟨nounphrase⟩	: = ⟨article⟩⟨adjective⟩⟨noun⟩
	/⟨article⟩⟨noun⟩
⟨relation⟩	: = to the left of
	/to the right of
	/in front of
	/behind
⟨article⟩	: = a
	/the
⟨noun⟩	: = cylinder
	/box
	/ball
⟨adjective⟩	: = ⟨adjective⟩⟨adjective⟩
	/large
	/small
	/white
	/grey

Reading down these production rules it becomes clear that there are three types of sentence that may be used in the language: questions, assertions and commands. Examples of these may be generated by going through a sequence of instances of replacements as indicated by the rules:

⟨sentence⟩   : = ⟨question⟩
                : = Is ⟨nounphrase⟩⟨relation⟩⟨nounphrase⟩ ?
                : = Is ⟨article⟩⟨noun⟩behind⟨article⟩⟨adjective⟩⟨noun⟩ ?
: =   Is a box behind the ⟨adjective⟩⟨adjective⟩ball ?
                : = Is a box behind the large grey ball ?

Similarly, an ⟨assertion⟩ may develop into:
          The white ball is to the left of a cylinder.
While a ⟨command⟩ may be:
          Place the small large white ball on the box.

The last of these does not appear to make any sense despite being grammatically correct according to the given rules. But 'sense' relates to meaning and we shall now see how the sentence generation rules may be used to generate meaning.

First, the state of the world in which the meaning is to be found needs to be represented as a data base within the machine:

LABEL	NAME	SIZE	COLOUR	(X, Y) POSITION
A	box	large	white	0,0
B	ball	large	grey	1,0
C	ball	small	white	2,0
D	cylinder	small	grey	2,1
E	box	small	white	0,2
F	cylinder	large	grey	1,2
G	box	small	grey	2,2

Each column in this data base gives rise to sets of objects with a common meaning:

All the objects: {ABCDEFG}

box   :   {AEG}
ball   :   {BC}
cylinder   :   {DF}

large   :   {ABF}
small   :   {CDEG}

white   :   {ACE}
grey   :   {BDFG}

The way in which the last, position, column is used to extract meaning from relations is also defined by sets. For example, 'to the left of' is taken to mean that set of objects for which the value of X is lower, and so on. This may be applied to sets of objects too. For example, 'behind {D}' is the set {EFG} (we choose not to interpret 'behind' as 'directly behind' but as 'generally behind'). Also 'behind {BD}' is taken to mean 'behind B *and* behind D' . So:

$$\text{behind } \{BD\} = \{DEFG\} \ \& \ \{EFG\} = \{EFG\}.$$

(& being the logical intersection operator).

Sequences such as ⟨adjective⟩⟨adjective⟩⟨noun⟩ are treated also as intersections of the relevant sets.

So 'large grey ball' evaluates as {ABF} & {BDFG} & {BC} = {B}. This explains how 'small large' would yield an empty set which the program can recognize as being impossible.

Using these simple set operations the meaning of a question may be extracted as follows:

Is a box behind the large grey ball ?
: Is a {AEG} behind the {ABF}&{BDFG}&{BC} ?
: Is a {AEG} behind the {B} ?
: Is a {AEG} & {DEFG} ?
: Is a   {EG}   ?

At this point the translation can go no further and the program recognizes that this is a question (from the non-terminal symbols used, especially the '?') and performs a test to see whether there is a non empty set in the curly brackets. Here this is the case, and through a simple lookup table the system can be made to answer 'yes E or G'.

Had the word 'white' rather than 'grey' been used in the question above, the last line of the computation would have been {empty} and the answer would have been simply 'no'.

The use of formal logic in these operations should be noted. This is another reason why the theory of logical programming as pursued in Chapter 8 is of great significance.

2.11 Expert systems

Many of the techniques mentioned in this chapter, so far, have contributed to the emergence of expert systems. An expert system is a data base consisting of rules and facts about a circumscribed area of human knowledge which can be interrogated in a natural way by a non-expert user. One of the strengths of these programs is that they must be able to retrace their steps over their own lines of reasoning and explain the rationale behind their answers to questions. Clearly, the concept owes much to work done on near-natural language interaction as described above and, yet again, the use of formal logic ensures that the knowledge bases are properly knitted together and presented in a clear way to the user.

In the context of robotics one should not look at expert systems too closely from the viewpoint of direct control of the robot. The benefits of such systems are more likely to impact on a wide variety of topics in the robot-oriented factory. These range from scheduling and planning problems, to more mundane matters such as the selection of appropriate machinery and materials. It seems inappropriate to try to provide more detail here on the operation of such systems since the aim of this chapter has been to present some of the milestones in the history of AI development which underpin the current development effort. The reader is directed towards some specific accounts of expert system development that exist in the current literature (eg Addis, 1985).

2.12 Conclusion

In this chapter we have surveyed the history of AI against a background of the need to improve communication between the human controller and the robot or a factory containing robots. Although the early history of the subject seems not to lead to a practical application, it is hoped that the point has been made that the research was not wasted. A clear set of advanced techniques is emerging and, although the third generation smart robot is still a target rather than an achievement, progress is taking place as a better understanding is being obtained through research into the all-pervasive nature of logical programming principles that are central to this book.

Chapter 3

Expert systems and knowledge-based languages

3.1 The place of knowledge-based languages in expert systems

The concept of the expert system primarily addresses a functional definition: this is presently based on software which takes on intellectual activities in areas where human expertise is considered to be either insufficiently structured to provide a precise, reliable and complete methodology, directly transposable on to a computer, or subject to revision or addition.

Expert systems are therefore created with the following objectives:

1. easy acquisition of 'grains' of knowledge, so as to facilitate the most direct expression possible for these grains, consistent with the way they emerge from experts.
2. exploitation of sets of grains, that is, (a) combining and/or chaining strings of the grains in order to infer new knowledge, such as judgements, plans, proofs, decisions, predictions, new grains and (b) where appropriate accounting for the way in which new knowledge has been inferred.
3. facilitating revision of the set of grains, that is, offering facilities for addition and subtraction of granules.

Two components can usually be distinguished in the structure of an expert system: the 'knowledge base' and the 'inference engine'. In fact, there is always a third fundamental component: the language used for the expression of knowledge which allows a general system (a knowledge-base shell) to be made specific or which allows an already defined expert system to be developed. The knowledge language plays an essential role in satisfying objectives 1, 2(b) and 3. When this knowledge language is sufficiently developed (particularly in terms of lack of constraint for use, and of flexibility), the term 'declarative programming' can be used.

3.2 Many languages, few comparisons

Several hundred expert systems have emerged in the literature of the last ten years, leading to a considerable collective experience of knowledge expression languages. Only a minimum of attention, however, has been paid to comparing the properties of these languages.

First, experiments concerning the processing of the same problem by different engines are very rare. Those that have been carried out have been based, without exception, on 'toy problems'. It must be admitted, however, that the same comment could be made with reference to traditional programming languages.

Second, unlike work with traditional languages, experiments on the processing of several problems by a single engine (that is, with a change of data base) are very few and far between. Among those that have taken place, however, can be cited the MYCIN/EMYCIN family, notably PUFF, SACON, DART, LITHO, SECOFAR, PDS and TOM, or the OPS family, notably R1/XCON, XSEL, ACE, AIRPLAN, AI-SPEAR and YES/MVS. Among the fifty or so inference engines built in France, only a few have given rise to several applications on any real scale. In addition to the specific example of PROLOG, which can actually be considered and used as a general system, mention must be made of SAM, SPHINX and PROTIS (with some three instances of each, one in the medical field, by the original authors), and SNARK (with seven instances in various fields by different teams).

Third, experiments concerning the updating of a data base related to a single problem (or a group of similar problems), progressing according to levels of expertise, are quite rare. R1 can be cited, with 800 rules in 1980, 1,000 in 1981, 1,500 in 1982, 2,500 in 1983 and 3,250 at the end of 1984.

Because of the difficulties involved in offering a general tutorial on the languages associated with expert systems, the following discussion will be restricted to a presentation of some of the differentiating characteristics of these languages (the differences between languages are, of course, related to differences between engines, not discussed here).

3.3 Categories of expert knowledge

Beyond the simple distinction, traditionally emphasized, between 'facts' and 'rules', the languages associated with expert systems often offer, and sometimes impose, other categories of knowledge.

3.3.1 FACTS

This common term is used both to denote expressions and interpretations of these expressions, of a highly varied nature. It is generally agreed that facts are:

 – grains of assertional information;

- usable for conditioning and exploitation of operational knowledge;
- capable of being created and discarded by the exploitation of operational knowledge.

in SNARK, a triple of 'constants' (see below), in the form:

object	attribute	value

2 examples:

journal X	no of subscriptions	11000
$7	nature	lichen

(or: the nature of object $7 is lichen)

in OPS5 and ARGOS-II, a list of constants,

2 examples: (tool-3 in (box (5 10)) appearance (blue metal))
(go-to (locations (10 12)))

in PROLOG-II, a 'literal' (predicative functional term) with 'variables' (see below),

1 example:

simplification (add,O,x,x,);
(or: the addition of O and x is simplified to x)

Figure 3.1 *Examples of the expression of facts*

In some systems, categories of facts can be distinguished, each one related to specific means of manipulation. For example, in systems capable of planning actions, 'facts' (established), 'problems' (facts to be established) and 'plans' can all be treated separately.

3.3.2 RULES

These are grains of operating knowledge. The 'activator' part of a rule describes the conditions for activation of the rule in terms of more or less completely specified facts. The expression 'associative compilation' of activators is used in this connection. The 'body' part describes the operations to be carried out in the event of activation.

Depending on the system, the possibilities for describing the activators and bodies of rules will vary. It is often possible to distinguish a sub-language for the activators and a sub-language for the bodies of rules.

3.3.2.1 Languages for activators

These play an essential role in making the 'associative compilation' of the rules more flexible, and therefore facilitating a style of 'declarative programming': definitions that are independent of each other, and of the grains of operational knowledge. Each system respects a compatibility model between the facts and the elements, called 'filters' which make up the activators. Figure 3.3 shows the rule activators for OURCIN, SNARK and PROLOG.

in SNARK:

```
JOURNAL-BASE (G)  =  (JB)
REARRANGEMENT (T)  =  NO
NO-NEIGHBOURS (TB)  =  (NB)
NO-NEIGHBOURS (TI)  <  (NB)
→
JOURNAL-BASE (G)  ←  (TI)
```

in PROLOG-II:

```
possible forms ('r'.'e'.'y'.x.q,crush,
                pres-ind(  <'e'.'i'.x.q,x.q>
                           <type-s-4,type-p-2>,press-i).
                imp-ind('y'.x.q,type-1,i-imp).
                ps-ind('y'.x.q,type-4,ps-i).
                fs-ind('e'.'i'.x.q,type-1,i-fs).nil)
         →    in(x,'o'.'u'.nil)
              do-not-start('o'.'v'.'n'.'e'.nil,x.q);
```

Figure 3.2   *Examples of rules. In both cases the 'activator' part precedes the separator* →

In OURCIN, a filter can be compatible only with one perfectly identical expression of fact (character for character), in which case the compatibility model respected in the identity, or with an expression of fact involving words declared as synonyms of words present in the filter, and of words declared as non-terminal. For example, the 'MULTIMODAL VARIABLES' filter is compatible with the 'MULTIMODAL TYPE UNKNOWNS' if UNKNOWNS is synonymous with VARIABLES, and if TYPE is a non-terminal word.

In SNARK, as in most inference engines, the compatibility model is semi-unification (that is, a specific example of 'unification' used in predicate logic). The rules, but not the facts of SNARK can explicitly include variables. In Figure 3.2 the symbols '(G)' and '(JB)' are identifiers of variables, and are compatible with any identifier of a constant or, more generally, with any expression without variables.

In PROLOG, the compatibility model is plenary unification; variables are admitted, both in the facts and in the rules; for example, the filter in Figure 3.3 is compatible with a fact such as: 'P(h(u),v,g(w));' where 'u','v' and 'w' are variables.

In most systems said to have variables, such as OPS5, ARGOS-II, SNARK or TANGO, only the rules explicitly admit variables, but not facts. The compatibility models respected by these systems, however, cannot always be reduced to semi-unification. In ARGOS-II, therefore, the activator language offers, apart from several types of variable, a range of filtering operators, filtering functions and rules specific to filtering (called 'theorems'). A few simple examples of this are given below.

Filters F2 and F3 in Figure 3.4 use the filtering operator '*', known as the 'absorbant operator'; this operator may appear anywhere in a filter; it is compatible with any sequence, possibly empty, of lists or ARGOS atoms.

In OURCIN:　　IF MULTIMODAL VARIABLES ... THEN ...
　　　　　　　　　　　a filter
In SNARK:　　JOURNAL-BASE(G) = (JB) ... → ...
　　　　　　　　　　　a filter
　　　　　　　　(G) and (JB) denote variables
In PROLOG:　　P(x,f(y),g(a),a) → ...
　　　　　　　　　　　a filter
　　　　　　　　x,y are variables

Figure 3.3　*Examples of part-activators*

It is possible to carry out logical operations (negation, disjunction and conjunction) on filters or elements of filters; for example, in filter F3, the ABSENT operator makes it necessary to verify that no fact of the base is compatible with the filter element following.

Procedures being filtered can be evaluated; for example, if the variable 'x' has already captured the list '(blue red white)', the filter: '((& class <x) >y)' will be compatible with the fact '((red blue white) france)' because first, the variable '<x' restores the list 'red blue white', second, the operator '&' commands the launch of the alphabetical classification procedure 'class' and returns the list '(blue red white)', and third, the variable '>y' is compatible with (and 'y' captures) the value 'france'.

It is possible to allocate a capture variable with a different value of the element filtered by this variable; for example, the filter '(?(FUNCRES >x price))' is compatible with the fact '(material sand)': the filtering operator '?' absorbs 'material', while '>x' is compatible with any expression; during filtering, 'x' captures the 'price' of 'sand' (for example: 'cheap') and not 'sand' itself, because the filtering function 'FUNCRES' launches the 'price' procedure on the argument filtered by '>x', in this case 'sand', and allocates the result to 'x'.

Normally, with ARGOS-II, a rule cannot be activated unless the activator is recognized as being compatible with the current state of facts and problems. It is sometimes convenient, in using it, to equip the system with 'theorems' which virtually extend the fact base to the moment of filtering. For example, consider the theorem T:

'((?blue) ← (? (& similar blue)))'

If a rule filter is '(blue block)' and is incompatible with the fact base, the ARGOS motor should reject the rule; nevertheless, it will first look in the 'theorem base' for a possible way of making the filtering more flexible. Here the preceding theorem T leads to the 'similar' procedure being launched on the 'blue' argument; let 'azure' be the result; the filter '(blue block)' will now be replaced by: '(azure block)' and a new

comparison with the fact base will be attempted. The theorems lend
themselves to recursion.

```
rule name          (r9  (
                F1        (take >x)
activator       F2        ( <x part >y *)
(3 filters)     F3        ABSENT ( <y * radioactive state *))
                   (
                C1        (EXECUTE (point in part ( <y) (>z)))
body            C2        (REPLACEPB (go <z) (approach <x))
                C3        (RECORD
                             (PLAN (grasp ( <x)))
                          (UPDATE
                             (MODIFY (robot *)(taken <x))))))
```

Figure 3.4   *A rule in ARGOS-II. The prefix > denotes variables being captured: the prefix < in*
<x is the command for restoration of the value ultimately captured by x. The upper case letters indicate
key words of the language

In certain systems, such as MYCIN and its descendants, compatibility
between the activator and the fact base is not reduced to taking only the
two values: absolute incompatibility or absolute compatibility, but rather
a degree of compatibility is evaluated (for example, a number between 0
and 1).

When categories of facts are likely to arise, the activators can refer to
each other. For example, the first filter (F1) of Figure 3.4 refers to the
'problem' base, whereas the subsequent ones (F2, F3) refer to the fact
base itself. From the point of view of the compiler of the rule, filter F1
characterizes the general opportunity of the rule, while F2 and F3
characterize the subsidiary conditions of applicability.

3.3.2.2 Languages for bodies of rules

The effects of rule activations are traditionally defined as transformations
of the fact base. In reality, it would seem more appropriate to distinguish
three sorts of effect, by making a comparison with the three standard
instruction types of programming languages:

- processing instructions: effects on the knowledge base;
- input-output instructions: external communications;
- control instructions: effects on the control of the engine.

The effects on the knowledge base concern, most importantly, the fact
base. These languages currently propose primitives to develop and insert
new facts in the fact base, even to delete facts in this base. In TANGO,
for example, it is only possible to add facts explicitly; nevertheless the

engine can, by its own authority, delete a fact if an addition should arise, concerning an object-attribute pair already present in the base. Sometimes the language authorizes recourse to filtering primitives, similar to those available for writing activators, to designate facts, groups or parts of facts associatively (see Figure 3.4). When the fact base is structured into sub-bases (for example: facts, problems, plans etc), specific primitives are available.

Sometimes (as with PAS-II, ADVISE or ARGOS-II, for example) primitives also allow modification of the rule base, or more generally, any part of the knowledge base. It is usual to classify any rule capable of modifying the state of the rule base in the category known as 'metarules' (see Section 3.3.3 below).

Some languages offer primitives to generate messages or to consult the environment: the user, data base and sensors, or more generally to launch processes external to the inference engine and the knowledge base (example: EXECUTE primitive in Figure 3.4).

Some languages (for example ARGOS-II, SNARK, ALOUETTE) make use of primitives that act directly on the behaviour of the inference engine, for example, abandonment of the base cycle in use, or stopping the engine. In ARGOS-II, a primitive in the form '(BACKTRACK ⟨filters⟩)' allows a reverse progress to be started, until a previous cycle can be found such that the fact base associated with this cycle is compatible with the ⟨filters⟩.

3.3.3 METARULES (OR RULES ON RULES)

These are grains of operational knowledge that can specify the style and manner of using the rules. In principle, metarules are invoked by associative access and therefore, like rules, they include an activator and a body.

Figure 3.5 shows a metarule from MYCIN. The second and third filters in the activator refer to the rule base, designated by RULES-OBJECTS. The rule is interpreted as: 'in case of pelvic abscess, if there are rules that mention ENTEROBACTERIACEAE in their context and others that mention BATONNETS-GRAM + , then place the former before the latter'. In MYCIN, in order to write the body of metarules, primitives are used to organize a group of rules relative to others or to fix the 'usefulness' of certain rules.

In other systems (for example ARGOS-II, SNARK) the metarule bodies can call primitives for inhibition and validation of rules, themselves designed associatively. Under ARGOS, inhibition or validation can sometimes be 'primed' during activation of the metarule without immediate execution; filters are associated, in the body of the metarule, with arming primitives: inhibition or validation will be executed automatically if the fact base comes to be compatible with the filters.

```
(($AND (SAME CNTXT PELVIC-ABSCESS)
       (THERE-ARE RULES-OBJECTS (MENTION CNTXT PREMISE
       ENTEROBACTERIACEAE) SET 1)
       (THERE-ARE RULES-OBJECTS (MENTION CNTXT PREMISE
       BATONNETS-GRAM + ) SET2))
CHAIN-LIST SET1 BEFORE SET2 MEASURE 0.4)
```

Figure 3.5 *A MYCIN metarule*

3.3.4 ASSERTIONAL/OPERATIONAL OBJECTS

In some systems (for example MYCIN and its derivatives, CENTAUR, MOLGEN and TROPICAID 2), the user is offered the possibility of structuring the assertional knowledge (facts) and/or operational knowledge (rules, procedures) into significant assemblies in the application domain. In different contexts, variants covering a range of complexities are offered by the 'frames' (which can be roughly translated as 'models') (Minsky, 1975) to the 'objects' of languages called 'object languages', such as SMALLTALK, passing through 'scripts' (Schank, 1977) and 'prototypes' (Bobrow, 1977). These variants are designated collectively here as 'assertional/operational objects'. A simple, currently used structure for an assertional/operational object is shown in Figure 3.6.

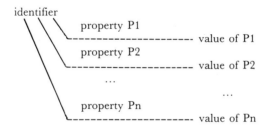

Figure 3.6 *A simple structure of an assertional/operational object*

This structure combines, in a single entity, a variable number of triples in the form: 'identifier-property-value', for a single identifier. The property values can be varied in type: constants, messages, procedures to be activated, etc. In MYCIN the significant assemblies have the name: 'clinical parameters' and 'context types'. An example of the 'clinical parameters' family is given in Figure 3.7. The 'category' property has as its value the constant 'ORGANISM'. The property 'area' has as its value a call from the 'AMONG' procedure, the argument of which is obtained by evaluation of the expression '(ORGANISMS)'. The property 'update-by' designates a list of rules to be activated to evaluate the clinical parameter IDENT (identity of a pathogenic agent).

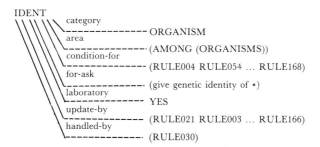

Figure 3.7   *An assertional/operational object in MYCIN*

To dedicate the EMYCIN system to an application domain, it is possible and indeed essential to provide such assemblies, and thus determine the objects, properties and values specific to the area. It is important to stress that the definition of the assertional/operational objects, which are notably 'clinical parameters' and 'context types', represents a large part of the effort involved in forming a knowledge base, over and above the definition of the expert rules.

Some assertional/operational objects can be developed, while the system is being used, as specific examples of more general, predefined objects. In MYCIN, when work is in progress, the engine produces structured objects, called 'contexts' as specific examples of other objects called 'types of context'. The assertional/operational objects can be organized into a network: the values of certain properties are pointers to predecessor or successor objects. For example, the value of the 'category' property in Figure 3.7 indicates an affiliation between the object 'IDENT' and the object 'ORGANISM'. The network structure can be used to allow an object to inherit the properties of predecessor objects and therefore simplify the representation of each object taken separately.

3.3.5 PROCEDURES

These are items of operational knowledge, judged by the experts as natural for explicit inclusion, and not by associative compilation (the procedures are known and are called by their names and not by their conditions of application). If it is known for a fact that particular knowledge, precisely determined and certainly present in the system, must be invoked without any possibility of alternative, then associative compilation has no role to fulfil.

Some languages, (for example, ARGOS-II and TANGO) allow procedure calls to be introduced into the rules or metarules, either in the body or activator part (procedures put into practice during filtering). It is also common to be able to use procedures in the compilation of the assertional/operational objects. For example, the procedure 'AMONG' in Figure 3.7 intervenes for the calculation of the value attached to the 'area' property of the object 'IDENT'. This technique is called 'procedural attachment'.

3.3.6 DEMONS

These are a type of operational knowledge generally written as 'associative compilations' in rules or metarules, but which are not subjected to the same basic cycles. This operational knowledge is automatically and immediately used as soon as certain events concerning the fact base (or sometimes other parts of the knowledge base) arise: additions, deletions and consultations. The use of demons tends to increase the capacity of what is known as the 'reactivity' of expert systems.

The user controls the demons, using specialized directives introduced into the rule bodies, as he would with a system of interrupts, in the sense of computer architecture. It is possible to 'prime' or 'release' a demon, conditionally or not. When an event of the type associated with a demon occurs during its definition, the demon, if it is primed, will carry out work of a type specified in advance. Here, however, unlike the standard use of interruptions, the purely logical events likely to cause 'interrupts', are described associatively.

For example, in the body of a rule written in ARGOS-II, a demon could be defined by an expression in the form:(DEFINE-DEMON add(lab-result $>x$) (EDIT $<x$ available)). This demon, when active, edits a message each time a fact compatible with the filter (lab-result $>x$) is added to the fact base (by the execution of any other operational knowledge, for example, a rule). If, for example, the fact added is '(lab-result hemoculture)', '$>x$' will capture the value 'hemoculture' which will then be restored by the symbol '$<x$', which gives rise to the message: (hemoculture available).

3.3.7 USE OF VARIABLES

A certain number of expert systems handle expressions of facts and rules without variables. This is the case with OURCIN (see Figure 3.3). More commonly (for example, PAS-II, MYCIN, OPS%, ARGOS-II< SNARK, TANGO and ALOUETTE), the languages associated with expert systems admit the presence of variables in rules but not in facts. Generally, the variables introduced in the rule activators are implicitly universally quantified. For example, the rule in SNARK, in Figure 3.2, must be interpreted as:

'whatever the specific values that can be substituted for the variables (G), (JB), (TI) and (NB), so that the conditions JOURNAL-BASE(G) = (JB), REASSEMBLY(TI) = NO, NB-NEIGHBOURS(JB) = (NB) and NB-NEIGHBOURS(TI) < (NB) are satisfied with regard to the fact base, TOUR-BASE of (G) can be allocated with the value of (TI)'

More generally, a rule like: $DEC(x) \rightarrow COR(x)$ is interpreted as:

'whatever the specific value of x that makes the activator $DEC(x)$ compatible with the fact base, the instructions defined in the rule body $COR(x)$ can be executed'

Some systems allow representation of the existential quantification. For example, in SNARK, the rule: 'MAN(X) = YES $\rightarrow$ CREATE(Y) FATHER-OF(X) $\leftarrow$(Y)' is a representation of 'for any man x, there exists y such that y is the father of x'.

Among inference engines, PROLOG occupies a place apart for a number of reasons, particularly because the use of variables is authorized both in the expressions that act as rules and in the expressions that act as facts. All the variables present in the PROLOG expressions are universally quantified. For example, 'A(x) :-B(x) C(x)' and 'C(y) :-D(y)' are rules that can be interpreted as: whatever the value of x, to establish A(x), B(x) and C(x) must be established whereas, whatever the value of y, to establish C(y), D(y) must be established. Another example is, 'B(z) :-' is a fact that can be interpreted as: whatever the value of z, B(z) is established. 'D(a) :-' is a fact that can be interpreted as: D(a) is established. ':-A(u)' is a problem that can be interpreted as: 'whatever the value of u, A(u) is not established', must be refuted, that is u must be found such that A(u) is established.

The use of variables allows several expressions of knowledge to be condensed into one, which is sometimes known as 'factorizing' knowledge.

3.3.8 REPRESENTATION OF UNCERTAIN OR IMPRECISE KNOWLEDGE

In the areas in which expert systems are being developed, the knowledge (facts and rules) processed and inferred is very often uncertain or imprecise. Among the expert systems that use or are capable of using, to very varied degrees, uncertain and sometimes imprecise knowledge can be cited: MYCIN (and all its derivatives: PUFF, HEADMED, DART, SECOFOR, LITHO, PDS and TOM, etc), PROSPECTOR, GARI, SAM, SPHINX, PROTIS, PLANT/ds (and its derivatives: PLANT/dc, BABY), SNARK/SUPERIKON, ELFIN, SPII, TROPICAID 2, DIABETO, MANAGER, CRIQUET, MEPRA and PILOTEX.

A fact is *uncertain* when it contains an assertion which cannot be confirmed as being true or false, although it must have one or other truth value. For example, 'the cause of the illness is, perhaps, pseudomonas'

A HEADMED rule:
if: 1) the diagnosis envisaged is: MAJOR DEPRESSION, and
         2) the intensity of this depression is: medium or light, and
         3) the current mental state of the patient is: psychotic, and
         4) there are no recent previous psychiatric problems
then: there is strong evidence (0.8) that the appropriate
         type of treatment is: antipsychotic

A LITHO rule:
if: 1) there are one or more plateaus on the curve FDC, and
         2) there are one or more plateaus on the curve CNL, and
         3) there are one or more plateaus on the curve BHC, and
         4) the overall porosity of the area is less than 10%
then: there is suggestive evidence (0.5) that the geological
         formation of the area is generally sunken.

An SPII rule:
if   the result of the intelligence test is, approximately,
         between 10 and 14 and
         the mark for English is, approximately, between 6 and 10
then   the test results are considered mediocre

Figure 3.8   *Rules involving uncertainty or imprecision*

(uncertainty is suggested by 'perhaps'). A rule is uncertain when it produces uncertain conclusions, even on the basis of certain premises. For example, 'if the patient presents a particular perfectly identified symptom, then it is likely he has a particular perfectly identified illness' (uncertainty is introduced by 'likely'). A fact is imprecise if it implies incompletely identified objects. For example, 'the patient has a temperature of about 39.5°C' (imprecision is introduced by 'about'). A rule is imprecise if it implies imprecise facts in premise or in conclusion. For example, 'if the temperature of the patient is high, then give him a large spoonful of a particular syrup'.

In practice, the language of an expert system concerned with inherent uncertainty or imprecision of facts or rules, must contain conventions and primitives to allow the user to modify the knowledge he transmits (only facts for ordinary users, rules for experts) with a degree of uncertainty or an area of imprecision. For example, to represent an uncertainty the ordinary user can attach a number to the facts (as in MYCIN and PROSPECTOR). In MYCIN, the 'attentuation coefficient' of a rule in the form 'P implies Q' represents the certainty that 'Q is true', when 'P is true' is certain. In PROSPECTOR the 'sufficiency factor' shows to what point 'P is true', is sufficiently certain for 'Q is true' to be certain, whereas the 'necessity factor' shows to what point 'P is true' needs to be certain for 'Q is true' to be certain.

3.4 Conclusion

According to Edward Feigenbaum, who played a leading role in the expert system breakthrough, '...to increase the performance standards of artificial intelligence programs, knowledge is power. Power does not reside in the inference procedure... practically speaking, any method of

inference would do the job. The power lies in the knowledge...'
(Feigenbaum, 1984). Actually, from a computing point of view, there is
no knowledge without a language of expression, and no knowledge
expression language without an engine capable of interpreting this
language. It is, therefore, vital to study the properties of languages, and
those of the engines associated with them, to use expert knowledge as fully
as possible. Among the subjects whose development should be considered
are the following: what can be expressed with existing languages? How?
What cannot be expressed? What must be expressed explicitly? What
risks are attached to the mode of expression?

Correspondence between systems mentioned and references:

ACE	(Vesonder, 1983)
ADVISE	(Michalsky, 1983)
AIRPLAN	(Masui, 1983)
AI-SPEAR	(Billmers, 1984)
ALOUETTE	(Mulet-Marquis, 1984)
ARGOS-II	(Farreny, 1980, Picardat, 1985)
BABY	(Michalsky, 1983)
CASNET	(Weiss, 1978)
CENTAUR	(Aikins, 1983)
CRIQUET	(Vignard, 1984)
DART	(Bennett, 1981)
DIABETO	(Buisson, 1985)
ELFIN	(Martin-Clouaire, 1984)
EMYCIN	(Van Melle, 1980)
GARI	(Descottes, 1981)
HEADMED	(Helser, 1978)
LITHO	(Bonnte, 1982)
MANAGER	(Ernst, 1985)
MEPRA	(LeFevre, 1984)
MOLGEN	(Friedland, 1979)
MYCIN	(Shortliffe, 1976, Buchanan, 1984)
OPS	(Forgy, 1982)
OURCIN	(Demonchaux, 1984)
PAS-II	(Waterman, 1975)
PDS	(Fox, 1983)
PILOTEX	(Husson, 1985)
PLANT/ds	(Michalsky, 1982)
PLANT/dc	(Michalsky, 1983)
PROLOG II	(Colmerauer, 1982)
PROSPECTOR	(Duda, 1979)
PROTIS	(Soula, 1983)
PUFF	(Aikens, 1983)
RI/XCON	(Mc Dermott, 1982a)
SAM	(Gascuel, 1981)

SECOFOR	(Courteille, 1983)
SNARK	(Laurriere, 1984, Vialatte, 1985)
SPHINX	(Fieschi, 1984)
SPII-I	(Martin-Clouaire, 1985)
SUPERIKON	(Lagrange, 1984)
TANGO	(Rousset, 1983)
TOM	(Cognitech, 1984)
TROPICAID 2	(Auvert, 1984)
XSEL	(Mc Dermott, 1982b)
YES/MVS	(Griesmer, 1984)

Chapter 4

Production-rule expert systems

4.1 Introduction

So far, mention has been made of knowledge representation and derivation systems, commonly known as 'formal logic', and this is detailed in Chapter 8.

In these systems, 'formulae', 'axioms' and 'inference rules' are all precisely defined, and the relationships that exist between formulae and their interpretations are carefully studied. Certain languages or systems arising from work in the field of AI, and which exist directly within the framework of this type of formal logic, are currently enjoying a rapid expansion in their use.

Generally speaking, study of formal logic has enabled methods of problem solving, that is methods for the discovery and justification of solutions, to be developed following a rigorous evaluation of the properties or limitations of these methods.

Nevertheless, many problem-solving systems have been constructed and have been found to be relatively satisfactory, without bearing a relationship to a particular formal logic needing to be established or postulated in advance. This has generally been the case with the 'production rule systems' to be considered in this chapter.

Attempts at logical formalization of production rule systems remain very limited (in France, Fargues (1983) can be cited); at a more fundamental level, the role of logic in inference and the representation of knowledge is the subject of some controversy (Newell, 1981; Moore, 1982).

The prominence of production rule systems goes hand in hand with the emergence of the concept of 'expert systems'. Since the mid 1970s, the term 'expert system' has been applied to some systems resulting from research carried out in AI. This software has excited great interest because it can be used to tackle, with relative success, particular types of task relating to diagnostics, prediction, design and planning hitherto generally uncomputerized.

Intellectual activities of this kind are often difficult to represent in definitive algorithmic form. This problem can be partly solved by applying expert system methodology: the structure and mode of operation is well-

suited to the reproduction of some human faculties of decision and judge-
ment, based not on complete algorithms, but elements of algorithms
specific to relevant areas of application, which may be sparse and ill-
defined, and supplied by human experts in the field considered.

In this chapter, the function and general organization of expert systems
will be considered first. Next, the common principles governing the
operation of production rule systems will be described, followed by a
general survey of various examples, with emphasis placed on the importance of this approach to advanced robotics. A number of characteristics,
important in the comparison and differentiation of systems will be introduced, and finally, a more technical insight will be given into 'filtering'
(or 'associative access'), in the same way as for 'unification'. This chapter
provides a relatively detailed introduction to production rule systems
oriented towards action planning.

General references on the subject of production rule systems can be
found in Waterman (1978); Michie (1979); Lauriere (1982); Barr (1982);
Stefik (1982); and Hayes-Roth (1983).

4.2 What is an expert system?

According to Edward Feigenbaum (Stanford University, USA) expert
systems are 'programs designed to allow skilled reasoning on tasks
thought to require considerable human expertise'.

This definition is actually not very revealing: could software representing a subtle mathematical algorithm, for example for the solution of any
equation of degree less than ten, be said to reason skilfully? The task
carried out by such an algorithm certainly requires considerable human
expertise, but is the term 'expert system' appropriate? What is the dimension introduced by this expression as compared to all the other reasonably
complex software produced by computer scientists?

Edward Feigenbaum's definition is all the more puzzling because
existing expert systems use only very simple reasoning methods: in fact,
modelling, with a view to computer applications of various forms of
'natural reasoning', is only in its infancy.

In order to try and define the concept of the expert system, the three
following complementary points of view will be considered:

- the role allotted to such systems in taking over some human intellectual activities;
- the type of organization available for the acquisition and use of
  expert human knowledge in particular fields;
- the method of eliciting knowledge used by experts to express their
  expertise for insertion into the system.

4.2.1 THE ROLE OF EXPERT SYSTEMS

When the intellectual process by which a person evaluates a situation or takes a decision is precisely modelled, it is relatively easy to program. This is the case, for example, in such areas as accountancy, scientific calculation or the numerical control of machine tools. It is not considered here, however, that the software resulting from programming of this type would constitute an expert system.

In certain large areas of application, such as medical diagnostics, educational orientation, the law, mineral prospecting and work organization, the available knowledge is often sparse, fragmented and of experimental or heuristic origin. In a considerable number of intellectual areas, ranging from engineering to human sciences and from social to life sciences, the knowledge of human experts is not sufficiently structured to allow representative algorithms to be developed.

In these areas, the specialist knowledge that is available appears more suitable for presentation as a set of work units, each one being appropriate to a particular class of possible situations. Several units may have bearings on the same type of situation, and each unit describes a possible stage in the reasoning of specialists in the area considered.

In these areas it is important to be able to complete and revise the set of units of knowledge easily, which leads to their being considered as a particular type of data to be used by a relatively general program, called the 'inference engine' or 'deductive machine'.

The inference engine, using various strategies, often largely independent of the area of application, searches through the units of knowledge, interprets them, and chains them so as to satisfy significant halting conditions (success or eventual failure).

An expert system is, then, a relatively general inference engine, using a separate collection of knowledge units, subject to revision, concerning a specific area of human expertise.

To facilitate the acquisition and revision of the knowledge units and the capture of the statement of problems, to ensure interaction during resolution with an operator, and to take account of the way in which the solution is reached, an expert system also provides, to a greater or lesser degree, the complementary functions of dialogue, training, and explanation of its behaviour.

4.2.2 BASIC COMPONENTS OF EXPERT SYSTEMS

An expert system always comprises:

- a *language* for the expression of knowledge;
- *structures* able to accept knowledge specific to an area of application, whether directly supplied by human experts or accumulated by the system itself in the course of experimentation;
- an inference *engine*.

4.2.2.1 A language for the expression of knowledge

Highly diverse conventions are used. For example, Figure 4.1(a) represents a unit of knowledge relating to the diagnosis of bacterial diseases.

Generally, from the point of view of the user, natural languages are the most comfortable form in which to communicate with an expert system, whether to instruct the system (as would be the case for an expert user) or to consult it (for an ordinary user). Some systems are capable of dialogue in natural language (usually English), intentionally restricted by the specificity of the area of application. Figure 4.1(b) shows the 'artificial' coding of the rule expressed in natural langauge in Figure 4.1(a).

If 1) the colour test of the organism
is positive,
and if 2) the structure of the organism
is cocci,
and if 3) the mode of development of
the organism is in colonies

then there is suggestive evidence (0.7)
that the organism is staphyllococcus
(a)

(($AND (SAME CNTXT GRAM GRAM +)
(SAME CNTXT STRUC COCCI)
(SAME CNTXT DEVEL COLONIES))
(CONCLUDE CNTXT IDENT
STAPHYLLOCOCCUS MEASURE 0.7))
(b)

Figure 4.1 *Two codings of the same unit of knowledge, in the MYCIN expert system (Shortliffe, 1976)*

4.2.2.2 Structures for the acquisition of knowledge

The elements of knowledge are organized in a 'knowledge base'.

In this, a distinction is generally made between 'declarative knowledge' describing situations considered as established or to be established, and 'procedural knowledge' which represents knowledge of the field: what consequences should be drawn or actions should be taken when a particular situation is established or is to be established?

This 'procedural knowledge' is usually represented by expressions of a sufficiently small range to allow them to be easily understood by a user, while corresponding to distinct, significant operations in the field: the expression 'grains' of operational knowledge is often used (introduced above as 'units of knowledge').

4.2.2.3 Inference engine

This is a program (perhaps in the future an integrated circuit) that applies general mechanisms for combining assertional and operational knowledge. Figure 4.2 shows the organic separation of the inference engine and the knowledge base.

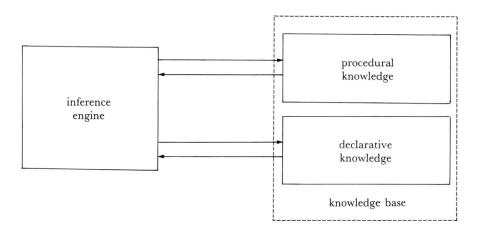

Figure 4.2 *Organization of expert system principle*

4.2.3 PATTERN MATCHING IN EXPERT SYSTEMS

The obvious importance of the most direct possible expression for the units of knowledge (grains) provided by experts, combined with the need to avoid time-consuming modifications to the processing structure of the expert system, following every addition or deletion of grains (new state of the operational knowledge), have tended to lead to designers adopting the 'associative access mode' to the knowledge base.

In associative access mode, the designation of a unit of information is not carried out by a label or pointer but by giving a fragment of the information content. For example, the unit of knowledge taken from the MYCIN expert system, shown in Figure 4.1(a), can be designated by giving a 'descriptor' or 'filter' such as: 'organism identity'; it may be that this filter designates several units of information collectively in the MYCIN knowledge base.

In a standard information system, the procedures (that play the role of units of knowledge) are each designated by a name and are called by an intermediary of their names. In this case, if a procedure is added or deleted, modifications must be made to all other procedures that use the added or deleted procedure.

Considerable flexibility can be built into the system if, in each procedure expression, a 'filter' is incorporated, describing the situations in which the procedure must be applied.

For example, the expression of a procedure P1 could contain a filter:(USEFUL-FOR (CHOICE (organism identity) (name class))) which means that the procedure can be used to establish either the identity of an organism or the name of the class to which it belongs. Consider the expression of another procedure P2, containing the sub-expression: (FIND (organism identity)) which means that P2 must establish an organism identity. When P2 is being compiled, it is not necessary to know and mention the names of the procedures (such as P1, but there could be others) likely to help in finding the organism's identity; it is simply assumed that the expression of these procedures includes one or more filters of the type given for P1. In this way, the procedures can largely be compiled independently of the effective existence of each other.

Generally, it is in this flexible manner that the units of knowledge assembled in an expert system can be made to refer indirectly to each other: with invocation via the filters. A còmmonly used term to designate expert systems is 'pattern-directed inference systems' (Waterman, 1978).

4.3 Production rule systems: organization and operation

Procedural knowledge (or units of knowledge or grains) is usually expressed as 'production rules'.

4.3.1 PRODUCTION RULES

Each production rule or simply 'rule', contains a 'conditions' part and an 'actions' part:

> if the conditions are satisfied by the current state of the assertional knowledge base (or fact base), then the actions can be carried out.

The actions generally consist of modifications to the fact base. They can also be modifications to the operational knowledge base (or rule base), communications with the environment or transformations to the environment. Examples of rules are shown in Figure 4.3.

4.3.2 BASIC CYCLE OF A PRODUCTION RULE SYSTEM

The inference engine chains work cycles each containing two phases: the *decision* phase and the *action* phase.

When the engine is set off, the fact base and the rule base contain information representative of the statement of the problem to be processed: an expression of given facts and facts to be established, and procedural knowledge in the field.

The engine is commanded to stop either in the decision or action phase.

TWO RULES FROM 'MYCIN' (MEDICAL DIAGNOSIS)

if 1) the site of the culture is the blood
and if 2) the organism has negative gram
and if 3) the organism is baton-shaped
and if 4) the patient is a host at risk,
then it is plausible (degree 0.6) that the
    organism is pseudomonas aeruginosa

if 1) the organism is a bacteroid
and if 2) the site of the culture was sterile,
then the recommended therapy must be chosen from
    the following: chloramphenicol, climdamycin,
    tetracyclin, lindomycin, gentamycin

A RULE FROM 'DENDRAL'
(DETERMINATION OF DEVELOPED CHEMICAL FORMULAE)

if there is a high peak at atomic number/charge 71
and if there is a high peak at atomic number/charge 43
and if there is a high peak at atomic number/charge 86
and if there is a high peak at atomic number/charge 58
then there must be an N-propylketone-3 radical

A RULE FROM 'PROSPECTOR' (GEOLOGICAL PROSPECTING)

if there is hornblend strongly altered with biotite
then there is strong evidence (degrees 320 and 0.001) for
    an area of potassic alteration

Figure 4.3 *Examples of production rules are compiled by experts in the fields considered. The systems 'MYCIN', 'DENDRAL' and 'PROSPECTOR' are discussed below*

4.3.2.1 Decision phase

The first stage of the decision phase, called *restriction*, consists of using, when possible, general knowledge on the distribution of the facts and rules in different families. For example, in a medical diagnostic context, it is possible to distinguish, a priori, the rules specific to childhood illnesses or the facts relative to blood analysis. The distinction into families of facts or rules often manifests itself in a division of each of the fact or rule bases into separate structures. The restriction determines which sub-sets (R1 in the rule base and F1 in the fact base) merit comparison, at a given moment.

In the second stage, known as *filtering*, the inference engine examines each of the rules of R1 relative to the set of facts F1: a sub-set R2 of R1 assembles the rules judged to be compatible with F1; R2 is called the 'set of conflicts'.

The third stage of the decision phase, called *resolution of conflicts*, deter-mines the rules (for example, a sub-set R3) that must be 'activated' (that is, effectively executed) among those that make up R2.

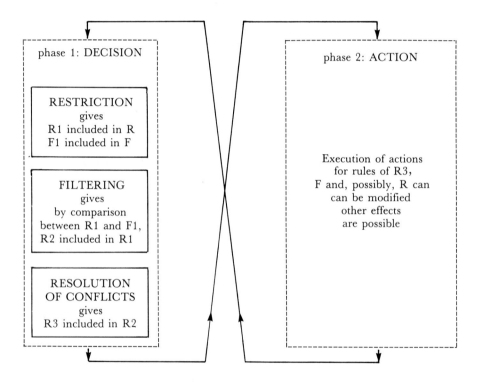

Figure 4.4 *Representation of the basic cycle of a production rule system. R and F denote the rule and fact bases respectively, as they are at the start of the decision. The inference engine commands the chaining of the stages in the decision phase, of the decision and action phases, and then of the complete cycles with each other*

4.3.2.2 Action phase

The action phase constitutes the second part of each cycle: the inference engine commands that the actions of each of the rules in R3 be carried out (if R3 is non-empty).

Figure 4.4 consists of a diagram indicating the progress of a cycle. In practice, of course, the basic cycle is managed according to a variety of strategies. The abstract, but simple example given in Section 4.3.3 illustrates the chaining of several cycles necessary to the solution of the problem.

4.3.3 OPERATION OF A PRODUCTION RULE MICROSYSTEM

Consider the rule base 1 to 6, shown in Figure 4.5(a). For example, rule 1 could mean: 'to establish hypothesis P give the result of a particular analysis, observation or measurement called B and establish the truth of hypotheses D and E. It is assumed that initially, the fact base includes the four symbolic facts shown in Figure 4.5(b): H, B, C, α. An underlined fact, such as H represents a hypothesis, the truth of which is to be established; for example: 'the patient is afflicted with a certain illness'. A non-underlined fact, such as B or α is considered as established or recognized, for example: 'a particular symptom was observed'.

4.3.3.1 Elementary work cycle

– *restriction* stage. During this stage, no restriction is placed on the rule base (or R1 = R). On the other hand, the fact base is reduced to the facts F that are not symbolized by Greek letters: at the current stage of activity of the rule system, the corresponding symptoms are assumed a priori to be of no interest. Here, therefore, during the first cycle F1 = {H,B,C}.

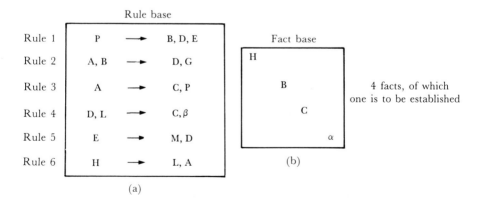

Figure 4.5 *An example of a knowledge base (facts and rules)*

– *pattern matching* stage. It is assumed here that it is the left hand member of each of the rules of R1 that is compared with F1. To activate a rule, each of the expressions making up its left hand member (two expressions, for example, A and B in rule 2) must be compatible with the facts of F1. In this case, this compatibility is defined as existing only when the expressions of the left hand member are present as such in F1. During the first cycle, therefore, only rule 6 is retained (set R2). Real inference engines use less strict compatibility models. For example, the general hypothesis: 'the organism is a bacteroid', present in the left hand member may be judged to be compatible with the hypothetical fact: 'the organism is the pseudomonas-aeroginosa'.

– *resolution of conflicts* stage. Within the framework of this example, only the first rule stored in R2 will be activated (it is assumed that the rules are subjected to pattern matching in the order 1 to 6). As a result, pattern matching will be halted as soon as a rule of R1 is recognized as being compatible with F1. This kind of strategy is often used in real systems; it is only reasonably acceptable if the inference engine is capable of 'backtracking': if the systematic choice of the first compatible rule leads to a situation in which no rule is applicable, the most recent previous choice is reconsidered (see Section 4.3.3.2 below).

– *action* stage. In this example, the action stage is limited to introducing symbols appearing in the right hand member of the activated rule into the fact base, while some facts in the base will not be used. The latter are the facts to be established that are also present in the left hand side of the activated rule. Here, after application of rule 6, H is not used whereas L and A are introduced: the fact base becomes $F = \{L,A,B,C,\alpha\}$. Naturally, if an established fact such as S appears in the fact base, it is advisable not to introduce S or S again. If S appears in the fact base, there is no point in introducing S; on the other hand, if S is in the fact base, and S is present in the right hand member of the rule, S must be substituted for S in F.

4.3.3.2 Chaining cycles with a view to verifying the initial hypotheses

This chaining is shown in Figure 4.6. A single hypothesis exists here: H.

After application of rule 6, the inference engine will execute other cycles that will transform the base until it only contains established facts. During the second work cycle starting from the fact base $F = \{L,A,B,C,\alpha\}$, rules 2 and 3 could be retained by the pattern matching. The resolution of conflicts chosen leads to rule 2 alone being retained. At the end of the second cycle, the fact base has become $F = \{D,G,L,B,C,\alpha\}$ (only A passed over, D and G introduced).

The third work cycle activates rule 4 and the fact base becomes $F = \{B,G,L,B,C,\alpha\}$. C is not introduced because C, an established fact, is present. The fourth work cycle leads to the conclusion that no rule is now applicable, therefore the chaining of rules 6, 2 and 4 has resulted in failure. The inference engine will reconsider this chaining. During the second cycle, rule 3, although capable of satisfying the pattern matching, was not retained for R2. It will now be retained and activated (fifth cycle), starting from the base arising from the first cycle: {L,A,B,C,α}, producing the fact base: {P,L,B,C,α}.

The sixth cycle activates rule 1, producing {D,E,L,B,C,α}. The seventh cycle activates rule 4, producing {β,E,L,B,C,α}. The eighth cycle activates rule 5, producing {β,M,D,L,B,C,α}. The ninth cycle activates rule 4 again, producing {β,M,L,B,C,α}. The inference engine then states that there are no more facts to be established, and stops.

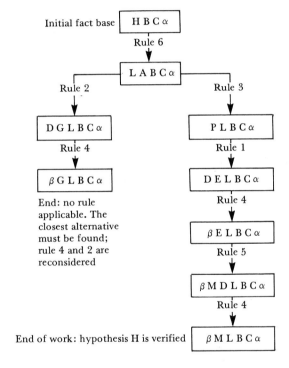

Figure 4.6 *Representation of successive states of the fact base, according to the transformations carried out by the activated rules*

Finally, rules 6 then 3, 1, 4, 5 and 4 allowed the initial hypothesis H to be justified, taking into account the already established facts B and C. During this process, several facts were established: β ,M and L. Fact L was the only one among them to be used for the justification of H.

4.3.4 GENERAL QUALITIES OF PRODUCTION RULE SYSTEMS

Through their principles of organization and operation, production rule systems present the following properties:

- the fact base is accessible, a priori, to all the rules;
- the rules do not call other rules directly;
- communication between rules takes place through the fact base.

These properties make expansion, refinement or transformation (by the expert user) of the set of rules as the experiment is carried out (by the ordinary user), a great deal easier. The rules introduced by different expert users are, in principle, both easily integrated and easily understood, particularly because the mode of rule invocation (pattern matching) allows rules to be created, revised or deleted without too much concern for those that depend on or use them. As a result, a rule can be applied when appropriate, with consideration for the other existing rules, and not only when its author has anticipated its application.

4.4 Examples of production rule systems

First a number of expert systems will be characterized relative to their various areas of application. Then a number of 'expert system shells' or 'general systems' will be mentioned. The dates indicate the period in which they were developed, and for each system one or two representative references are given.

4.4.1 EXPERT SYSTEMS

4.4.1.1 Chemistry

-   'Heuristic DENDRAL' (Stanford University, USA, 1969) (Buchanan, 1969; Buchanan, 1979; Lindsay, 1980)
Finds the formula of an organic body derived from the basic formula and the mass spectogram of the body considered. Production rules, an example of which is given in Figure 4.2, are used for two purposes: first, to represent the knowledge of chemists which allows the presence or absence of chemical radicals to be deduced from the spectograms to the point of determining a number of possible developed formulae; second, to represent the knowledge of chemists which allows the spectogram to be predicted from a developed formula. The second set of rules is applied to formulae produced by the first.
- 'SECS' (Stanford University, USA, 1978) (Todd, 1978)
Helps the chemist in designing plans for the synthesis of complex molecules.
- 'CRYSALIS' (Stanford University, USA, 1979) (Engelmore, 1979)
Finds the structure of proteins from the results of crystallographic analysis.

4.4.1.2 Biology

– 'MOLGEN' (Stanford University, USA, 1977) (Friedland, 1979)
Produces a plan of genetic manipulation for the production of a given
biological entity.

4.4.1.3 Geology

– 'PROSPECTOR' (SRI International, Stanford, USA, 1978)
(Konolige, 1979; Duda, 1981)
Helps geologists to evaluate the importance of a site with a view to mine
prospecting. Note that it contains 1,600 rules, one of which is shown in
Figure 4.2.
– 'LITHO' (Schlumberger-France, Clamart, 1981) (Bonnet, 1982)
Concerned with determining the most plausible possible lithofeatures as
a function of parameters recorded during sample boring (500 rules).
'DIPMETER ADVISOR' is produced for similar tasks by
Schlumberger-USA (1981).
– 'SIMMIAS' (ELF-Aquitaine, Pau, 1981) (Lauriere, 1981; Perrot
1983). Finds migration routes of hydrocarbons from mother-rocks to
reservoir rocks, taking account of the relative geological parameters in the
sub-soil.
– 'SECOFOR' (ELF-Aquitaine, Pau, 1982) (Courteille, 1983)
Intended for diagnostics in drilling accidents (250 rules).
– 'ELFIN' (ELF-Aquitaine, Pau, LSI, Toulouse, 1984) (Martin-
Clouaire, 1984)
Treats same problem as SIMMIAS, mentioned above, but is capable of
approximate reasoning.

4.4.1.4 Mathematics

– 'AM' (Carnegie-Mellon University, USA, 1977) (Davis, 1982)
Discovers mathematical concepts and formulates conjectures concerning
them (500 rules).
– 'LPS' (Keio University, Japan, 1979) (Anzai)
Specializes in the solution of geometric problems.

4.4.1.5 Electricity

– 'SOPHIE' (Stanford University, USA, 1975) (Brown, 1975)
A system to assist in teaching, by computer, detection of faults in elec-
tronic circuits.
– 'PEACE1' and 'PEACE2' (CERT, Toulouse, 1981) (Dincbas, 1983)
Systems for the analysis and synthesis of passive electronic circuits, using
inference engine 'METALOG' (an extension of the PROLOG system).

4.4.1.6 Organization

– The system by R B Wesson (Austin, USA, 1977) (Wesson, 1977)
Using parameters characterizing the environment of a control tower, it produces plans for radio intervention for the various aircraft concerned (and follows the execution of the plans).
– 'MANAGER' (CERFIA, Toulouse, 1983) (Ernst, 1984)
Intended for the real-time management of paramedical personnel in a large hospital.

4.4.1.7 Medicine

– 'MYCIN' (Stanford University, USA, 1974) (Shortliffe, 1976)
This is a system to assist in the diagnosis and treatment of bacterial blood diseases. The production rules (450, of which two examples are given in Figure 4.2), are used to represent the relationships between certain groups of symptoms and the various possible diseases (with about one hundred possible diagnoses). MYCIN attempts to measure the suitability of its diagnosis in each case considered and can dialogue with the doctor it is assisting, in natural language (a sub-set of English, comprising about 900 different words). With the ancillary system TEIRESIAS (Davis, 1982b), MYCIN can explain its reasoning to the consulting doctor, and interactively acquire new knowledge (facts or rules).
– 'CASNET' (Rutgers University, New Brunswick, USA, 1978) (Weiss, 1978)
A system to assist in the treatment of glaucoma.
– 'SAM' (University of Paris VI, 1981) (Gascuel, 1981)
Gives opinions on a pre-recorded medical file, for the treatment of hypertension (200 rules), cerebral vascular accidents (35 rules), and cancers of the larynx (32 rules).
– 'TOUBIB' (IBM-France, Paris, 1982) (Fargues, 1983)
A system for assisted diagnosis for emergency medicine (300 rules, Boat Without Doctor project).
– 'SPHINX' (Aix-Marseille Faculty of Medicine, 1982) (Fieschi, 1982)
Intended for the diagnosis of icterus (400 rules) and for therapeutic prescription in diabetology (about 300 rules).
– 'PROTIS' (Aix-Marseille Faculty of Medicine, 1982) (Soula, 1983)
Intended for the treatment of icterus, hypertension and, recently, diabetes.
– 'DIABETO' (Laboratory of Endocrinology and Laboratory LSI, Toulouse, 1984) (Buisson, 1985)
Intended to assist in the diagnosis and treatment of diabetes (currently 150 rules); the system is accessible to the Minitel videotex network, and will be available to GPs for consultation from their surgeries.

4.4.1.8 Data processing

– 'RI' (DEC, USA, 1980) (McDermott, 1982)
Assists in the design of specific configurations of the VAX-11/780 computer (several thousand rules). A system for a similar use is being developed under the name 'SPEC' by BULL (Louveciennes, France, 1983) (Recoque, 1984).
– 'DART' (IBM, USA, 1981) (Bennet, 1981)
Designed for diagnosis of computer failures (190 rules).

4.4.1.9 Mechanical construction

– 'GARI' (ENSIMAG, Grenoble, 1981) (Descottes, 1981)
Generates manufacturing ranges from geometric and mechanical specifications.
– The system designed by J C Bocquet and S Tichkiewitch (ENSET, Cachan, 1982) (Bocquet, 1982)
Constructs perspective views from industrial plane drawings.

4.4.1.10 Motor vehicle repair

– The system by P P Bonissone (General Electric, USA, 1982) (Bonissone, 1982)
Assists in the diagnosis of motor failures (140 rules).
– 'CAMA' (Politecnico, Milan, Italy, 1982) (Gini, 1982)
Oriented towards automatic repair of complex mechanisms. Unlike other diagnostic systems, such as MYCIN, DART and SECOFOR, which study a state pre-existing the consultation, without modifying it, CAMA admits that the state of the mechanism observed develops during repair. CAMA has been used experimentally in the context of motor vehicle repair (100 rules).

4.4.1.11 Agriculture

– 'PLANT/ds' (University of Illinois, USA, 1982) (Michalski, 1982)
Intended for the diagnosis of diseases in the soya plant. In addition to the rules supplied by experts, it uses automatic rules derived by generalizing the cases.

4.4.2 GENERAL SYSTEMS (SHELLS)

When only the following are predefined in a production rule system:

– the language for writing the rule;
– the representation structures (specific forms for the rule base and fact base);

- the inference engine;
   without a particular set of rules being considered, then the system is said to be a 'general system' or 'shell'

A number of general systems are described below:
- 'PAS-II' (Carnegie-Mellon University, USA, 1975) (Waterman, 1975)
Constructed with the intention of evaluating the extent to which production systems are suited to forms of training. Several sets of rules were defined to illustrate, for example, the solution of 'intelligence tests' of the type involving the continuation of numerical or alphabetical sequences.
   'EMYCIN' (Stanford University, USA, 1974) (Melle, 1979)
This is 'shell' MYCIN, and has been applied to areas of medicine other than that of bacterial blood diseases, and has given rise to other expert systems, such as 'PUFF' (diagnosis of pulmonary illnesses, 60 rules) (Kunz, 1978) and 'HEADMED' (psycho-pharmacology, 275 rules) (Helser, 1978). It has also been applied to problems of mechanical design: 'SACON' (160 rules) (Bennett, 1979), and to the diagnosis of computer failures and drilling accidents (see 'DART' and 'SECOFOR', mentioned above).
- 'PROLOG' (University of Marseille, 1975) (Roussel, 1975)
Represents facts and rules in the form of specific expressions of first order predicate logic called 'Horn clauses'. The inference engine is a theorem demonstrator which uses the inference rule, by Robinson, called the 'resolution principle', according to a strategy from the 'linear strategies' family. It was stated above that an extension of PROLOG, called METALOG, was used as the inference engine for the expert systems PEACE1 AND PEACE2.
- 'OPS' (Carnegie-Mellon University, USA, 1977) (Forgy, 1980)
This is a general experimental system, and constitutes a development of 'PS', which was successfully used to rewrite, in production rule system form, several well-known programs, including 'STUDENT' (Bobrow, 1964), 'EPAM' (Feigenbaum, 1964), 'GPS' (Ernst; Newell, 1969) and 'SHRDLU' (Winograd, 1972). The R1 system mentioned above results from a specialization of the version 'OPS5' of OPS.
- 'NOAH' (SRI, Stanford, USA, 1977) (Sacerdoti, 1977)
Represents the decision function of a robot: a human operator executes the physical tasks of assembly and dismantling with advice from the robot. NOAH generates plans with progressive degrees of detail, according to the demands of the 'apprentice'. The plans may include parallel branches and their execution is supervised by NOAH. It has been applied to examples of electromechanical parts assembly.
- 'TROPIC' (ENSIMAG, Grenoble, 1977) (Latombe, 1979)
Oriented towards computer-assisted design, it has been applied to the design of electrical transformers (350 rules).

– 'ARS' (MIT, USA, 1979) (Stallman, 1979)
This was completed as an expert system for the analysis of electrical circuits ('EL' system), for the demonstration of plane geometric theorems and for the modelling of management in an agricultural business.
– 'ARGOS-II' Laboratory LSI, Toulouse, 1980) (Farreny, 1980)
Oriented towards the control of third generation robots. It comprises a generator for plans of action and a monitor for execution of the plans. Experiments have been carried out using it in the context of parts assembly in flexible workshops.
– The 'SAM' (1981), 'SPHINX' (1982), 'PROTIS' (1982) and 'CAMA' (1982) systems, presented above as expert systems (to illustrate applications in medicine and motor vehicle repair) are also general systems.
– 'SNARK' (University of Paris VI, 1982) (Lauriere, 1982)
This was used experimentally, particularly for the calculation of function primitives (250 rules) and in the field of archaeology (100 rules). There are several versions, the first of which derive from the SIMMIAS inference engine (see above).
– 'TANGO' (Laboratory LRI, Orsay, 1982) (Cordier, 1982)
Oriented towards computer-assisted education.
– 'SASCO' (Laboratory CERFIA, Toulouse, 1982) (Dalle, 1981)
Oriented towards scene analysis.

4.4.3 GENERAL COMMENT

In some cases, the areas of application of the systems presented above do not have the characteristics mentioned in Section 4.2.1. In the analysis or synthesis of electrical circuits, the design of electric transformers, and the transformation of drawings, therefore, it is possible to model the activities of human experts with precision. None the less, the use of rule systems (on the one hand separating the inference engine and the expert knowledge, and on the other facilitating the independent expression of this expert knowledge) lends itself to heuristic experimentation or substitution strategies.

4.5 Differentiation of production rule systems

Five criteria for differentiation between systems are adopted here.

4.5.1 STRATEGIES FOR CHAINING PRODUCTION RULES

NB: The concepts of forward chaining and backward chaining are often the subject of controversy. The definitions given here are those adopted by the majority of authors. Producing new facts from those already possessed is a question of 'inferring' new facts. There are two main categories of inference, depending on the way in which the inferred and starting facts are interpreted.

In the first, the inferred facts are 'logical consequences' of those from which they are inferred; that is, the starting point is that of the fact-axioms, interpreted as true in the area of application, whereas the inferred facts are considered as true once the inference has been carried out; then the set of true facts (old and new) obtained is used to infer new facts, considered in their turn as true, and so on. This method of proceeding is known as forward reasoning, or data oriented reasoning.

In the second, the facts from which inferences are made are interpreted as hypotheses, which must be established as true in the area of application; the inference is interpreted as follows: if the facts inferred are recognized as true, either directly (fact-axioms) or by other inferences, then the facts from which the inferences are made are considered to be true. This method of proceeding is known as backward reasoning, or goal oriented reasoning.

4.5.1.1 Forward chaining

This idea corresponds to the first inference mode mentioned above. A production rule system operates with pure 'forward chaining' when the facts in the fact base, to which the conditions of the rules apply, represent information which is of direct significance in the area of expertise, and the truth value of which has already been established. The rules are called 'forward rules'.

Among the examples in Figure 4.3, forward chaining is used for the second rule taken from MYCIN, and for the rules taken from heuristic DENDRAL and PROSPECTOR.

Note that when handling this type of rule, the MYCIN, DENDRAL and PROSPECTOR engines know that the conditions of the rules are in the 'if' part of the representations suppied by the rule compilers. So if the facts: 'the organism is a bacteroid' and 'the site of the culture was sterile' are established (which is witnessed by the presence of those expressions in the fact memory), the MYCIN engine can record in the fact memory: 'the therapy recommended should be chosen from the following: chloramphenicol, climdamycin, tetracyclin, linomycin and gentamycin'.

4.5.1.2 Backward chaining

A production rule system is said to function with pure backward chaining when certain facts in the fact base are considered as still to be established or evaluated (they are often called 'problems'), and the conditions of the rules apply solely to such problems (backward rules).

The first rule taken from MYCIN, shown in Figure 4.3, is processed by backward chaining (MYCIN uses two classes of rule, one using backward chaining and the other using forward chaining).

Note that when handling a rule of this type, the MYCIN engine knows that the conditions of the rule are described in the 'then' part of the representation provided by the rule compiler. It must, therefore, be established that: 'the organism is a psuedomonas aeruginosa', that is, if such a 'problem' exists in the fact base, it will be able to execute the rule, or record three new facts to be established (three 'problems') in place of the previous one, in this case: 'the site of the culture is the blood', 'the organism has negative gram' and 'the organism is wand shaped'.

4.5.1.3 *Other chaining*

Other strategies for chaining, with forward chaining and backward chaining can be superimposed on the standard scanning strategies: 'in breadth', 'in depth', 'ordered search', etc.

In the case of MYCIN, backward chaining is combined with depth-first scanning: the problems introduced most recently, as sub-problems of a previous problem, are given priority consideration. This is known as 'necessity chaining'.

Some production rule systems operate with 'mixed chaining'; in this case, certain facts in the base are considered as having to be established (these are 'problems'), others are considered as established (these are facts proper). The conditions of the rules can apply to facts of one or the other sort, simultaneously.

The microsystem of rules analysed in Section 4.3.3 (above), is governed by a strategy of this sort. This is also the case with 'IPS' (Rychener, 1978), which is a derivative of OPS and ARGOS-II.

For systems that use on the one hand forward rules, and on the other backward rules, the term 'bidirectional chaining' is used, rather than 'mixed chaining', used above.

4.5.2 INVOKING RULES AND FACTS BY PATTERN MATCHING

Most of the rules presented so far use a simple method of pattern matching: the compatibility between a rule filter and a fact (whether already established or not) is modelled according to the identity relationship: the expression of a fact in the template is the same as that of the fact in the fact base.

Many rule systems use richer compatibility models. The rule presented in Figure 4.7, written in the language of the general system ARGOS-II, includes 'pattern-matching variables' and 'pattern-matching operators'.

The words in capital letters are specific to the vocabulary of the general system ARGOS-II, whereas the words in lower case letters concern a

[ACTIVATOR]
$$(((\text{ take } >x \text{ near } >y)$$
$$(<x \text{ position } >q1) (<y \text{ position } >q2))$$

$$((\text{RECORD (PLAN (roll } (<q1))$$
$$(\text{grasp}(<x))$$
$$(\text{roll } (<q2))$$
$$(\text{release}))$$
$$\text{UPDATE (MODIFY}$$
$$((<x *)$$
$$(\text{position } <q2))))))))$$
[BODY]

Figure 4.7   *A rule from ARGOS-II. The general form is [ACTIVATOR] [BODY]*

particular application. The notation $>x$, $>y$, $>q1$, $>q2$, $<x$, $<y$, $<q1$ and $<q2$ represent 'pattern matching variables'. The rule is in the form:

$$([\text{ACTIVATOR}] \ [\text{BODY}])$$

The [ACTIVATOR] is a list of templates, the compatibility of which must be verified with the current situation, as described in the fact base. It is a convention that the first filter in this list will apply to a part of the fact base called the 'memory of resolution' (or MR), which assembles all the relevant problems. Here, this filter is:

$$F = (\text{take } >x \text{ near } >y)$$

A possible example of this problem is:

$$P = (\text{take box5 near block2})$$

It is agreed that the other filters possibly concern part of the fact base called the 'memory of facts in planning' (or MFP). The MFP stores the information established as true at the current stage of processing carried out by ARGOS-II. The following is an example of such information:

$$(\text{box5 position14})$$

$$(\text{block2 position8})$$

The prefix $>$, in $>x$ indicates that the variable x is in a situation of 'capture'. If the previous filter F is applied to the problem P, it can be seen that F and P are compatible term for term: the homologous terms in row 1 and 3 are the same, the term $>$x 'captures' the homologous term box5, and the term $>$y captures the homologous term block2.

The prefix $<$ in $<$x orders the 'restoration' of the value just captured by the variable x. After application of F to P, everything takes place as if the second filter had become:

(box5 position $>$q1).

The templates may include 'pattern-matching operators', for example, the operators ? and *. The operator ? is compatible with any atomic term (such as: block2 or box5) or any list of terms, for example:

(block4 (on block2) free)

The operator * is compatible with any finite sequence, possibly empty, of terms; for example:

block4 (on block2) free

In ARGOS-II and other systems, there are also 'pattern-matching functions' that provide the filters, and therefore the knowledge-writing language, with a powerful facility for expression.

4.5.3 MONOTONY OR NON-MONOTONY OF KNOWLEDGE

If the rule represented in Figure 4.7 is activated, stages of the plan such as: (roll (14)), (grasp (box5)), (roll (8)) and (release), will be added to the partial plan already formed by the rules previously activated. In order to follow the planning, the effects associated with these new stages must be represented. The activation of this rule will bring about the recording in the MFP memory of a fact, such as:

(box5 position 8)

None the less, in the case of backwards movement in the chaining of the rules, as seen in the example illustrated in Figure 4.6, the facts memorized can be questioned again (deleted). In systems that allow this deletion of facts (see rules), the knowledge - or the system - is said not to be 'monotonic'. Often, in existing diagnostic systems, the knowledge processed is monotonic; when the truth value of information is established, it does not change again. MYCIN is a monotonic system; CAMA is not. In most systems intended to generate plans of action, knowledge is not monotonic.

4.5.4 METHODS FOR THE RESOLUTION OF CONFLICTS

This stage of the basic cycle for the inference engines (see Figure 4.4) often consists of activating a rule, chosen arbitrarily from the 'set of conflicts' (called R3 in Figure 4.4), with the possibility of later backward scanning to activate another rule taken from the conflict set. Other systems may use a heuristic function representing the importance of the conflict rules, to determine the rule or rules to be activated. Systems like MYCIN execute all the rules of the conflict set in each cycle; generally, for MYCIN, the order of activation of the rules is unimportant, but not always.

4.5.5 IMPRECISE OR UNCERTAIN KNOWLEDGE; APPROXIMATE REASONING

In many areas of application of expert system methodology, the knowledge processed or inferred is imprecise or uncertain. Among the expert systems that use such knowledge (with various models, generally empirical) are: MYCIN, PROSPECTOR, PUFF, HEADMED, DART, SECOFOR, GARI, LITHO, SPHINX, PROTIS, PLANT/ds, ELFIN, DIABETO and MANAGER. In MYCIN, for example, 'factors of certainty' are associated with each fact. These factors are numbers of interval $[-1,1]$: 1 when a fact is absolutely certain, -1 when the negation of this fact is absolutely certain, 0 in cases of absolute uncertainty. These numbers are either provided by the doctor-user of MYCIN, or derived by application of the rules. An 'attentuation coefficient' is associated with each rule, and is representative of the confidence invested in each rule, between 0 and 1. Figure 4.8 is a symbolic representation of a rule from MYCIN.

Symbolic text of the rule:
      IF F1 AND F2 THEN (0.8) F3
Equivalent schema:

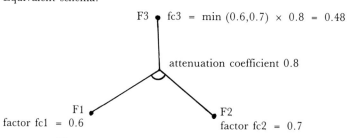

Figure 4.8 *A MYCIN-type rule and its execution*

The factor of certainty of F3 is calculated as the minimum of those of F1 and F2 multiplied by the attenuation coefficient of the rule.

Let it be supposed that two rules from MYCIN (see Figure 4.9) are each capable of concluding with regard to fact F3. To establish the factor

Two rules:

IF F'1 and F'2 THEN F3
IF F"1 AND F"2 THEN F3
Equivalent schema:

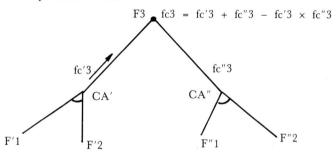

Figure 4.9 *Two MYCIN rules leading to F3*

of certainty of F3, taking into account the two rules, MYCIN will proceed as follows:

– each rule will be applied separately producing the partial factors of certainty fc'3 and fc"3; let these two numbers be positive;

– fc'3 and fc"3 are combined to establish the definitive factor of certainty according to the formula:

$$fc3 = fc'3 + fc"3 - fc'3 \times fc"3$$

Note: fc3 will be, like fc'3 and fc"3, between 0 and 1.

Chapter 5

Introduction to search techniques

5.1 Introduction

Inference and problem solving systems (PSS) may be broken down into
three components:

1. a data base describing the specific area of the problem to be solved
   and specifying the initial situation as well as the objective to be
   attained;
2. a set of decision rules which are operators for situation transformation (change, breakdown);
3. a control procedure that guides the solution and specifies at each
   stage what must be done next.

The various characteristics of the first two components (problems of
representation, types of rule, unification, validation and transformation
of state, etc) have been discussed. This chapter will concern itself with the
methodological study of PSSs, and specifically with the analysis of their
third component.

The procedures and methods of control that allow the solution of a
problem to be organized and guide the search for the answer can generally
be grouped under the title 'heuristic search algorithms'. This is one of the
areas of AI that has been thoroughly studied and formalized, with abun-
dant literature and a good base of methods for mathematical analysis.
Paradoxically, the introduction of these methods into existing PSSs, as an
effective control tool is still very limited. These systems often have rather
diffuse control structures, and rudimentary and inefficient solution
strategies. This is due to the fact that control algorithms are not currently
widely known, except in the context of simple applications, and their
practical use outside these cases still raises many problems, demands and
certain conditions difficult to fulfil.

5.2 Formulation of the problem

The problems presented by the control of a PSS are formulated in terms
of searching within a discrete space. For a control procedure, the first two
components of a PSS (beyond the difficulties underlined in Chapter 2, of
finding a suitable form of representation) can be reduced to the following
simple conceptual framework:

- a discrete set U, finite or infinite, which is the problem representation space;
- a particular element $u_0 \epsilon U$, which is the initial state of the problem;
- a sub-set $T \subseteq U$ of terminal states (objectives to be attained);
- a set of state transformation rules, each one considered as a partial application (defined or valid in certain states only) of U in itself, or in P(U). It is assumed that for each state $u \epsilon U$, there is a corresponding finite sub-set of valid rules in u, no pair of these rules resulting in two identical transformations from u.

Depending on whether each of these rules is a biunivocal or multivocal application (that is, leads to a single state v, or a sub-set $v1, \ldots, vn \; n > 1$ state corresponding to u) the problem of control comes down to search in a graph or in a hypergraph. These are two representations by graph of the state space (with the rules as change of state operators), or by an AND/OR graph of the problem space (the rules correspond to problem decomposition operators).

In both cases, the aim is to progress from the initial stage u_0 to a terminal state or sub-set of states. For a graph, a solution will consist of a linear sequence of rules corresponding to a line on the graph leading from u_0 to a state $w \epsilon T$. In the case of a hypergraph, the solution will be a slightly more complex rule structure (a tree or a sub-graph without loops), which always starts from u_0 and ends at the states of T.

Generally, the set U and its sub-set T are not known explicitly. Using u_0 and the set of rules, U will be defined as the set of all the states attainable from u_0 by any number of applications of rules (image of u_0 by transitive closure of the set of rules), and T will be characterized by a particular property valid only for the terminal states.

A search procedure will therefore have to clarify (the terms 'explore' and 'create' are also used) a sub-set of states of U necessary to attain a solution, starting from u_0. This is basically achieved through the operation of development of a state: developing the state u consists of determining all the valid rules in u, and explicitly creating all the image states of u by these rules, called *successor states* of u. One or more of these states may already have been generated as successors to other states developed before u. Depending on the case, the search procedure may or may not have the means of recognizing them as such. In the latter situation, the search will be said to be *redundant*: the same state could be generated as many times as there are ways of attaining it from u_0, which would give rise to particular difficulties, discussed below in detail. It will also be seen that certain search algorithms carry out partial development of states, that is, they generate only one, or an incomplete sub-set of successors; the same state can, therefore, be developed several times.

A search algorithm basically works with successive developments of states, which continue until the sub-set of the states created contains a solution. The basic difficulty that this type of procedure must solve at each stage relates to the selection and choice, from the set of known states suitable for development, of the one that actually will be developed. This choice corresponds directly to what was referred to above as the 'resolution of conflict' in a PSS.

5.3 Convergence

If the search problem formulated above admits a solution, it is rare for there to be only one. In many applications, any solution can be admitted. The property required of a search procedure will then be convergence, in the particular sense described below: this procedure should provide, at the end of a finite period, a solution if one exists; if not, in the case of a finite space U, it should indicate the absence of any solution. It is not expected to stop the procedure for search in an infinite space not containing any solution. Note the similarity between this definition and that of semi-decidability in first order predicate logic (if a logical expression is valid then a demonstration of the corresponding theorem can be found at the end of a finite period of time, but if it is invalid, there is not algorithm that can establish this is all cases). The difference results from the fact that decidability is an intrinsic property of a problem (which may or may not be decidable), whereas the aim here is to characterise a research procedure. The semi-decidability of the problem is, of course, a necessary condition but is not sufficient for the convergence of the search procedure applied to it.

Note that the rules of a PSS (in fact, schemas of rules) are of necessity finite in number. Because of the quantified variables, a rule can have an infinite number of instances, but the data associated with a state u are of finite number, and therefore the number of instances of valid rules in u is also finite.

5.4 Admissability

In other applications, stricter demands must be made, and convergence alone is not enough: an elementary cost will be linked to the instance of each rule, and by using a certain criterion, an overall cost will be associated with any solution. For problems of control of PSSs, only the additive criteria and the positive or nil elementary costs will be considered. The search is aimed at obtaining a good solution, and preferably the optimal one. Even if the application considered does not impose any constraint of cost and all the solutions appear to be of equal merit, if the convergence of the research is to be guaranteed, it is often advisable to introduce costs and simple criteria and to demand an optimal solution.

In either of the above cases, the desirable characteristic for a search algorithm will be admissibility, that is, being a procedure that converges towards the optimum, if a solution exists.

5.5 Complexity

The difficulty with the problem, both in obtaining any solution and in reaching an optimal solution, is very often such that any method of systematic or quasi-systematic search will tend to end in failure. The dimension of the sub-space of U, explored by such methods, is prohibitive: each stage of the search generates a large number of alternatives, leading very rapidly to a combinatory explosion. To be in any way capable of containing this explosion, the research algorithm must have a low complexity, that is, it must explore only a small number of alternatives. There are two concepts involved here. The more important is qualitative: beyond a certain threshold of complexity an algorithm is often unusable, even if it has all the desired theoretical properties. Beyond this threshold, a concept of qualitives intervenes. Two types of cost can be associated with a PSS:

1. the cost of applying a solution (for example the cost in terms of energy or the time of execution of a plan by a robot), which corresponds to the property of admissibility introduced above;
2. the cost of searching (in calculation time) for this solution, which can be divided between:
   - the cost of development of states (mainly those due to the pattern-matching and rule instantiation operations);
   - the costs of resolution of conflicts, linked directly to the execution of the control procedure.

The complexity of the search algorithm corresponds to the costs mentioned in 2. In many applications, these are far greater than the cost of type 1. This is very often the case in robotics, when the characteristics of task variability and robot flexibility mean that the solution of a given problem can only be used once or a limited number of times.

5.6 Heuristics

The three key concepts of convergence, admissibility and complexity lead quite naturally to that of heuristics, and allow it to be introduced (in this particular context) with a preliminary definition: a heuristic is any means of diminishing the complexity of a search algorithm (which will then be referred to as a heuristic search algorithm, if it uses such a method), by reducing the alternatives and/or restricting their choice.

A number of nuances (on which authors are far from being agreed) should, however, be introduced. The main ones apply to the ad hoc, imprecise and non-infallible characteristics of this method for reducing complexity.

A heuristic uses information specific to the problem in hand. It will generally be pertinent and effective only for that particular problem, and cannot be immediately generalized to other problems. It does not, therefore, constitute a means of reducing complexity in a methodological way, and is not an inherent part of the search method: the same control procedure can use different heuristics, depending on the problem. Some authors draw a distinction by referring to algorithms that only differ formally by the heuristic properties they use, by different names (algorithms A^* and A for example). They are distinguished here only by the base of organization and research strategies applied.

General techniques for the development of heuristics have, however, been categorized for large classes of problem (Gaschnig, 1979); this is a kind of 'meta-heuristics' that must be instanced for a specific problem. Information specific to the problem considered is not, in fact, used by a heuristic on the basis of a strict and precise formalization. It is based more on unformalized knowledge, on the 'rules of the art' and the experience of the person describing the problem. It should be noted that if a general PSS is called upon, it is probably because there is no specific method available, and/or the problem is hard to represent. For the resolution of a well-characterised mathematical problem of low complexity (a linear equation represent, for example), it would be preferable to use a specific algorithm rather than general heuristic search techniques.

The third aspect is the most controversial. For some authors, the heuristic method is synonymous with an absence of guarantees for the eventual solution of the problem, and is far from being an infallible technique; other authors insist, however, on the necessity of retaining the properties of convergence and admissibility, whilst reducing complexity. The former correctly state that, for search problems, complexity is not a preoccupation of a quantitative type (obtaining a slightly faster algorithm), but primarily qualitative: the solution of a practical problem can only be achieved with a search procedure of very low complexity. The reduction in complexity is obtained by the elimination, at each stage, of the largest possible number of alternatives. To demand that none of the alternatives eliminated should reduce access to the solution (or to the best solution) could only impoverish the possibilities for reduction in complexity.

These authors feel it preferable to have a probable but unguaranteed solution to the problem, rather than a theoretical guarantee at the cost of increased complexity in finding a solution (or the optimum), and therefore little practical chance of reaching it. This is particularly the opinion of H.A. Simon, who compares it with a mental solution process:

'Research progress in some areas of problem solving has been slowed down by an excessive preoccupation with the completeness of selection rules (ie, the guarantee that they will not eliminate all solution paths if one or more exist)...there is no reason to suppose that the problem solving process used by creative mathematicians, or other professional human problem solvers, possess any completeness properties (even when they are solving problems in decidable domains). That being the case, I see no reason for imposing such restriction on artificial intelligence systems. Probably the best attitude is to regard questions of heuristic as more or less orthogonal to the question of its heuristic power.' (Simon, 1977).

A synthesis of these two positions is now becoming possible, as concerns the property of admissibility, because of the development of quasi-admissible systems: this allows the user to find a compromise between the guarantee of a degree of optimality (difference from the optimum) and a decreased complexity (Pearl, 1982; Ghallab, 1983). A similar synthesis in the convergence property is far more difficult to produce: it requires models of probability, convergence and of the complexity of search procedures as a function of various heuristics. Some approaches are starting to be used in simple cases (Karp, 1983).

5.7 Strategies for search organization

As mentioned above, the basic difficulty solved by a search algorithm concerns the stage of choice (resolution of conflict) between the set of known states suitable for development, to find the best one. This choice is determined primarily by the organization strategy for the search that uses the algorithm, and second by the heuristic (or heuristics) it applies. With certain variations, the main known strategies operate by combining one of the two types of state development and one of the three types of organization of the following alternatives.
At each stage, the chosen state will be:

(a) completely developed: all its successors will be generated, and all the alternatives arising from this stage and those preceding are completely listed for participation in the following choice;

(b) partly developed: in general only the first successor is generated; it is noted for future searching that this stage has not been entirely explored, and the new state or states are added to the known alternatives.

The choice of the state to be developed is made relative to the order in which the alternatives are encountered, or else, if a cost criterion is considered, relative to an evaluation of the cost of the potential solution associated with each state encountered. The set of alternatives is therefore organized into a stack, with three basic types of organization possible:

1. 'last in first out' (LIFO): the search is continued on the last alternative in the date found;
2. 'first in first out' (FIFO): the first alternative in the date generated is developed from among the set of alternatives;
3. ordered search (organization in order of increasing cost): the state chosen will be the one for which the evaluation of cost function is minimal.

Algorithms using type (a) strategies are most commonly described in literature on the subject; but those encountered in the PSSs are more often based on strategies of type (b). This is due to the very long calculation time required, in existing systems, for the complete development of a state. Strategies of type 1 represent a mode of 'depth-first search' which leads to a successor to the state just developed being pursued. They are generally very easy to implement.

Type 2 strategies are generally only encountered in the formulation 2(a). They correspond, in this case, to a broad search: all the successors of a state must be developed before one of *their* successors can be. These strategies are less effective because of their complexity and more arduous to apply than those mentioned above.

For the purposes of this discussion, however, the type 3 strategies are of most interest. They alone allow the properties of convergence and admissibility to be admitted in certain situations (redundant research, for example). In addition, these strategies have been demonstrated as performing better than the others in many classes of problem, because they are in a position to use heuristic information far more efficiently.

5.7.1 CHOICE OF STRATEGY

The various strategies introduced only restrict the choice stage to a subset of alternatives. They do not completely define the state that will be chosen; and with a greater or lesser degree of flexibility, they leave space for the use of heuristic information. Strategies 1 and 2 do not specify the order in which the newly developed state successors should be stored in the stack. Any information specific to the problem will be used to introduce an order of preference between these successors: one may be preferred to another because it is thought it will lead to a solution more quickly, or to a better solution in terms of cost, or that it combines both advantages.

In the case of breadth-first search, this information is hardly used at all, because all the successors must be developed (in the order indicated by the heuristic) before any further progress can be made: the heuristic will be more effective if variants of strategy 2, such as 'pruning' of certain successors, are introduced.

The order of preference of the successors is, however, essential for depth-first search: in the ideal situation where the heuristic information is perfect, a solution could be reached by developing only those states that feature in this solution. Outside of this case (highly improbable, in practice), strategy 1 has the drawback of limiting the heuristic information to a partial order between successors in a single state, and does not allow a comparison between any two states suitable for development to be made.

Strategy 3 overcomes this inconvenience because it defines a complete order of all the existing alternatives, by intermediary of a cost function. The heuristic information intervenes specifically in the estimation of the cost associated with a given moment in the state.

This cost will include several components reflecting what has been spent to reach a state, in a certain way, and what remains to be spent to reach a terminal state from its current state. The first of these components will not be an estimate, and can be calculated precisely as a function of the elementary costs of the rules which allowed a state u generated by the search to be reached from u_0: these rules correspond to a partial solution (but not necessarily the best for reaching u), with which a cost is associated. The second component is an estimate of the cost of the best solution between u and one or more terminal states. A process of balancing (indicating various factors, such as the degree of confidence in the heuristic estimate) will intervene between these two components. A third component, estimating the number of stages necessary to reach a solution starting from u (a number reflecting the remaining complexity), could also intervene, with a certain amount of balancing, in the cost function ordering the search. The type 3 strategies seem to be the richest, and will tend to be preferred over the others.

Note that in all the cases considered above, the heuristic information is used to define a relationship of order in one part of the representation space; this could be obtained by the intermediary of a partial application of U to a totally ordered set. Because only criteria of additive cost are being introduced, and for reasons of convenience, all heuristics will henceforth be considered as applications of U in $\mathbb{R}^+$ (the set of positive or nil real numbers).

5.8 Further discussion

As stated above, there is no fundamental distinction between search in a graph and in a hypergraph. A unified development of the principles and strategies applied by these two types of search will continue to be adopted in the rest of the text. For reasons of clarity and ease of reading, however, they will be discussed in two distinct chapters, with algorithmic details being presented for search in a hypergraph as an extension of search in a graph.

In each of these sub-chapters, a set of algorithms will be described and analysed as a function of their strategy, the functions of the heuristics they use, the redundant or non-redundant nature of the search, and the structure and properties specific to the representation space. Their properties of convergence, admissibility and complexity will be discussed (the proofs of these properties are often long, and will only be given as illustrations), as will the practical difficulties involved in their implementation. In each case, the most general algorithm of that particular class will be given, with mention of how restrictive hypotheses (such as the absence of cost criteria, or redundant search) affect its properties. Simple examples will be used to illustrate the behaviour of these algorithms.

5.9 Notes

1. Many problems of discrete optimization can be formulated in terms of PSSs, and the algorithms for their solution designed as control procedures. In addition, techniques for heuristic control may be similar, on more than one level, to the techniques for combinatory optimization developed in operational research. Readers familiar with this domain will find many analogies, in particular with the procedures for progressive separation and evaluation (Branch and Bound). For formal comparisons, the reader is referred to Ghallab (1982) or Kumar (1983).

2. In most texts on AI, the expression 'heuristic search' is also taken to cover all the techniques of development and exploration of game graphs: the algorithms $\alpha\beta$, SSS^*, or B^* for example (Knuth, 1975; Stockman, 1979; Berliner, 1979). These techniques will not be discussed here for the following reasons:

- they do not enter into the framework of the PSS control problem, but are more concerned with the solution to the problem: in a given situation of a game with two adversaries where each plays in turn with a view to attaining a conflicting objective state (one which cannot be attained by both), the aim is to find out what will be the best following move for one of them to play, whatever the response of the adversary and whatever happens in the rest of the game.
- the application of this problem to robotics, involving as it does the concept of active adversity in systematic opposition to the achievement of the objectives assigned to a robot, and requiring planning as a function of this adversity, is only significant as a development tool for search programs.

Chapter 6

Heuristic graph searching

In this chapter, the following will be considered:

—algorithms involving complete developments (strategy a);
—algorithms involving partial developments (strategy b);
—algorithms involving redundant search;
—ε-admissible algorithms.

6.1   General statement of the problem

Let U be the finite or infinite representation space of a PSS, each rule of
which is a state change operator; $u_0 \varepsilon U$ is the initial state of the problem,
and $T \subset U$ is the sub-set of terminal states.

Consider a pair of states (u, v), where there exists a valid rule in u
which, applied to this state, leads the system to v. A positive or nil real
number is associated with the couple $k(u, v)$, and reflects the cost of the
change of state from u to v (that is, the cost of application of the corresponding rule).

The problem consists of determining a sequence, if it exists, of states
$(u_0, u_1, u_2, \ldots, u_r)$ such that:

1. $u_r \in T$;

2. for any i, $1 \leqslant i \leqslant r$, there is a rule which allows the system to be led
from state u_{i-1} to state u_i;

3. the sum of the costs $\Sigma_1^r k(u_{i-1}, u_i)$ is minimal over all the sequences
verifying 1. and 2.

This problem is equivalent to that of searching a route of minimal cost
in a simple, oriented graph $G = (U, s)$. G is defined implicitly by the value
of $u_0 \varepsilon U$ and by the successor relationship s. This relationship expresses
the rules of the PSS: $v \varepsilon s(u)$ (that is, G comprises an arc from u to v, of
cost $k(u, v)$) if, and only if, there is a rule transforming state u into v.

The following notation is used: $s(u) : \{v_1, \ldots, v_k r\}$ the sub-set of successor states of u (also known as sons of u); $\hat{s}(u)$: the sub-set of all the
descendents of u (transitive closure of s); $s^{-1}(u)$: the sub-set of the state
of which u is the successor (also known as the fathers of u); $\hat{s}^{-1}(u)$: the
sub-set of all the ascendents of u. By hypothesis, $\forall \sim \in \mu$, the number

$|s(u)|$ of sons is finite. By definition, the cost of a route in G is the sum of the costs of its arc, and the following is established: $k^*(u, v)$: minimum of the cost of routes from u to v if there exists one between these two states; if not, the convention is $k^*(u, v) = \infty$. The three applications g^*, h^* and f^* of U in R^+ are also defined:

$-g^*(u) = k^*(u_0, u)$: minimum of cost for routes from u_0 to u;

$-k^*(u) = \min\{k^*(u, v) \mid v \in T\}$: minimum of cost for routes from u to any terminal state;

$-f^*(u) = g^*(u) + h^*(u)$: minimum of cost for routes passing through u and leading from h_0 to a terminal state.

Note that $g^*(u)$, $h^*(u)$ and $f^*(u)$ are infinite by convention if the corresponding routes do not exist, and that $f^*(u_0) = h^*(u_0)$ corresponds to the cost of an optimal route solving the previous problem.

Except in a very few cases, none of the three applications f^*, g^* or h^* is known a priori. To help in solving the problem in hand, heuristic information is used in the form of an application h, of U in R^+: $h(u)$ is an estimate of the cost $h^*(u)$. It is stated that $h^*(u)$ corresponds to the perfect information on the position of u relative to the objective T and that $h(u)$ is an approximation of it.

The quality of this heuristic estimator h is measured by the difference $[h(u) - h^*(u)]$, and is validated on the basis of one or more of the following properties:

1. h is an almost perfect heuristic if, and only if, it defines, in U, a relationship of identical order to that defined by h^*; that is, $\forall u, v \in U: h(u) < h(v) \Leftrightarrow h^*(u) < h^*(v)$;

2. h is a consistent heuristic if, and only if, $\forall u, v$ such that there exists a route from u to v: $h(u) - h(v) \leqslant k^*(u, v)$;

3. h is a monotonic heuristic if, and only if, $\forall u, v \varepsilon s(u): h(u) - h(v) \leqslant k(u, v)$;

4. h is a reducing heuristic if, and only if, $\forall u: h(u) \leqslant h^*(u)$;

5. h is a coinciding heuristic if, and only if, $\forall u \in T: h(u) = 0$.

The first property is extremely strong; it can guarantee as effective a search as one guided by perfect information. It is unlikely that an almost perfect heuristic could be found for a practical problem.

Contrary to appearances (and to what has been written in some literature on the subject), the two properties of consistence and monotonicity are strictly equivalent. Only monotonicity will be discussed in the following.

The property of reduction is also easy to establish, but does not always guarantee a good heuristic (in the sense of reduction of complexity).

The property of coincidence assumes the existence of the faculty of recognizing and testing for terminality of a state, which will later be accepted.

To appreciate the importance of a state u in the solution of a problem, the heuristic search algorithms will also need an estimate of $g^*(u)$. Since for any state u generated explicitly by the research, one or more routes from u_0 to u are explicitly known, and the cost of the best of these routes will be taken as the estimate of $g^*(u)$. The following notation is used: $g(u)$: minimum of the cost of routes from u_0 to u, explicitly known at a given moment in the search; $f(u)$: $g(u) + h(u)$.

Notes:
—for any u such that $g(u)$ is defined, there is $g(u) \geqslant g^*(u)$;
—g is not an application of U in R^+. $g(u)$ is an algorithmic variable associated with the state u and updated gradually as the new routes from u_0 to u are known. The same applies for f, but g and f can also be seen as applications of $U \times J$ in R^+, with J as the set of states of the search algorithm;
—in certain applications, it may be of interest to make the heuristic h depend not only on the state u, but also on the current state of the research at the moment when h is evaluated. This example will not be considered again.

6.2 Complete development algorithms

6.2.1 SEARCH ORDERED BY THE EVALUATION OF COST f: THE A* ALGORITHM

This algorithm appears with many variations throughout the relevant literature (Hart 1968, 1972; Martelli 1977; Pohl 1977). It will be described here in a simple form first, and then in relation to various extensions and specific examples. A* partitions the set of explicitly generated states (the only ones known) into two sub-sets:
—P: the set of states suitable for development or redevelopment, called pending states (or 'open states' in some literature);
—Q: the set of states already developed, and which are not candidates for development.

P is the set of alternatives from which the algorithm must choose the next state to develop. This state is totally ordered (stack structure), in order of increasing values of f, then in order of decreasing values of g for states with the same f, and finally with priority for the terminal states in cases of equality in f and g simultaneously. Any new state established or re-established as pending is stored in P (without duplication, of course), in the above order. At any time, $\hat{u}$ will designate the first pending state (at the top of the stack).

For any state u of P or Q, the algorithms will retain only one route from u_0 to u, by associating with u a pointer father (u) to the state to which u is successor on this route. The notation is: route (u) = u_0, . . . , father (father(u)), father(u), u) the corresponding route.

6.2.1.1   Algorithm A*

Input data; graph $G = (U, s)$ implicitly defined by u_0 and s; relationship of cost k on the arcs of G; application h of U in $\mathbb{R}^+$.
1. Initializations $P \leftarrow \{u_0\}; Q \leftarrow \phi; g(u_0) \leftarrow 0; u \leftarrow u_0$
2. Iterate while ($P \neq Q$ and $u \notin T$)
2.1 Delete u from P and put it in Q
2.2 Iterate on $\{v \varepsilon s(u)\}$
2.2.1 If $(v \varepsilon PUQ)$ or $(g(v) > g(u) + k(u, v))$ then do:
  $g(v) \leftarrow g(u) + k(u, v)$
  $f(v) \leftarrow g(v) + k(v)$
  father $(v) \leftarrow u$
  Store v in P, in order of increasing f, then decreasing g
  End iteration 2.2
2.3 If $[P \neq 0]$ then $u \leftarrow \hat{u}$ state at the head of stack P
3. End iteration 2
Output data: If $(P = \phi)$ then the problem admits no solution;
        If not, give route (u) solution.

This algorithm uses a strategy of type (a3). The iteration (2.2) corresponds to the complete development of the pending state, of which the evaluation f is minimal. All its successors are reviewed, and those encountered for the first time $(v \notin PUQ)$ are stored in P after calculation of the estimated $f(v)$. Those already encountered, but for which the new routes leading to them are better in terms of cost than the ones known previously $(g(v) > g(U) + k(u, v)$ are re-established as pending with the new route retained (updating of $g(v)$, $f(v)$ and father (v)) and stored once more in P, according to their new values of f and g.

The algorithm halts, either because there are no further pending states $(P = \phi)$ in which case there is no solution to the problem or at the first terminal state at the top of P.

Example 6.1. To illustrate the behaviour of the algorithm, the problem shown in the simple graph below (Figure 6.1) can be solved. The terminal states are $T = \{u_{15}, u_{16}\}$; the costs of the arcs and the value of the application h are shown in the figure, $Ch (u_0) = 17, h(u_1) = 15, K(u_0, u_1) = 4, \ldots)$ The sequence of developments carried out by A^* is given in the opposite table.

The properties of convergence, admissibility and complexity of the algorithm are analysed below.

6.2.1.2   Convergence of A*

This is established for virtually every function of heuristic estimation, and for every search space G with positive or nil costs, which may be a finite

State u developed	$g(u)$, $f(u)$, father(u)	Successors of u in P (unmodified)	Set giving P: $u_i(g(u_i), f(u_i))$
u_0	0, 17	u_1; u_3; u_5	$u_5(2, 17)$; $u_1(4, 19)$; $u_3(5, 21)$
u_5	2, 17, u_0	u_7; u_8	$u_8(7, 14)$; $u_7(4, 17)$; $u_1(4, 19)$; $u_3(5, 21)$
u_8	7, 14, u_5	u_3	$u_7(4, 17)$; $u_1(4, 19)$; $u_3(5, 21)$
u_7	4, 17, u_5	u_{10}	$u_1(4, 19)$; $u_3(5, 21)$; $u_{10}(19, 25)$
u_1	4, 19, u_0	u_2; u_4	$u_2(5, 20)$; $u_4(9, 21)$; $u_3(5, 21)$; $u_{10}(19, 25)$
u_2	5, 20, u_1	u_3	$u_4(9, 21)$; $u_3(5, 21)$; $u_{10}(19, 25)$
u_4	9, 21, u_1	u_3; u_5; u_7; u_6, u_9	$u_9(13, 20)$; $u_3(5, 21)$; $u_6(12, 23)$; $u_{10}(19, 25)$
u_9	13, 20, u_4	u_{10}; u_{11}; u_{12}; u_{15}	$u_{10}(14, 20)$; $u_3(5, 21)$; $u_{12}(16, 22)$; $u_6(12, 23)$; $u_{11}(15, 24)$; $u_{15}(25, 25)$
u_{10}	14, 20, u_9	u_{12}, u_{13}	$u_{12}(15, 21)$; $u_{13}(20, 22)$; $u_6(12, 23)$; $u_{11}(15, 24)$; $u_{15}(25, 25)$
u_{12}	15, 21, u_{10}	u_{13}; u_{15}; u_{16}	$u_{13}(18, 20)$; $u_3(5, 21)$; $u_6(12, 23)$; $u_{15}(24, 24)$; $u_{16}(24, 24)$; $u_{11}(15, 24)$
u_{13}	18, 20, u_{12}	u_{16}	$u_3(5, 21)$; $u_{16}(22, 22)$; $u_6(12, 23)$; $u_{15}(24, 20)$; $u_{11}(15, 24)$
u_3	5, 21, u_0	u_4, u_6, u_8	$u_{16}(22, 22)$; $u_6(12, 23)$; $u_{15}(24, 24)$; $u_{11}(15, 24)$

$u_{16} \in T$: halts A* with the solution: $(u_0, u_1, u_4, u_9, u_{10}, u_{13}, u_{16})$ of cost $f(u_{16}) = 6$

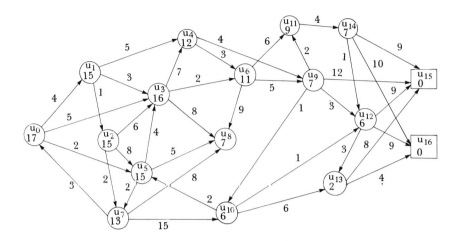

Figure 6.1 *Graph showing a problem to be solved by the algorithm*

graph, or an infinite δ-graph containing at least one route from u_0 to a terminal state. By definition, a graph valued in $\mathbb{R}^+$, containing no route of infinite length (in the number of arcs) and of restricted cost is a δ-graph (that is, any sequence of arcs of infinite number with an unrestricted infinite cost).

Assertion 6.1: for any h application of U in $\mathbb{R}^+$, and for any finite graph G with positive or nil valuations, A^* will stop either on a terminal state, or because of the absence of a pending state $(P = \phi)$ if there is no route from u_0 to a terminal state.

Proof: a developed state (εQ) cannot be re-established as pending (εP) unless a new route leading to it is found, strictly better in terms of cost than the one known previously. In addition, a circuit in the graph can only be followed once, because of the positive or nil costs. Eventually, all the routes leading to a state will be explored, and when the best is found, the state will stay in Q definitively. If G contains a route from u to a terminal state, it will appear at the head of stack P and A^* will stop with $\hat{u} \in T$; if not, A^* will stop with $P = \phi$.

In the case of infinite graphs, convergence will occur through the establishment of the following lemma:

Assertion 6.2: for any finite or infinite G containing at least one finite route from u_0 to a terminal state; and for any h application of U in $\mathbb{R}^+$; with each of the iterations (2) of A^* any optimal route from u_s to T will have at least one pending state u_i such that $g(u_i) = g^*(u_i)$.

Proof: let $(u_0, u_1, \ldots u_r)$ be an optimal route in G between u_0 and

$u_r \varepsilon T$. u_0 is developed initially, its successor u_1 is either pending or developed; in the latter case, u_2 can also either be in P or in Q, ... etc. Since the state u_i is terminal, it cannot be developed by A^*. At any moment, therefore, there is at least one pending state in this sequence. Let u_i be the first (in the order of the sequence) to be pending: the states $u_0, u_1, \ldots, u_{i-1}$ having been developed, the route $(u_0, u_1, \ldots u_i)$ is known by the algorithm or by hypothesis, and the route is optimal, so $g(u_i) = g^*(u_i)$.

Assertion 6.3: if G and h verify the following hypotheses:
—G is a finite or infinite δ-graph with positive or nil valuations in which there is at least one route of finite length between u_0 and a terminal state;
—h is an application of U in R^+ such that there exists an increase η with $h(u_i) \leqslant \eta$ for state u_i on an optimal route $u_0 \ldots u_i \ldots u_r$ from u_0 to a terminal state $u_r \in T$;
A^* then converges: it stops after a finite number of stages and provides a solution route from u_0 to T.

Proof: this is based on the following argument: A^* can only develop states of a sub-graph G′ of G, which is finite and includes at least one of the solution routes of G. The existence of a minimal cost solution route can be demonstrated. By hypothesis, G admits at least one route of finite length between u_0 and T. Let K be the cost of this route, and ζ the set of routes from u_0 to T of cost less than or equal to K. Since G is a δ-graph, any route of γ is of finite length. In addition, any state $u \varepsilon U$ will admit only one finite set of successors. So ζ is a finite set (it is easy to demonstrate that there is a maximum of $(p^{q+1} - 1)/(p - 1)$ states attainable from u_0 by a route with a maximum of q arcs, with $p = \max\{| s(u)| \}$ on these states). The cost function of a route therefore admits a minimum on the finite set ζ, which is $f^*(u_0)$, the cost of the optimal route from u_0 to T. Starting from this proof, G′ can be defined as the sub-graph of G restricted to the states u such that $\{u \in U \mid g^*(u) + h(u) \leqslant f^*(u_0) + \eta \}$.
—G′ is a finite sub-graph: the application g^* to the set of states u of G′ is limited, so for each of these states there exists a route between u_0 and u of finite length; or the set of states attainable from u by a route of finite length is finite.
—G′ includes at least one of the solution routes contained in G: if $(u_0, u_1, \ldots, u_r)$, $u_r \varepsilon T$ is a route of optimal cost in G, for any u_i on this route, there applies: $g^*(u_i) \leqslant g^*(u_r) = f^*(u_0)$, and by hypothesis on **h**: $h(u_i) \leqslant \eta$ so $g^*(u_i) + h(u_i) \leqslant \eta + f^*(u_0)$ and u_i appears in G.
—A^* does not develop any state external to G′: if the state u, not featured in G′, is pending to a certain iteration, then: $f(u) = g(u) + h(u) \geqslant g^*(u) + h(u) > f^*(u_0) + \eta$ by definition of G′; but following on from the previous assertion, there exists, for this iteration, a state u_i in

P on an optimal route with: $g(u_i) = g^*(u_i) \leqslant f^*(u_0)$, and $h(u_i) \leqslant \eta$; therefore $f(u_i) < f(u)$, the state u placed after u_i in the stack P will not be developed. To sum up, the search is restricted to the finite sub-graph G'_{q-1} which contains at least one solution; therefore assertion 6.1 applies to G'.

Notes:

1. The hypothesis on h of the previous assertion is unrestrictive: h limited in every direction can simply be used.

2. The algorithm halting with $P = 0$ (absence of solution) cannot occur except in the case of a finite graph. There is no convergence for an infinite δ-graph which does not contain a route from u_0 to a terminal state (the concept of semi-decidability, from first order predicate knowledge, applies here). To rediscover this convergence, an estimate of the cost of each (if any) solution would be required in advance, and the algorithm would have to be modified to allow only those states where the evaluation of cost f is less than the estimate to be established as pending.

6.2.1.3 Admissibility of A^*

The same hypotheses on G are adopted as for assertion 6.3. The admissibility will, however, only be established for reducing heuristics. An intermediate lemma is required.

Assertion 6.4: If h is a reducing estimator, then at the end of each of the iterations of A^*, the state û at the head of pile P verifies $f(û) \leqslant f^*(u_0)$.

Proof: the state û is defined by $f(û) = \min\{f(u) \mid u\varepsilon P\}$. But according to the lemma (6.2), there is, at any time, a state u_i in P, on an optimal route such that $g(u_i) = f^*(u_i)$; since h is reducing: $h(u_i) \leqslant h^*(u_i)$ so that: $f(u_i) = g(u_i) + h(u_i) \leqslant g^*(u_i) + h^*(u_i) = f^*(u_i) = f^*(u_0)$ and $f(û) \leqslant f(u_i) \leqslant f^*(u_0)$.

Assertion 6.5: for any finite or infinite δ-graph G with positive or nil values in which there is at least one route from u to a terminal state, and for any **h** reducing estimator, the algorithm A^* is admissible: it stops by providing an optimal route between u_0 and a terminal state.

Proof: since the algorithm is convergent, it always ends by encountering a pending state û such that $û \in T$. But $f(û) \leqslant f^*(u_0)$, and by definition $f^*(u_0) = \min\{f^*(u) \mid u \in T\}$ which gives $f(û) = f^*(u_0)$, and the route $(u_0, \ldots, û)$ is optimal.

Note:

For a reducing heuristic, the finite sub-graph G' to which the search is limited is restricted to the states u, such that: $\{u\varepsilon u \mid g^*(u) + h(u) \leqslant f^*(u_0)\}$.

Algorithm A* using a monotonic heuristic is equally admissible. It is, in fact, very easy to establish.

Assertion 6.6: If h is a monotonic and coincident heuristic, h is also reducing.

6.2.1.4 Complexity of A*

The analysis of the complexity of A* consists, as for any algorithm, of establishing the decomposition of the number of simple operations that will be carried out as a function of the size of problem to be handled (quantity of input data). As a preliminary approximation, the number of developments achieved by A* is determined as a function of the total number of states in U, or more precisely as a function of the number N of states in the finite sub-graph G (the only states suitable for development).

The results found from this are as follows:

1. Generally speaking, A* can achieve $\theta(L^N)$ state developments in the least favourable situation: each state u will be developed as many times as there are distinct routes from u_0 to u.

2. For a reducing heuristic, and with the addition of a simple test, the maximal complexity of the algorithm can be reduced to $\theta(N^2)$ developments (Martelli 1977). This test applies to the choice of the state to be developed at each iteration:

—If $f(\hat{u}) \geqslant \max\{f(v)|\, v\varepsilon Q\}$;

—If not, then from all pending states u such that $f(u) < \max\{f(v)|\, v\varepsilon Q\}$, then develop the one with minimal g(u).

—If the heuristic h is monotonic, for any state u developed by A*, $g(u) = g^*(u)$. It follows that u cannot be developed more than once, and therefore that A* carries out a maximum of N developments (Nilsson 1971).

It should be noted that this result of complexity in $\theta(N)$ is far from being satisfactory for an algorithm like A*. Part of the input data is not in an explicit graph G, but a set of rules defining the successor relationship; in addition, in almost all practical applications, the values of N far exceed any realistic possibility of carrying out N developments (even for highly academic examples: N = 9! = 936880 states for the simple game Nim, and $N = 4.3 \times 10^{19}$ for a sub-set of states of Rubik's cube). Complexity in $\theta(N)$ does not, therefore, reflect an algorithm that is practically applicable, and polynomial in the dimension of its input, in this case. A more interesting characterization of the complexity of A* determines the number of developments as a function of the number of arcs in the optimal route leading to a terminal state (dimension of the output data). Let M be this number. The main results found are as follows:

1. A^* guided by an almost perfect heuristic to a complexity in $\theta(M)$(Ibaraki 1976).

2. If h is monotonic, and for a simplified model of a search in a K-nary uniform tree containing a single solution in rank M, A^* is of exponential complexity if $\theta(K^M)$.

3. For a reducing heuristic, Pohl (1977) and Gaschnig (1979) have considered the complexity of A^* as a function of the difference between h and the perfect information h^*. For the same model in the uniform K-nary-tree (with r constant $\varepsilon\sqrt{K} + :$

    a. if $(1-r)h^* \leqslant h \leqslant h^*$, then A^* is exponential in $\theta(K^{rM})$;

    b. if $h^* - \sqrt{h^*} \leqslant h \leqslant h^*$, then A^* is exponential in $\theta(\sqrt{MK})$;

    c. if $h^* - \log h^* \leqslant h \leqslant h^*$, then A^* is polynomial in $\theta(M^{\log k})$;

    d. if $h^* - r \leqslant h \leqslant h^*$, then A^* is linear in $\theta(MK^r)$.

It is extremely rare to use an estimate that is marred only by an absolute or even logarithmic error (as with c and d). A heuristic with constant relative difference (case a) is the best that can be hoped for in most problems (cf. discussion on the construction of heuristics). It follows that the previous results on the maximal complexity of A^* are negative. The average behaviour of the algorithm could be hoped to be fairly far from this maximum. The analysis, mainly carried out by Huyn (1980) and Pearl (1983) shows that this is not the case.

In fact, Pearl's general theorem establishes that, for search in a uniform K-nary tree, with a heuristic such that the estimation errors $(h^*(u) - h(u))$ in the various states are independent random variables with, if they exist: $\varepsilon > 0, \delta > 0$ and a function ϕ with $\lim x \to \infty \phi(x)/x <$ such that for any state u of the tree: $(h^*(u) - h(u))/\phi(h^*(u)) \leqslant \delta$; and probability $[(h^*(u) - h(u))/\phi(h^*(u)) > \varepsilon]$ $> 1/K$, then the average complexity of A^* is an exponential function of $\phi(N)$. In other words, this theorem shows that if there is no heuristic h available, that in every state it is very close to the perfect information, that is, with logarithmic difference: $(h^* - h) \leqslant \delta(\log h^*)^n$, then the algorithm A^* will develop, on average, a number of states exponential on the length of the solution length. Outside these examples, the area of practical application of A^* will be limited to those in which the desired solution is a sequence of, at the most, twenty or thirty states.

The last result to be quoted here shows that this limitation applies to all classes of admissible algorithms. Hart (1972), and with extensions Gelperin (1977), established that any state developed by algorithm A^*, using a reducing heuristic h, will be developed by any other admissible algorithm using a heuristic **h'**, less informed than **h** (that is, such that $\forall u: h'(u) < h(u) \leqslant h^*(u)$). Any algorithm of this class that does not have available better heuristic information than A^* will be relegated to having a degree of complexity at least as high as that of A^*. This result is often referred to as corresponding to the 'optimality' of A^*, in that the algorithm has minimal complexity in this particular class of algorithm.

To conclude this section on A^*, it should be added that despite what has been said above on the subject of its complexity, this algorithm is still very popular. In robotics, for example, most of the searches for routes free of obstacles, both for mobile robots (Chatila 1982) and for manipulators (Lozano-Perez and Gouzene 1982) make use of A^*. The reasons for this fairly wide-spread use are based partly on the complexity of all the other admissible search algorithms, which is at least equal to that of A^*, and partly on the relative ease of implementing A^*.

This can be achieved in a general way, and independent of any particular application. The A^* program will, for example, call on two external procedures:

    1. successors (u): it supplies the list s(u) of successors to a state u and the costs k(u, v) corresponding to them;

    2. heuristic (u): it evaluates h(u).

Two distinct types of data structure should be associated with each state: (i) the first can simply be the number, in order of appearance, of a state generated by A^*. If the index i corresponds to u, tables such as son(i) and father(i) will provide the indices of the corresponding states. F(i) and G(i) will give the costs f(u) and g(u); (ii) the second should include all the data characterizing a state of the search, in the application considered. When the successors procedure returns a structure for a state v, before it can be allocated with an order number in the new state, a test must be made to ensure that it has not already been stored (test 2.2.1 for A^*).

The information associated with the states will be used to simplify the development of those states already developed (deletion of the call to successors, and of the previous test).

6.2.2 DEPTH-FIRST SEARCHING†

The order in which the states are stored in P by A^* corresponds to a search in order of increasing values of cost f. This order can be modified to implement other strategies, so for depth-first searching the pending states will be stored as they are encountered at the head of stack P.

An interesting variation consists of organizing the successors of the developed state u in order of increasing values of f(v), then storing them at the head of P in that order: the state that will be developed in the following iteration will be the successor to u with minimal f.

To obtain a stopping condition similar to that of A^*, however, and to guarantee a solution to the problem presented under similar circumstances, the algorithm must be provided with an estimate (preferably

---

† Corresponds traditionally to an exhaustive search without evaluation. A slightly more general presentation with an admissible algorithm is given below.

increasing) of the cost $f^*(u_0)$ of an optimal solution.

In addition to the notation given above, the following data structures will be used to define the algorithm:

1. P': list of successors to the state u in development, that are established or re-established as pending, P' is organized by increasing value of f;

2. Solutions: set of all routes from u_0 to a terminal state, known by the algorithm at a given moment;

3. y_0: estimate of cost $f^*(u_0)$ of an optimal solution, provided a priori;

4. Y: estimate of cost for routes in the set of solutions;

5. y: minimum $\{f(u) \mid u \in P\}$.

6.2.2.1 *Depth-first search algorithm*

Input data: graph $G = (u, \Gamma)$, costs K, application h, estimate Y_0

1. Initialization: $P \leftarrow \{u_0\}; Q - \phi; g(u_0) \leftarrow 0, f(u_0) \leftarrow h(u_0)$
    Solutions $\leftarrow \phi; y \leftarrow y_0; u \leftarrow u_0; y \leftarrow f(u_0)$
2. Iterate while $[P \neq \phi$ and $Y > y]$
2.1 Delete u in P and place in Q
2.2 Iterate on $\{v \in s(u)\}$
2.2.1 If $(v \notin P \cup Q)$ or $(g(v) > g(u) + K(u, v))$ then do:
2.2.1.1 $g(v) \leftarrow f(u) + K(u, v)$
2.2.1.2 $f(v) \leftarrow g(v) + h(v)$
2.2.1.3 father $(v) \leftarrow u$
2.2.1.4 If $(v \in T)$ then do:
            Place v in Q
            Store Route (v) in Solutions
            $Y \leftarrow \min\{Y, g(v)\}$
2.2.1.5 If not If $(g(v) \leqslant Y)$ then do:
            Store v in P'
            $y \leftarrow \min\{y, f(v)\}$
2.3 End iteration 2.2
2.4 Add stack P' to head of P
2.5 If $P \neq \phi$ then $u \leftarrow$ state at head of stack P
3. End iteration 2

Output data: if Solutions $= \phi$ then there is no solution of cost less than or equal to Y_0
If not supply route of minimal cost in solutions

At each iteration, the algorithm develops the best son pending from the state just developed. This 'in-depth descent' continues until a terminal state is encountered, or a state without a pending successor or with all successors of cost $g(v) > Y$ is encountered.

In one of these cases, the organization of stack P means that the algorithm will backtrack to the second best pending son, most recently encountered, and starts another in-depth search from that point. The algorithm halts when the estimate of the cost of the best pending state (y) is greater than or equal to the cost of the best known solution (Y) or to the estimate provided a priori (Y_0), if no solution has been reached; or else when there are no more pending states.

The following properties can be demonstrated for this algorithm:

1. Convergence: whatever the properties of the heuristic h (application of U in $\mathbb{R}^+$) the algorithm will stop. It is not guaranteed to find a solution unless there is at least one with cost $f^*(u_0) \leqslant Y_0$.

2. Admissibility: if h is a reducing heuristic $\forall_u$: $h(u) \varepsilon h^*$ and if Y_0 is an increasing estimate of the optimal cost ($Y_0 \geqslant f^*(h_0)$) then the algorithm is admissible. Note that if h is reducing, the algorithm can be improved by only establishing the successors v as pending, such that $f(v) \leqslant Y$ (instead of $g(v) \leqslant Y$ in test 2.2.1.5).

3. Complexity: at least equal to that of A^*.

Depth-first search is, in some implementations, very economical of memory space. Apart from this fact, its importance for A^* can be accounted for mainly by the fact that it allows several solutions to be reached, often before the optimal one has been found. If admissibility is not absolutely necessary, the search can be stopped far earlier, as soon as the first terminal state has been generated. The way in which this property is used by ε-admissible research will be shown later.

6.2.3 BREADTH-FIRST SEARCH

This corresponds to the pending states being stored, as they are encountered, in a queue in stack P. Development takes place in order of increasing rank, starting from u: all the successors of u are developed, then the successors of these successors, etc. As before the successors to the developed state can be organized before they are stored in P, but this does not allow their systematic development to be avoided, and is therefore not of great interest.

It is not necessary to test the extent to which the cost exceeds the limit Y, and to supply an a priori estimate Y_0. The conditions for halting are similar to those for DF search: when the cost Y of the best known solution is less than or equal to the estimate f of the best pending state. A non-admissible search will stop at the first terminal state encountered, and will generate a route of minimal length. The BF search converges, and is admissible if h is reducing. Its complexity is, however, always greater than or equal to that of the DF search, or of A^*, since it corresponds to an exhaustive and systematic enumeration: all the states of rank n are developed before any state of rank n + 1. For this reason, it is not widely used.

6.2.4 NON-EVALUATED SEARCH

In many applications, no function **h** of U in $\mathbb{R}^+$ is known to allow estimation of h^*. In other cases, the calculation time required to evaluate the known function h is too high, or not justified by the quality of the estimate it provides. It is, therefore, necessary to carry out a non-evaluated search (NES), that is, one without heuristic information.

The previous algorithms can be used for this with $h(u) = 0$ for any state u. The traditional methods for route research, discussed in relation to graph theory, are then reintroduced. The algorithm A^*, called uniform cost in this case, is therefore reduced to the Moore–Dijskstra algorithm.

It should be noted that $h(u) = 0 \,\forall u$ is a monotonic heuristic. The lack of heuristic in A^* gives rise to an admissible algorithm, carrying out N state developments, whereas in the general case with a reducing heuristic there may be $0(N^2)$ developments. The introduction of any heuristic function does not, therefore, reduce complexity automatically, and the use of NES is calculably costly.

6.2.5 SEARCH ORDERED BY THE HEURISTIC **h**

The control of a PSS must take into account the idea of cost for the stages of the solution it generates, principally when this solution takes the form of a plan actually carried out by physical parts of the system. Although this is the general case in robotics, in some situations no criterion of cost is imposed to favour one solution over another. This might be so, for example, when particular information is to be identified as having been deduced from that explicitly present in a data base (demonstration of theorems). In such cases, the aim is to reach any solution as rapidly as possible. A heuristic h will be adopted in relation to the sole criterion of the complexity of research, to evaluate the proximity, in the number of arcs, of a state u from a terminal state, that is, h(u) estimates the number of iterations (state developments) necessary to converge from u. With $g(u) = 0$, and $f(u) = h(u) \,\forall u$, the specific case of the previous algorithms is again encountered. For the algorithm A^*, for example, the same formula can be adopted, but without the test on g (that is, $g(v) > g(u) + k(u, v)$). Note that, unlike the general case, this leads to already developed states never being replaced in P (as was the practice for improving the cost of a route leading to a state, and which is clearly not applicable here).

In the absence of a cost criterion, the only properties of interest are convergence and complexity. Search ordered by h is, unfortunately, not convergent for infinite graphs. The heuristic h may be reducing and limited, but can, nonetheless, lead the search to infinite routes: not taking account of the costs (or lengths) of the routes will not allow research to be restricted. This is borne out by the proof of the convergence of A^*, and the hypothesis that a strictly increasing function g* is essential to the definition of the finite sub-graph G'. The following counter-example of the infinite binary tree can also be considered:

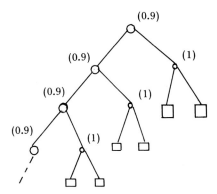

The right-hand son of the root has two terminal successors; the left-hand son is identical to the root. With the values of **h** indicated in the figure (h is decreasing for the unitary costs k(u, 0)), the search continues to infinity.

It may seem intuitively that an admissible algorithm searching for a cost criterion would be more complex than one not concerned with this optimization, and attempts to reach any solution as quickly as possible. Some results, both theoretical and empirical, have established that this is not always true: a search ordered by **h** can be more complex than one ordered by f = g + h.

Pohl (1970, 1977) has demonstrated this in the following example: if h is at an absolute difference with limited h^*, that is, $\forall u$: $h^*(u - r) \leqslant h(u) \leqslant h^*(u) + v$, then the complexity of the search ordered by h in a K-nary uniform tree is $\theta M.k^{2r}$. The algorithm A^* with the same heuristic and on the same tree, with unitary costs, is only $\theta(M.K^r)$.

As suggested by Vanderburg (1976) an infinite number of weightings can be introduced between f = g + h and f = h. The experimental study by Gaschnig (1979) explores this possibility. It covers almost 30,000 tests of a search ordered by $f = \alpha g + (1 - \alpha)h$ with $\alpha \varepsilon [0, 1]$, for three distinct heuristics on the game of Nim (unitary costs). The results can be summarized as follows:

1. for all problems of intermediate size (M < 20), complexity is minimal for $\alpha = 0.5$; the value $\alpha = 0$ can lead to searches up to ten times more costly;

2. for more difficult problems (M $\simeq$ 25, noting that the maximum possible for this game is M = 30) the search ordered by h($\alpha = 0$) becomes

less complex, although it still gives routes of between two and six times
longer than the optimum;

3. in all cases, the values $\alpha > 0.5$ are less interesting, and reducing the
weighting of **h** will at least consist of taking account of the heuristic and,
in general, exploring the graph more thoroughly in breadth. For $\alpha = 1$
and unitary costs on the arcs, broad research is the best solution.

In conclusion, it should be noted that the absence of heuristic information in certain applications leaves no choice other than to attempt a blind
search ($\alpha = 1$). The situation is very different for applications without cost
criteria: unitary costs can be introduced, taking account in the function
f ordering the search, of a component g (possibly with less weighting than
that of **h**, if the heuristic can be used with great confidence). The advantage in this will be that convergence can be guaranteed and exploration
limited with, very often, reduced complexity.

6.2.6   SEARCH WITH 'PRUNING'

In most cases the processing time associated with each state generated by
heuristic research will be more of a constraint on the available resources
than on the memory space required to store the states. Sometimes,
however, the maximum number of states stored must be limited: when
the data base (DB) associated with each state is very large, and is not
encoded in an economical way, and/or when the maximum number of
states generated is far higher than the number of states developed. In
order to respect these memory limitations, the technique of 'pruning' will
be used, based on increasing estimates of the costs.

In the most simple case, A^* could be formulated as follows: Y is an
estimation of $f^*(u)$, given a priori; each time a terminal state u is attained,
this estimate is updated with Y min Y, f(u); any state v generated by the
search such that $f(v) > Y$ will not be taken into account. If Y is increasing
($Y > f^*(u)$) and if h is reducing, then the algorithm will still be
admissible.

The 'bandwidth search' suggested by Harris (1974) is based on a
heuristic h, verifying: $uh^*(u) - d < h(u) < h^*(u) + e$; with e and d as
positive or nil constants. Any state v generated such that $f(v) > f(u) +
(e + d)$ can be pruned. The algorithm will not be admissible, but will
remain convergent by providing a solution of absolute distance from the
limited optimum: $f(u) < f^*(u) + e$.

An admissible alternative would be to use, in addition to a reducing
heuristic h, a second increasing heuristic h for the pruning: u: h(u) >
$h^*(u) - d$. Any state v generated such that uP with $f(v) > g(u) + h (u) - d$
can be pruned. The evaluation of h will be restricted, for example, to u,
the state at the head of stack P.

Note that, whatever the technique used, a pruned state v can be found by another route, and possibly retained if its evaluation f(v) is lower than the pruning threshold.

6.2.7 SEARCH WITHOUT REDEVELOPMENT

Another interesting modification that can be made to A^* consists of avoiding the redevelopment of the same state several times. In a previous example it was shown that a state v, already developed, was re-established as pending if the cost of the route leading to it was strictly better than the one known before: $(g(v) > g(u) + k(u, v))$. The resulting improvement in cost can eventually be propagated among the successors of v, using the same mechanism for redevelopment. Instead of this, a simpler updating procedure can be used for the propagation. The iteration (2.2) of A^* will become:

2.2′ Iterate on v s(u) v $P \cup Q$ or $g(v) > g(u) + k(u, v)$
        $g(v) \leftarrow g(u) + k(u, v)$
        $f(v) \leftarrow g(v) + h(v)$
        father (v) $\leftarrow$ u
        If v Q then Store v in P
        If not then Update (v, g(v))
    End iteration 2.2′

The updating procedure is recursive with two arguments; a state v and the cost g of the known route $(u_0 \ldots v)$:

Update (v, g)
  Iterate on $\{w \in S(v)\}$
    If $g(w) > g(v) + k(v, w)$ then do:
    $g(w) \leftarrow g(v) + k(v, w)$
    $f(w) \leftarrow g(w) + h(w)$
    father (w) $\leftarrow$ v
    If $w \in Q$ then Update (w, g(w))
    If not restore w in P
    End iteration

In relation to the redevelopment, the update basically avoids having to restore in P the states of Q re-established as pending. It does, however, systematically propagate an improvement in the cost of all the descendants concerned, which is often an advantage, except when this propagation reaches a terminal state, and accelerates the convergence of the algorithm.

6.2.8 BIDIRECTIONAL SEARCHING

This technique was proposed and developed principally by Pohl (1971), who starts from the statement that, in some applications, the two concepts of forward-chaining and backward-chaining are equivalent, differing only in their representation.

In fact, for all cases where the search is aimed at attaining a single, completely described terminal state, $T = \{t\}$, and where change of state rules can be interpreted in both directions ('modus ponens' type: 'if a particular state is reached, it is possible to go to another'; or 'modus tollens' type: 'to attain a particular state, it is possible to start from another'), two search procedures can be carried out simultaneously, one from u_0 to t, and one in the opposite direction, from t to u_0, stopping the two search procedures simultaneously as soon as they have a developed state in common.

The objective behind this type of procedure is to replace a unidirectional search, the exponential complexity of which is $\theta(K^M)$, by two similar searches which, if they meet 'halfway', will each be $\theta(K^{m/2})$. The gain will be exponential in $\theta(K^{M/2})$ and should compensate very rapidly for the additional calculation required for the test of intersection of the two procedures.

A formulation for a bidirectional search algorithm is given below. The same notation: $P, Q, f, g, h, \hat{u}$ and father, is used as for A^*; with index a, $P_a, Q_a, f_a, g_a, h_a, \hat{u}_a$, and father $_a$ to designate the data associated with the search by forward chaining from u_0 to t; and index t, $P_t, Q_t, f_t, g_t, h_t, \hat{u}_t$, and father $_t$ to designate the data associated with the search by backward chaining from t to u_0.

The variable X is equivalent to 'a' when the following iteration will be a development by forward chaining; X = 't' when the development is by backward chaining; and X = 0 when the stopping condition is satisfied.

Bidirectional search algorithm

Input data: $u_0, t, s, s^{-1}, h_a, h_t$, costs K, estimator y_0
1. Initialization: $P_a \leftarrow \{u_0\}; g_a(u_0) \leftarrow 0; f_a(u_0) \leftarrow h_a(u_0); Y \leftarrow Y_0$
   $P_t \leftarrow \{t\}; g_t(t) \leftarrow 0; f_t(t) \leftarrow h_s(t)$
   If $u_0 \neq t$ then do: $u \leftarrow u_0; X \leftarrow$ 'a'
   If not $X \leftarrow$ nil

2. Iterate while $[(P_a \neq \phi \text{ or } P_t \neq \phi) \text{ and } X \neq 0]$
2.1 If X = 'a' then do:
2.1.1 Remove u from P_a and place it in Q_a
2.1.2 Iterate on $\{v \in s(u)| v \notin P_a \cup Q_a\}$ or $g_a(v) > g_a(u) + k(u_1v)$

   $g_a(v) \leftarrow g_a(u) + k(u, v)$
   $f_a(v) \leftarrow g_a(v) + h_a(v);$ father $_a(v) \leftarrow u$
   Store v in P_a

End iteration 2.1.2

2.2 If not do: (in this case X = 't')

2.2.1 Remove u from P_t and place it in Q_t

2.2.2 Iterate on $\{v \varepsilon s^{-1}(u) | v \varepsilon P_t \cup Q_t\}$ or $g_t(v) > g_t(u) + k(v, u)$

$g_t(v) \leftarrow g_t(u) + k(v, u)$

$f_t(v) \leftarrow g_t(v) + k_t(v)$; father $_t(v) \leftarrow u$

Store v in $f_t(v) \leftarrow g_t(v) + k_t(v)$ P_t

End iteration 2.2.2

2.3 If $(u \varepsilon Q_a \cup Q_t$ and $Y > g_a(u) + g_t(u))$ then do:

$Y \leftarrow g_a(u) + g_t(u)$; route $\leftarrow (u_0, \ldots, u_1 \ldots t)$

If $Y \leqslant \max\{fa(\hat{u}_a); f_t(\hat{u}_t)\}$ then $X \leftarrow nil$

2.4 If $X \neq nil$ then do:

If $|P_a| < |P_t|$ then do: $u \leftarrow \hat{u}_a$; $X \leftarrow$'s'

If not do: $u \leftarrow \hat{u}_t$; $X \leftarrow$ 't'

3. End iteration 2

Output data: If X = nil then take Route solution for cost Y; If not there is no solution of cost less than or equal to y_0.

At each iteration, this algorithm chooses to pursue the development with forward chaining if there are less pending states in the corresponding search than there are for backward chaining (that is, $|P_a| < |P_t|$), and vice versa in the opposing situation. Other strategies are, of course, possible; for example, forward and backward chaining can be applied in turn. The idea is to maintain a balance, in the number of states explored, between the two types of search, with a view to satisfying the condition of meeting halfway. Any state that is u developed by both types of search (that is, $u \in Q_a \cap {}_\alpha$) corresponds to a complete route from u_0 to t, passing through u, which can be found simply by setting up the two father pointers in both directions, starting from u. The algorithm stops when the cost of this route drops below the minimum estimation of cost f for a pending state in one or other of the two searches.

With this stopping condition, the algorithm is convergent (if there is a solution of cost less than or equal to Y_0, it will be found and admissible (if h_a and h_t are reducing). The stopping condition is far simpler in the case of non-admissibility.

For the complexity, Pohl (1971, 1976) shows in his analysis that bidirectional research is only really an advantage in cases where unidirectional research is very inefficient; in particular, when there is no heuristic, non-evaluated bidirectional search can be four times more efficient in some applications than non-evaluated unidirectional research. Unfortunately, once a good heuristic is available, bidirectional research becomes far more costly than unidirectional, so for the heuristics h verifying: $(1 - \delta)h^* \leqslant h \leqslant (1 + \delta)h^*$ twice as many states would be developed using the first instead of the second. This is mainly due to the fact that the 'meeting halfway' condition is easily verified by blind research, which corresponds, in practice, to scanning through the breadth of the graph, whereas using heuristics focuses and guides both searches in a specific direction, not bringing about their meeting until each has almost attained its objective.

Given the difficulties of implementation that accumulate, the need to use two heuristics h_a and h_t (except in certain cases, where the same heuristic can be used in both directions), and the previous complexity results, bidirectional research is very rarely used.

6.3   Partial development algorithms

So far, the complexity of a search algorithm has been considered to be equal, to within a constant factor, to the number of developments it carries out, given that this state development operation is carried out in a constant time. In most PSSs, this hypothesis cannot be verified. The length of a development depends, in particular, on the degree of each state. This concerns the determination, by pattern matching, of the set of valid rules ('conflict set'), generating the successor state for each one by this rule (with suitable encoding for the data base associated with the state), testing whether the state has already been encountered, evaluating the corresponding heuristic and storing it in the stack of states that are candidates for development.

This processing can only be achieved in practice if:

1. the conflict set is always very restricted (five rules maximum) and easily determined;

2. the data base characterizing each state can be encoded very efficiently, particularly to facilitate the test comparing two states;

3. the heuristic evaluation is very rapid (possibly carried out incrementally: $h(v)$ is calculated, without the state v having to be generated explicitly, from $h(u)$ and the rule leading from u to v).

In robotics, for example, the problem of generating trajectories that are free of obstacles very often corresponds to these constraints, whereas the problems of planning are generally outside them.

The issue here is to determine what control procedures can be used in all the PSSs when it is not possible to carry out complete developments.

The best known algorithm for this purpose corresponds to a depth-first search, generally called 'backtrack search'. The normal recursive formulation given below does not involve a heuristic function:

Algorithm BSG(u)
  If $u \in T$ then Return ('success')
  If not If $g(u) > Y_0$ then return ('failure')
    If not do:

Iterate on $\{v \varepsilon s(u) | v \notin Q \text{ or } g(v) > g(u) + k(u, v)\}$
    put v in Q
    $g(v) \leftarrow f(u) + k(u, v)$
    father $(v) \leftarrow u$
    If BSG(v) = 'success' then do:
    Route $\leftarrow$ (v, route)
    Return ('success')
  End Iteration
  Return ('failure')
End

The BSG algorithm uses the overall variables Y_0, Route and Q: Y_0 is an a priori estimate of the cost of an optimal solution; Q is the set of states already encountered; and Route is the sequence of states in the solution being constructed.

Initially, $BSG(u_0)$ is called with Route = empty list and $Q = \{u_0\}$. The algorithm will return either: 'success', in which case Route corresponds to the sequence of states $(u_0, \ldots, u_r)$, $u_r \in T$, found; or 'failure', in which case there is no route from u_0 to T of cost less than or equal to u_0.

During any call to state u, recursion will stop if u is terminal, or if g(u) exceeds the threshold Y_0; if not the recursion continues on a successor v of u not yet encountered $(v \notin Q)$, or one in which the cost g(v) has improved. If the call BSG(v) succeeds (finds a route from v to T), then the other successors of u will not have to be generated, and all the previous calls will terminate by concatenating the state corresponding to the Route sequence every time. Thus the iteration will not actually take place (and the development of u will not be complete) unless the explorations of all the successors of u end in failure. If this is the case, the BSG(u) call will also have failed, and 'backtracking' will take place towards a brother of u. Note that the idea of a pending state is no longer used here: any state generated is immediately explored.

One method of using heuristic information in this algorithm consists, first of all, of choosing from the set $\{v \varepsilon s(u) | v \notin Q \text{ or } f(v) < g(u) + k(u, v)\}$ the state that will have 'the best chance' of resulting in a route being found from v to T: the successors of u will therefore be ordered, in a way, without their having to be generated. In the formulation proposed, the algorithm converges: if Y_0 is an increasing estimate of the optimal cost $f^*(u_0)$ and if a solution exists, then BSG (u_0) will return successively a solution route (the test $g(v) > g(u) + k(u, v)$, which leads to the same state being explored several times, is essential to this convergence). The algorithm is not, however, admissible. An admissible formulation would demand that the call BSG(u) should not give rise to a return, unless an optimal route from u to T is known, or there is no solution. The examination of all the successors of u will be necessary, even if a heuristic function h is used, and a situation of complete development will arise.

The following algorithm avoids this problem, while ensuring admissibility:

Algorithm A^*DP
Input data: u_0, s, costs k, heuristic **h**
1. Initialization: $P \leftarrow \{u_0\}; Q \leftarrow \phi; f(u_0) \leftarrow 0; u \leftarrow u_0$
2. Iterate while $[P \neq \phi$ and $u \notin T]$
      $v \leftarrow$ Choose-Successor (u)
      If v = nil then remove u from P and place it in Q
      If not do:
          $g(v) \leftarrow f(u) + k(u, v)$
          $f(v) \leftarrow f(u) + h(v)$
          father (v) $\leftarrow$ u
          store v in P
      If $P \neq Q$ then $u \leftarrow \hat{u}$ state at head of stack P
3. End iteration
Output data: if $P \neq Q$ then the problem has no solution
               If not ($*u \in T*$) provide the solution Route (u)

This algorithm is formulated in a similar way to that of A^*, with an additional category of states: those that have only been partially developed. A partially developed state is not transferred, as in A^*, from P to Q; it remains in P for as long as it has pending successors. Only the completely developed states are placed in Q.

The algorithm A^*DP calls the non-determinist procedure Choose-Successor, which can be defined as follows:

Choose-successor (u)
If the set of successors of u verifies

$s \leftarrow \{v \in s(u)| v \notin P \cup Q$ or $g(v) > g(u) + k(u, v)\}$
If s = 0 then Return (nil)
If not choose a particular state v in s and
   Return (v)

The implementation of this procedure must, of course, be carried out avoiding an extensive definition of the set s(u) and the corresponding tests for each of its elements. This could be achieved as described below.

Let it be supposed that heuristic information is available (in addition to the function h), which allows the importance of a specific rule R_i to be appreciated a priori, in a state u and relative to the objective T, without having to determine the conflict set and generate all the successors of u. The Choose-Successor (u) procedure will then ask the Pattern-matcher: is the rule R_i valid in u and for which instances? If the instance found allows a state v, corresponding to the test, to be generated then that state will be returned. If not (R_i is not valid or does not allow a satisfactory state to be generated) then another rule R_j is chosen, and the process of inquiry and test is repeated with the new rule.

Another approach can be envisaged in the case of applications where the conflict set is easy to determine and where the heuristic h(v) can be evaluated without v being made explicit, either directly or based on u and the rule R_i leading from u to v. The states v would be generated and tested in increasing order of f(v), stopping with the first to respond to the test.

These approaches will be advantageous if they allow a state v to be attained by testing, on average, fewer alternatives than a complete development would require. Note, also, that if several successor states $v_1, v_2, \ldots, v_i$, close in quality, are known, the Choose-Successor procedure could return them all, and the algorithm A^*DP would carry out partial developments, not limited to the generation of a single successor each time.

It should be mentioned, in conclusion, that the algorithm A^*DP is convergent and admissible. In terms of the number of partial developments, its complexity is, of course, greater than or equal to that of A^*. It can be less advantageous than A^* even in the number of states generated, if the Choose-Successor procedure directs the search clumsily. If, on the other hand, it systematically provides the successor state v to minimal f(v), then any state, developed even partially by A^*DP will also be developed by A^* (but not necessarily the same number of times). Note that if h is monotonic, then $\forall u, vtS(u): f(v) \geqslant f(u)$; as a result, the order on P will impose that no state v be developed before the complete development of its father u: A^*DP will be identical to A^* if, at each iteration, the state u with minimal f continues to be developed. It will be seen (Section 6.5) that it is possible to modify the order on P to add a 'depth-first' component to the search, and accelerate its convergence.

6.4   Redundant search algorithms— tree searching

As was explained in the previous section, the development of a state is a complex and costly operation. Algorithms for partial development attempt to reduce the cost by limiting, as far as possible, the number of successors generated and tested. Redundant search algorithms are intended to simplify the development stage still further, by suppressing the operation that tests the successors: if the conflict set is known, the generation of successors to a state u is not very costly (each one is generally obtained by a small number of very simple modifications to the data base characterizing u); on the other hand, the state identification test $[v \in ?P \cup Q]$ can be so complex that even the partial development techniques will be impracticable.

The data base (DB) associated with each state u is the most complete description possible of everything known explicitly in that state. It may correspond, in size, to a (non-ordered) set of several hundred items of structured data (or relationships between simple data). Evaluating the test $[v \in ?P \cup Q]$ implies that it would be necessary to:

1. retain in memory all the DBs associated with all the states encountered up to the present by the search (that is, states of P and those of Q);

2. compare the DB associated with v with each of those stored, to establish equality or difference.

To date, this has only been carried out in a direct way in cases where the search graph could be made entirely explicit (for example, the generation of trajectories free from obstacles), or in simple academic applications (such as Nim's game or a state that could be characterized by a single whole number in a machine word). For complex applications, the test of identification of a state u requires recourse to highly sophisticated encoding of the DB, and high-level tri-ordinate techniques for forming comparisons.

One way of handling this would be to code each DB in terms of its difference relative to that of state u_0, and to structure it into classes of data (by unification with the conditions); each class of data would be organized alphabetically by the instances of the variables. Each DB would, therefore, be characterized by a list of discriminant information, such as the number of data in each class, which would be used as a 'key' for the comparison of DBs with each other. Although this type of approach does not present any conceptual difficulties, there is no known practical application which would allow the benefit to be established for the search algorithm, or in relation to the overhead cost it involves.

In the absence of methods such as the one suggested above, most PSSs that handle large DBs have their control reduced to the use of one of the redundant search algorithms.

Starting from any of the partial or complete development algorithms described in this chapter, a redundant search algorithm can be obtained by simply suppressing the set Q and the test $[v \notin P \cup Q$ or $g(v) > g(u) + K(u, v)]$ (note that inequality has no meaning unless v has been recognized as identical to one of the states of P or Q, since otherwise $g(v)$ would not be defined). So for redundant A^*, the developed state u will be removed by P, and in its place will be stored all its successors without any concern for which ones are already present, or have already been eliminated by previous developments. The search will be redundant because of the duplication, not only of the same information several times in the memory, but also of the same iterations doing exactly the same thing. There is a risk, therefore, of obtaining a non-convergent algorithm as well as that of suffering a loss in efficiency. The conditions for this are analysed below.

If the search finds a state v', identical to v already encountered, on a route $(u_0, \ldots, v')$ that does not pass through v, then v' will eventually be redeveloped, but the process will only repeat itself a finite number of times: at the most as many times as there are distinct routes from u_0 to v and of lower cost than a particular increase (see definition of the finite sub-graph G' in the proof to assertion 6.3). If, however, v' is found by a route passing through v: $(u_0 \ldots v \ldots v')$, a loop on graph G will have been followed, and will be transformed into an infinite iteration if, and only if, the cost of the loop $(v \ldots v')$ is nil. If this loop is of nil cost, then $g(v') = g(v)$ and v' will be stored in P in the same relative position as that of v before its development: v' will be redeveloped in the same way, as will all its descendants with the same cost, and v" identical to v will be found by the route $(v, \ldots, v', \ldots, v'')$ of nil cost. Reciprocally, if the algorithm iterates to infinity on a loop of the search graph and, taking the example to the point of absurdity, if the cost of the circuit is nil, states of infinite cost will be developed. This cannot occur if there is a route from u to T, and if h is limited all around, except in the states that do not lead to T.

It is important to remember that the δ-graphs do not exclude the possibility of a circuit of nil cost. A ω-graph will therefore be defined as a finite or infinite graph, the arcs of which are valued on $\mathbb{R}^+$, containing no route of infinite cost and length, or any circuit of nil cost, and the result will be stated.

Assertion 6.6: for any G ω-graph in which there is at least one route from u to T, and for any application h of U in $\mathbb{R}^+$, such that if $h(u) = \infty$ there is no route from u to T, the redundant A* algorithm is convergent.

The assertion 6.5 can easily be generalized to establish the admissibility of redundant A* in the ω-graphs and for reducing heuristics.

It is possible to deduce from the above that a redundant search algorithm, organized by **h** (most frequently encountered control procedure) is not convergent: if the cost of the routes is not taken into account, and the identity of the state is not tested, there is no means available for protecting against circuits being followed to infinity. Note that in relation to complexity, a redundant search will develop and generate more states than a non-redundant search. It will, however, profit from the economy of tests for state identification. The authors know of no comparative study between these two alternatives.

It is a particularly fortunate case in which the absence of redundance in the search can be guaranteed a priori, without having to test the identity of the states. This concerns all the problems of searches in which the rules of the PSS (that is, the successor relationship s) define a tree, rather than a general graph. Between any two states in a tree, there will exist at most one route, and therefore the possibility of finding a previously encountered state is excluded.

The formulation of an algorithm for search in a tree is equivalent to that of a redundant search algorithm. The properties of convergence and admissibility are demonstrated with the same hypotheses (knowing that a tree has no cycle). It should be remembered, finally, that all the complexity results given above are established in the simplified model of search in a tree (taking into consideration only the number of state developments and not the complexity of each development), and are therefore valid here.

6.5 ε-admissible algorithms

With the same heuristic information, no admissible search algorithm will be better in terms of its complexity than A^*, which has an exponential style of behaviour for the length of the route found. A non-admissible search, ordered directly by heuristic **h**, will not only have convergence problems, but will not guarantee, in some cases, a level of complexity lower than that of the admissible search.

In most cases, however, the minimization of the solution cost (admissibility), and the minimization of the cost of searching for it (complexity) will be two contradictory objectives, between which an intermediate solution must be established. This is all the more relevant because for many applications, particularly in robotics, the costs associated with a solution are comparable in order of magnitude to the costs related to the search. For example, for a plan executed once only, the execution cost of the plan may be of the same order as the cost of the search. The intermediate solution between these two approaches, admissible and non-admissible, is provided by the ε-admissible search.

The search algorithm, which for any parameter $\varepsilon \in \mathbb{R}^+$ given a priori, provides an output of a solution of increased cost: $f(u) \leqslant (1 + \varepsilon) \ f^*(u_0)$, is said to be an ε-admissible algorithm. The parameter ε is the maximum of the difference relative to the optimum tolerated by the user in the solution he is searching for.

The basic principle of ε-admissible search is based on the idea of acceptability of a pending state. A state u is said to be acceptable relative to the objective of ε-optimality if, and only if: $u \in P$ and $f(u) \leqslant (1 + \varepsilon) f^*(u_0)$. Since, in general, $f^*(u_0)$ is not known, a reducing estimator will be used as the acceptability threshold.

Instead of being constrained, like A^*, to develop the state $\hat{u}$ at the head of P (with minimal f) at every iteration, an ε-admissible algorithm can develop any acceptable state. In this way, a large choice of states is available for pursuing the search at each iteration, and it is hoped that the one eventually selected will reduce the complexity of the algorithm.

To guide this choice, a second heuristic function $h_c(u)$ is defined: this is the estimate of the minimal number $h_c(u)$ of iterations necessary to attain a terminal state from u. It is, therefore, an indication of the length, in numbers of arcs, of the shortest route between u and a terminal state. This estimator is, in general, independent of the distribution of cost K.

The various possible strategies for choosing the acceptable pending node for development are briefly analysed below:

1. Opportunist strategy: this consists of developing the acceptable state with minimal h_c at each iteration. This strategy is carried out by the algorithm A^*_ε (Pearl 1982). In the ideal situation of a perfect heuristic $h_c = h_c$, any state will have at least one successor v, such that $h_c(v) = h_c(u) - 1$. If u is developed with iteration j, the next iteration successor v of u being developed, while v remains acceptable. The algorithm pursues the development of a single route through the graph and will not abandon it, except for one of the two following reasons:

a. either that the acceptable successors v of u are such that $h_c(v) > h_c(u)$; this will be the case if h_c is not locally consistent;

b. that u has no acceptable successor.

If there were no direct correlation between cost and length of a route, the first situation would arise frequently. The opportunist strategy will therefore lead to the algorithm changing this route, and will force it, a few iterations later, to abandon this second route as soon as another is believed to be any shorter. The tendency to favour backtracking will be more pronounced when the heuristic h_c is imperfect.

The problem with the opportunist strategy is that it may lead to the exploration of many different routes, and to a large number of iterations on a single route, and so may be inconveniently complex.

2. Depth-first development strategy: this consists of pursuing the development of a single route for as long as the cost remains acceptable. Among the acceptable successors to the state just developed, a choice can be made between trying one with minimal f, one with minimal h_c, or a successor offering a compromise between f and h_c.

The strategy of in-depth development allows the first method of backtracking in the opportunist strategy to be avoided. The second case (absence of acceptable successor) can also be avoided in many cases. The threshold of acceptability uses the largest known reducer of $f^*(u_0)$, which will often be $f(\hat{u})$. It will often be possible to raise the threshold of acceptability simply by developing u, and this gives rise to:

3. Perseverance strategy: if u, a newly developed state, has no acceptable successor, but the distance from the acceptability threshold of the best of them is small, then the perseverance strategy consists of developing u, and going back to the previous explored route if one of the successors of u has become acceptable relative to the new threshold of acceptability.

It is, of course, possible to develop a sequence of several preliminary pending states $\hat{u}$, with a view to making a new route acceptable. This acceptability is all the more plausible in the case of a monotonic heuristic h, since in such a case the sequence $f(\hat{u})$ is non-decreasing.

Note that development of the state $\hat{u}$ is not the same in the perseverance strategy as it is in the other developments, in that the object is not to attain a terminal state, but to raise the threshold of acceptability. This is an investment in relation to reducing the complexity of the algorithm, but is also useful to the progress of the search: the development of û will not be lost if the route being explored does not lead to success, and back-tracking has to be introduced.

For algorithm A_ε, a formulation of which is given below, the two strategies 2. and 3. can be implemented. It uses the following notation, as well as that defined for A^*: P_ε, set of acceptable successors to the newly developed state u; Solutions, sets of terminal states attained by the algorithm; Threshold $= (1 + \varepsilon)_x \max\{f(\hat{u})\}$: largest known reducer of $(1 + \varepsilon)_x f^*(u_0)$. To simplify the explanation, the algorithm will call four procedures: Develop, Choice-in-P, Choice-in-P_ε and Persevere.

Algorithm A_ε
Input data: u_0, T, s, costs K, heuristic h, parameter $\varepsilon \geqslant 0$
1. Initialization: $P \leftarrow \{u_0\}$; $Q \leftarrow \phi$; solutions $\leftarrow \phi$; $g(u_0) \leftarrow 0$; $f(u_0)h(u_0)$
                    Threshold $\leftarrow (1 + \varepsilon) \times f(u_0)$
                    Develop (u_0)
                    $P_\varepsilon \leftarrow \{v \varepsilon s(u_0) | v \in P$ and $f(v) \leqslant$ Threshold$\}$
2. Iterate while $[P \neq \phi$ and $\forall t \varepsilon$ solutions: $f(t) >$ Threshold$]$
2.1 If $P_\varepsilon \neq \phi$ then $u \leftarrow$ Choice-in-P_ε
2.2 If not $u \leftarrow$ Choice-in-P
2.3 Develop u
2.4 Iterate while $[$Persevere and $P \neq \phi$ and $\forall v \varepsilon P \cup s(u)$: $f(v) >$ Threshold$]$
        Develop $(\hat{u})$
2.5 End iteration 2.4
2.6 $P_\varepsilon \leftarrow \{v \in s(u) | v \in P$ and $f(v) \leqslant$ Threshold$\}$
3. End iteration 2
Output data: If $P = 0$ then there is no solution
    If not for state t in Solutions with minimal $f(t)$, take out Route(t) and

$$\varepsilon' \leftarrow [(1 + \varepsilon)/\text{Threshold}] f(t) - 1$$

The development of a state u is carried out by the procedure:

Develop (u):
1. Suppress u in P and place it in Q
2. Iterate on $\{v \in s(u)\}$
        If $[v \notin P \cup Q$ or $g(v) > g(u) + K(u, v)]$ then do:

    $g(v) \leftarrow g(u) + K(u, v)$
    $f(v) \leftarrow g(v) + h(v)$
    father $(v) \leftarrow u$
    Store v in P
    if $[v \in T]$ then place v in Solutions
3. End iteration 2

4. Threshold $\leftarrow$ max {Threshold; $(1 + \varepsilon)f(\hat{u})$}}

The initialization of the algorithm develops the root u_0, and the iteration (2) is the main loop. After the development of a state u (in 2.3) and if there is no acceptable successor to u, the possibility of applying the perseverance strategy is tested (iteration 2.4). If u has already acceptable successors, or if they have become so after 2.4, then the following iteration will develop one, chosen by Choice-in-P_ε. The same route will then be followed. If not $P_\varepsilon = 0$, and backtracking will be applied (in 2.2), along another route, chosen by Choice-in-P. Apart from a termination test, the development of a state is identical to that carried out by A^*. Any terminal state attained is placed in Solutions, and the Develop procedure updates the Threshold variable.

Both the main loop of A_ε and the internal loop (2.5) stop when there are no further pending states, or when the cost of the best known solution is acceptable. The latter condition arises either as a result of pursuing an acceptable route until the end, or by raising the acceptability threshold. The three procedures used by A_ε are examined below:

1. Choice-in-P: selects from P the acceptable state from which A_ε will continue the search in the case of backtracking (the first iteration will be started). The choices are:

—the pending state $\hat{u}$ (the one with minimal $f(u)$), this choice takes the algorithm as 'high' up as possible in the search graph, in the hope of starting on a good route (that will remain acceptable for a long time, because the acceptability threshold will be raised);

—the acceptable pending state with minimal h_c, which moves the search to the first acceptable bifurcation, with the risk of leading to a broad development at that level (frequent backtracking and development of short routes);

—the acceptable pending state minimizing a sum such that $[\alpha f(u) + \beta h_c(u)]$; this solution demands a thorough knowledge of the problem to determine the weighting factors, which may not be constant (α should be larger at the start of the search, and at the end the weighting of h_c will be of greater importance).

2. Choice-in-P_ε: selects the acceptable successor on which the route being explored can be pursued. The same alternatives arise as for the previous procedure: the choice is, however, less crucial for the complexity of the search.

3. Perseverance: returns a {true, false} logical value, determining the possibility of applying the perseverance strategy. The following considerations can form the basis:

—the maximal number of successive iterations of (2.4) must remain low (2 or 3);

—the route being developed is almost acceptable (that is, there is a successor v such that $[f(v) - \text{Threshold}]$ is low;

—this route is sufficiently close to a solution to merit perseverance on it (that is, $h_c(u)$ is low);

—there may exist an almost acceptable solution, that is: ε solution such that $[f(t) - \text{Threshold}]$ is low;

—$\hat{u}$ corresponds to the largest actual reduction of $f^*(u_0)$, that is, $\text{Threshold} = (1 + \varepsilon)f(\hat{u})$;

—the heuristic h is monotonic;

—the first pending state $\hat{u}$ is sufficiently 'isolated' at the head of P, that is, the development of $\hat{u}$ will raise the acceptability threshold to a considerable degree.

It is interesting to compare the halting conditions of A_ε with that of A^*. Algorithm A^* stops when, at the moment of development of the best pending state, it notices that the state is terminal. A_ε on the other hand, surveys the terminal states at the moment of their generation (or reorientation of their father pointer).

By retaining the best solution attained at a certain stage, this algorithm can not only stop as soon as the estimate of the optimum guarantees the acceptability of this solution but, in addition, it can use the heuristic information (h and h_c) which is available for it to orient its search towards a particular stop. In imagining the comparison, it can be said that A^* halts by arriving at a solution somewhat surprisingly when A_ε directs itself towards it as a result of a differing view of the explored space. Another advantage of A_ε is that it can provide, if necessary, several solutions for the price of one (more than one of which may be acceptable).

The algorithm can also be asked to provide a solution without backtracking (simple in-depth search, developing only the vertices in the solution route): for this $\varepsilon = \infty$ must be fixed. Note that the algorithm A_ε provides as output not only the solution found, but also a value which is the smallest increase in the difference between this solution and the optimum, taking into account all the information acquired during the search.

The main properties of A_ε are:

1. for any finite value $\varepsilon \geqslant 0$, the algorithm converges (with the same hypotheses on G and h as those in assertion 6.3);

2. if the heuristic h verifies for any u: $0 \leqslant h(u) \leqslant (1 + e)h^*(u)$, e constant positive or nil, A_ε returns a solution t and a value $\varepsilon' \leqslant \varepsilon$ such that: $f(t) \leqslant (1 + e)(1 + \varepsilon')f^*(u_0)$.

Taking $e = 0$, and noting that in all cases $\varepsilon' \leqslant \varepsilon$, then if h is reducing, A_ε is ε-admissible.

On the subject of complexity, to the authors' knowledge no analysis of the average behaviour of the ε-admissible search has yet been published. Comparative, empirical results are available (Pearl 1983; Ghallab 1983), however, and concern the problem of the 'travelling salesman' in the plan (search of the minimal cost Hamiltonian cycle in a complete graph). The two following curves (Figure 6.2) give, for various values of ε, the proportion of the number of states developed by A_ε^* and A_ε, respectively, relative to the number of states developed by A^* (these algorithms being used to solve the problem of the commercial traveller in nine cities, with the same heuristics h and h_c, without perseverance strategy for A_ε).

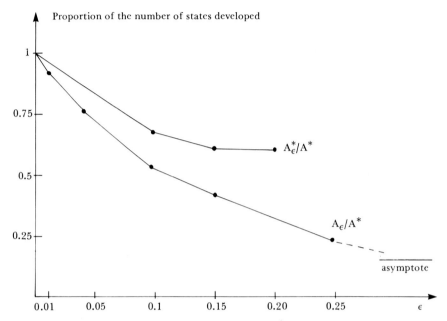

Figure 6.2 *Proportion of states developed by A_ϵ^* and A_ϵ relative to those developed by A^**

The extensions made by A^*, such as search with pruning, without redevelopment, or redundant research, can be generalized easily for A_ε. The search with partial development is particularly advantageous in the ε-admissible case, if the Choose-Successor procedure systematically returns the state v with minimal f (the updating of the acceptability threshold would have to be modified slightly).

To conclude this section, it would appear that the results of the behaviour illustrated in Figure 6.2, as well as interesting properties such as greater flexibility of use, diversity of strategies and choices, or the additional methods of using heuristic information (h_c, persevere), indicate ε-admissible research as a very promising approach. Despite their slightly more difficult implementation, these properties should eventually lead to a wider use.

Chapter 7

AND/OR graphs

7.1 The search problem using an AND/OR graph

The difference between searching a graph and searching an AND/OR graph resides in the fact that, in the latter case, the PSS rules are no longer bi-univocal applications (transforming a state u into one other state v), but multivocal applications (transforming u into several states $v_1 \ldots v_K$). For this reason, the expression 'state decomposition rule' is introduced. The search problem here is formulated in a similar way to that in the previous chapter. It is based on finding a method that, starting from an initial state u_0, for which several decomposition rules are valid, will choose one in particular for application to u_0, start at each of the states obtained by this rule, and continue in the same way until all the states that have not been broken down are terminal.

Each state, in fact, actually corresponds to a problem that must be solved. A valid rule for a problem can be to break it down into several sub-problems, each simpler to solve than the one it originated from. The solution of the initial problem cannot be found unless it is decomposed into sub-problems, all of which must be solved. The resolution of terminal states then becomes a trivial problem.

This formulation is very common in plan generation, and corresponds to solution by backwards chaining: the initial problem is the objective to be reached, and is described in terms of a particular situation or a set of conditions; the terminal states are sub-objectives and can be attained directly by applying planning operators. The order of the sub-problems, into which a given problem is broken down, is very important. The final plan will correspond to the sequence of operators solving the terminal sub-problems, determined by this order. An example of a plan generator, applying this type of approach, can be seen in the ARGOS-II system (Farreny 1981), which is discussed in detail later in this chapter.

As an illustration of the graphic representation used in this search, consider the simplified example of the seven following rules:

Example 7.1
R1 : a → b, c
R2 : d → a, e, f

R3 : d → a, k
R4 : f → i
R5 : f → c, j
R6 : f → g, h
R7 : k → e, l

Rule R2 states that the solution of problem 'd' is equivalent to the solution, in order, of sub-problems 'a', then 'e', then 'f'.

Let it be assumed that the terminal sub-problems are T = {b, c, e, j, l}
and that the initial problem 'd' is to be solved; the space corresponding
to this search will be represented in the following way (Figure 7.1):

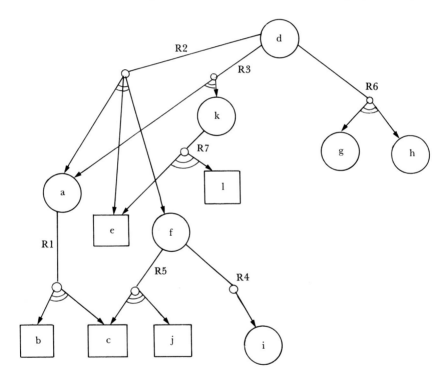

Figure 7.1 *Representation of a search space*

Starting from a node associated with a problem 'p' , there are as many
arcs as there are valid rules for p. Each of these arcs is labelled with the
name of the corresponding rule R_i, and leads to a decomposed node, from
which start as many arcs as there are sub-problems broken down from 'p'
by R_i. To distinguish these arcs from those mentioned above, a double
line is used to link them together, signifying that all the sub-problems they
lead to must be resolved before 'p'. The resulting graph is known as an
AND/OR graph, because it has two types of node: the OR nodes

associated with the problems (disjunction of the valid rules for a problem), and the decomposed AND nodes (conjunction of all the sub-problems). The terminal nodes (rectangular in the figure) are specific OR nodes.

Another type of representation (Figure 7.2) is more economical with its breakdown nodes. Only two entities are used: nodes associated with the problems, and connectors, a set of arcs linked with a double line, associated with the rules. As before, there are as many connectors starting from the node 'p' as there are valid rules in 'p'. Each connector R_i leads to the nodes into which R_i breaks down 'p' (in the order shown by the rule).

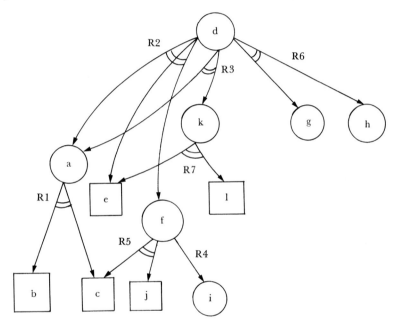

Figure 7.2 *Representation of a search space using fewer breakdown nodes*

This representation corresponds to a specific hypergraph (the basic relationship is no longer the binary arc between two nodes, but a K-nary relationship: a hyperarc called a 'connector' links several nodes together in a particular order).

Whereas for searching in a graph a solution corresponds to a specific route in the search graph, here a solution to the problem will be a particular sub-graph of the AND/OR graph; the sub-graph will include the root node; and, for any non-terminal node, a single connector in the AND/OR graph, and all the nodes to which this connector leads. The only two possible solutions in this example are shown in Figures 7.3 and 7.4:

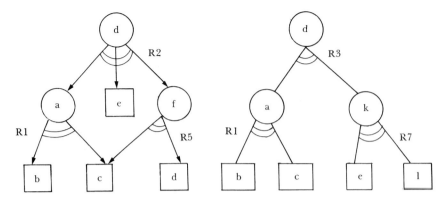

The two solutions to a search in Figure 7.2

Figure 7.3   Figure 7.4

In the case of plan generation, a purely sequential interpretation of a solution such as the one shown in Figure 7.3 would lead to the following plan: apply in order the operators that solve the terminal sub-problems: b, c, e, c, then j. Note that stage c appears twice.

A broader interpretation allows a certain level of parallelism in the plan represented by a problem solution modelled with an AND/OR graph. This interpretation consists of seeing each rule as a STRIPS type operator, with a precondition and action modifying the validity of certain data (Add and Delete list for the data added and deleted, respectively, in the base).

The rules from the previous example can be applied here, with slight modifications. The following operators apply:

R1 : if (b ∧ c) then Add {a}
R2 : if (a ∧ e ∧ f) then Add {d} etc.

The interpretation of the search graph (Figures 7.1 or 7.2) will be as follows: a plan will be found to validate the condition 'd' on the basis of the data {b, c, e, j, l}; three operators can produce 'd': R2, R3 or R6; the preconditions of R2 are 'a', 'e' and 'f'; to produce 'a', the operator R1 can be used with the data 'b' and 'c'; etc. The parallel interpretation sees the solution sub-graph as a partial order on the operators. The only sequencing constraint imposed by the solution in Figure 7.4 is: the operator R2 must take place after operators R1 and R5 have produced the data 'a' and 'f', which R2 needs; R1 and R5 can be executed in parallel since their preconditions are verified in the initial state.

To sum up, sequential interpretation considers the rules for decomposing problems into sub-problems, and associates an operator (action of the plan) with each terminal node of the solution graph. Parallel interpretation models the action of each operator (with transformation of the DB) with a rule that reappears as a connector in the solution graph. This latter interpretation becomes more complex when the effect of an operator is not restricted to simple addition of data, but also involves deletions. The interaction of the resulting rules can be managed in two phases: 1. by finding a potential solution without taking account of the deletions; and 2. by finding a partial order for the operators of this solution, guaranteeing the validity of each operator in relation to those preceding it in the plan produced (see, for example, the DCOMP system (Nilsson 1979).

Representation with an AND/OR graph is not limited to plan generation, with the interpretations introduced above. In the field of robotics, there are other types of application for this search model, including:

1. Generation of classifiers, in the form of decision trees, for iden-tification of objects by their overall characteristics;

2. Identification of partly observed objects, with syntactic methods (a context-free grammar is equivalent to an AND/OR;

3. Deduction of implicit information from a data base describing the state of the environment for robot development (that is, demonstration of theorems). The simplified example given above can be applied in the following way: rule R1 would correspond to the logical implication $b \wedge c \rightarrow a$. Figure 7.3 would be the search graph used to deduce the conclusion 'd' from the conjunction of facts $(b \wedge c \wedge e \wedge j \wedge l)$ initially pre-sent in the memory (a connector in this graph is a logical conjunction).

In this interpretation, the rules must be of type $\psi \Rightarrow L$, with L as an elementary literal and ψ as any logical formula. The starting data corres-pond to a conjunction of literals; the conclusion to be established is also a logical formula, itself represented by part of the AND/OR graph on which the search is based. The demonstration of the formula: $(a \wedge d) \vee (g \wedge f)$ would correspond to the following search space (Figure 7.5).

A proof-solution would be a specific sub-graph, as before, in which all the nodes without successors are elementary facts. In the same application, and for the same type of rules, Vanderburg (1971) can be used as a reference for the construction of the search graph using facts. Nilsson (1976) contains an extended development of this question with, in particular, a rather different second interpretation: the search is forward chaining: the rules are of the Horn clause type $L \Rightarrow \psi$. A logic formula is used, expressing the starting data (in the form of part of an AND/OR graph), and the idea is to establish a conclusion which is a disjunction of literals. The connectors in the search graph are logic disjunctions. A sub-graph solution will have as its terminal nodes all the conclusion literals, as well as the starting data required for the proof.

It should be noted, finally, that apart from its applications in the field of robotics, representation with AND/OR graphs forms the basis of many

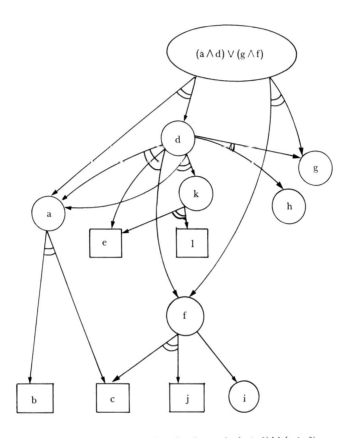

Figure 7.5 *Search space for the formula (a ∧ d) ∨ (g ∧ f)*

PSSs and is used in most expert systems (see Section 2.11). In addition, this representation is very close to that used in game trees (see Kumar (1983) for a formal comparison).

To sum up, representation using AND/OR graphs corresponds to the search problems in which stages involving the choice of one alternative from many, and stages requiring several different cases to be taken into account at the same time, both appear. Even for this type of problem, representation by a space of the state graph is still possible. A typical example of this is the generation system for the STRIPS plan: a state of the search space in STRIPS is made up of the couplet: current situation (initial, or resulting from the application of certain operators); and list of current sub-objectives to be attained. For example 7.1, the equivalent of Figure 7.1 is represented by the search graph in Figure 7.6.

A terminal state is one for which the list of sub-objectives is empty. There are four solution routes in this graph, corresponding to Figures 7.2

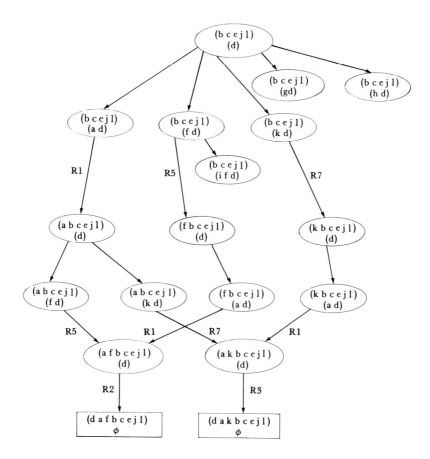

Figure 7.6 *STRIPS representation of Example 7.1*

and 7.3, each with two possibilities for sequentialization of the operators R1, R5 or R1, R7.

The technique used by STRIPS (of associating the objectives-situation couplet with a state) is very general, and can be implemented in a procedure for automatic transformation from an AND/OR graph to a graph (Vanderburg (1976) suggests a similar algorithm). The inverse transformation is even more immediate (because a graph appears as a specific case of an AND/OR graph in which all the connectors are reduced to simple arcs).

The question then arises of knowing which representation to choose: a simple graph or an AND/OR graph. The criteria for choice are, on the one hand, the algorithmic complexity of solving the problem in the representation adopted, and on the other hand, the ergonomic quality of a representation for the person modelling and formalizing the problem in this representation, and who may have to add or modify rules, translate non-formalized knowledge using heuristics, and provide parameters and estimates for cost. Since these two criteria are, for different reasons, very difficult to appreciate, it is not only impossible to reply to the question in a general way (by delimiting, for example, a class of problems for which a particular choice of representation is most suitable), but it is sometimes even difficult to answer specifically for a particular problem. The choice is often justified by reference to such ideas as that of the 'natural' character of representation for a problem.

Note, in the example given, that the representation of STRIPS in Figure 7.6 seems heavy and 'unnatural' compared with that of Figure 7.1. The reader is, however, encouraged to consider a slightly more complicated case in which the operators would carry out not only addition, but also deletion of data (for example, each of the seven operators would delete the preconditions), in which it would become clear that the representation of STRIPS is far easier to handle than that of the AND/OR graphs (see also Chapter 8).

These considerations can be concluded by mentioning the fact that if the two criteria for the choice of representation are divergent, it is entirely possible (although we know of no examples) to handle several representations simultaneously, chosen independently for their ergonomic or algorithmic quality, with procedures for automatic transfer from one to the other.

7.2   Algorithms for non-evaluated search

Consider a PSS in which each rule is a state decomposition operator and for which: U is the representation space; $u_0 \varepsilon U$ is the initial state; $T \subset U$ is the sub-set of terminal states; and $\{R_1, \ldots, R_M\}$ is the set of breakdown rules.

The search space associated with this PSS is an AND/OR graph, known as $H = (U, s)$, with $s = \{s_1, \ldots, s_M\}$, such that, if $I(u) = \{i, i', i'', \ldots\}$ is the set of indices of the valid rules in the state u, $I(u) \subset \{1, \ldots, M\}$, then:

—$s_i(u) = \{v_1, \ldots, v_9\}$ is the set of successor states to u, in which the rule R_i breaks down u (the set can be ordered under some conditions); $s_i(u)$ is a connector of H;

—$s(u) = \cup s_i(u)$, for $i \in I(u)$; $s(u)$ is the set of all possible successors to u in H, by all its connectors; it is accepted that $s(u)$ is a finite set, which implies that both $I(u)$ and all of the values $s_i(u)$ are finite;

—$s^{-1}(u) = \{v \varepsilon U \mid \exists i \in I(v) : u \in s_i(v)\}$ is the set of all states to which u is the successor;

—$\hat{s}(u)$ and $\hat{s}^{-1}(u)$ are the transitive closures of relationships s and δ^{-1}, that is, the set of all the descendants and ascendants, respectively, of u in H.

At this level, the following restrictive hypothesis is admitted: the search space H is an AND/OR graph without circuit, that is, $\forall u \in U : u \notin \hat{s}(u)$.

One solution to the search problem is a particular sub-graph of H, found in state u, and noted $G(u_0)$, defined by:

1. u_0 belongs to $G(u_0)$;

2. for any state v of $G(u_0)$, either v is terminal, or there is a single connector $s_i(v)$ in H, such that: (a) for any $w \in s_i(v)$, w is the successor to v in $G(u_0)$, and (b) v has no successor in $G(u_0)$ other than the states of $s_i(v)$.

A partial solution can be provided by a sub-graph defined as before, but which can admit the states v that are non-terminal and have no successor. In the same way a sub-graph G(u) can be defined to provide a solution (total or partial) from any state u. Note that, because there is no circuit in H, G(u), if it exists, is a latticial (that is, a graph without circuits, and in which all the states are descendants of u).

In the absence of a cost criterion, the solution of the search problem modelled by H consists of finding a solution sub-graph $G(u_0)$. A non-determining algorithm can be introduced for this search:

Define–Solution (u_0): Non-deterministic procedure
1. Initialization: $B \leftarrow \{u_0\}; G(u_0) \leftarrow (\{u_0\}, \phi)$ graph reduced to single state u_0
2. Iterate while $[B \neq \phi]$
2.1 Take state u at head of stack B and delete it from B
2.2 If $I(u) = \phi$ then Return ('Absence-of-solution')
2.3 $\hat{i} \leftarrow$ Non-deterministic-choice $(I(u))$
2.4 Iterate on $\{v \in s_i(u)\}$
    If $[v \in T$ and $v \in G(u_0)]$ then store v in B
    Add to $G(u_0)$ the state v and the arc (u, v)
2.5 End iteration 2.4
3. End iteration 2

This algorithm progressively extends a partial solution $G(u_0)$ until a complete solution is obtained. With the current iteration, B is the list of all the states of $G(u_0)$ which have no successor in $G(u_0)$ and are not terminal. If several connectors in H $(I(u) \neq \phi)$ start from u, the state at the head of list B, then a non-deterministic choice of one of them is made (the choice is assumed, by definition, to be the best, that is, the one that leads to a solution, if one exists), and all the successors of u along the chosen connector $s_i(u)$ are added to $G(u_0)$. If u has no successor in H and is not terminal, then there is no solution.

Basically, Define–Solution carries out a depth-first exploration in H: the construction of the same partial solution if pursued to the stopping point. The order of storing of the states in B means that this construction can be carried out either depth- or breadth-first relative to $G(u_0)$. These two alternatives correspond to the states being stored, as they are generated, at the head or tail of B, respectively. This variation in the in-depth search strategy (which did not appear in the previous chapter, because the desired solution is a linear sequence) may be important to the complexity of the search.

The previous non-deterministic procedure has no practical use on its own in the form given here. It does, however, serve a purpose in the Backtrack Search in a Hypergraph (BSH) recursive algorithm with partial development, to be introduced below, and in the algorithms that follow it, when a means of fixing the non-deterministic choice will be defined.

Ideally, BSH should behave like Define–Solution: choosing a connector in each state and pursuing the search along this connector. If, however, this results in failure (encountering a terminal state without successor) the previously made choice must be reconsidered, and other alternatives explored.

In order to manage this backtracking, two sub-sets are defined among the states of H, generated by the search:

—SOLVED: set (i) of the terminal sets, and (ii) of the sets u such that there exists a connector $s_i(u)$, $i \in I(u) : s_i(u) \subset$ SOLVED (that is, for any $v \varepsilon s_i(u)$, v is in SOLVED).

—INSOLUBLE: set (i) of the non-terminal states without successor in H, and (ii) the states u such that for any connector $s_i(u)$, $i \varepsilon I(u) : s_i \cap = \phi$ (that is, there exists $v \varepsilon s_i(u)$, v is in INSOLUBLE).

There is a constraint to ensure the convergence of the algorithm, and to limit the space explored by a certain increase. In the absence of a cost, an increase will be used on the rank of the states. By definition (generalizing for simple graphs) the rank of a state in an AND/OR graph is: $\forall_u \varepsilon U$ rank $(u) = 1 + \max\{rank(v) \mid v \in s^{-1}(u)\}$; and rank $(u_0) = 0$. On the basis of an estimation of rank(u), noted rg(u), BSH includes any state, with rank above a threshold, in INSOLUBLE.

The algorithm is as follows:

BSH(u)
1. If $u \varepsilon T$ then Return ('Success')
2. If $[I(u) = \phi$ or rg(u) $>$ Threshold] then Return ('Failure')
3. Iterate on $\{i \in I(u)\}$
3.1 Flag $\leftarrow$ true
3.2 Iterate on $\{v \in s_i(u)\}$ while [Flag]
     If $v \notin$ SOLVED then do:
     If $v \in$ INSOLUBLE then Flag $\leftarrow$ false
     If not do:
     rg(v) $\leftarrow$ 1 + rg(u)
     If BSH(v) = 'Failure' then do:
     place v in INSOLUBLE

Flag ← false
If not place v in SOLVED
End iteration 3.2
3.3 If [Flag] then do:
place u in SOLVED
$\hat{i}(u) \leftarrow i$
Return ('Success')
End iteration 3.
4. Place u in INSOLUBLE
5. Return ('Failure')

During a call to state u, the recursion halts if u is terminal, if u has no successor, or if the rank of u is greater than Threshold. If not, the recursion continues along a connector $s_i(u)$ and on a state $v \varepsilon s_i(u)$ which appears neither in SOLVED nor in INSOLUBLE. If BSH(v) succeeds (manages to place v in SOLVED), or if v was already in SOLVED, then the search continues on the other successor states to u, along the same connector $s_i(u)$; u will itself be placed in SOLVED if all the elements of $s_i(u)$ are; a pointer $\hat{i}(u) \leftarrow i$ will be retained for u on this particular connector $s_i(u)$. If, however, the search BSH(v) fails for one of the states v of $s_i(u)$, or if v was already in INSOLUBLE, then it is useless to continue the iteration on the other states of this connector (the logical variable Flag ε {true, false} indicates this situation), and another connector $s_i(u)$ must be explored. Because of the recursive structure, the BSH algorithm carries out an in-depth search, both relative to H and to the solution $G(u_0)$ being constructed.

In making a comparison with the BSG algorithm, it is important to note the presence of two iterations in BSH: one external (3) on the connectors (corresponding to the disjunction in the AND/OR graph), and one internal (3.2) on the states of a single connector (corresponding to conjunction). The internal iteration (3.2) must always take place completely if u is to be SOLVED, and it is immediately interrupted in case of failure. Iteration (3), however, will not actually take place (and the development of u will not be complete) unless explorations of all connectors from u fail. If this is the case, the BSH(u) call will also fail, the analysis of the connector in which u appears will be interrupted, and there is a return to a 'brother' connector, if one exists.

As in BSG, the idea of a pending state does not exist in BSH; any state generated is explored immediately. In addition, the hypothesis on the absence of any circuit in H provides an interesting property: during the call BSH(u), any state $v \in s(u)$, previously generated by the search, is either in SOLVED or in INSOLUBLE (the only other alternative is that its exploration is still taking place, in which case the stack for recursion from the call BSH(v) would constitute a circuit in H).

Note that the limitation of the search space is not carried out exactly on the basis of the state ranks, but on a decreasing estimation of these ranks: $\forall_u rg(u) \leqslant rank(u)$. This allows the algorithm to be simplified, while guaranteeing that the sub-space explored will include only that to which access is allowed by the limitation using rank (if $rg(u) >$ threshold then $rank(i) >$ threshold). This also makes it possible to avoid entering an infinite loop, when the hypothesis of absence of circuit in H could not be verified. Initially, $rg(u_0) = 0$ is adopted, with a value being fixed for the overall variable Threshold, and $BSH(u_0)$ is called. The algorithm will return either:

—'Failure: there is no solution sub-graph $G(u_0)$ in H, with all states of rank lower or equal to Threshold; or
—'Success': a solution $G(u_0)$ has been found. To make $G(u_0)$ explicit, the part of H generated by the search must be scanned, starting from state u_0, and following the length of each connector $s_i(u)$ on which the pointer $\hat{i}(u)$ has been retained, for each state u (the notation should strictly be: $s_{\hat{i}(u)}(u)$, since both the pointer and the connector are specific to u, but the notation used does not introduce any confusion).

This scanning of H is carried out by the Define–Solution (u_0) procedure: the instruction (2.2) and (2.3) must simply be deleted from the previous non-determinist formula, since the choice of $\hat{i}(u)$ in each state of $G(u_0)$ is fixed in a determinist way by BSH.

If heuristic information is available, it can be used by the BSH algorithm in the order in which the various connectors of $I(u)$ are examined by the iteration (3): the valid rules in u are ordered a priori, according to their desirability, without there being any need to generate and analyse the successors into which u is broken down by each rule. It can also be used to interrupt the recursion on certain states u, the appearance of which in a solution is judged unlikely: they will be placed in INSOLUBLE without otherwise verifying the conditions of instruction (2).

If H is an AND/OR graph (finite or infinite) without circuit, containing at least one solution $G(u_0)$, and if Threshold is an increasing estimator with rank of any non-terminal state of $G(u_0)$, then BSH converges and finds a solution of this kind.

For any state u in H, the call $BSH(u)$ is made once at the most. The complexity of the algorithm is therefore in $O(M)$ calls, if M is the number of states in H, with rank lower than or equal to Threshold.

Finally, because of the recursion, the implementation of BSH is very simple (a single pointer structure to manage: $\hat{i}(u)$; algorithms AO^* and AO_ε which will follow.

7.3　Admissible search: the AO^* algorithm

This section is concerned with the search, in an AND/OR graph, for an optimal solution in relation to a cost criterion.

As for searching in a simple graph, a positive or nil cost is associated with each state decomposition rule: if R_i is valid in u, the connector $s_i(u)$ will have a cost $k(u, i) \geqslant 0$. A cost $k(v) \geqslant 0$ can also be made to correspond to any terminal state $v \varepsilon T$. These costs are assumed to be additive. Unlike the case of a linear route solution, however, in a solution $G(u_0)$ which is a graph, a state u may be accessible from u_0 by several routes. In this way, the cost of a solution $G(u_0)$ will be defined recursively as $\zeta(G(u_0)) = k(u_0, \hat{\imath}) + \Sigma_{v \varepsilon s_i(u_0)} \zeta(G(v))$ with $s_i(u_0)$, set of successors to u_0 in $G(u_0)$ and $G(v)$, sub-graph of $G(u_0)$ generated by v and all its descendants in $G(u_0)$, taking $\zeta(G(v)) = k(v)$ if v is terminal.

In this definition, the cost $k(u, \hat{\imath})$ (or $k(u)$) intervenes in $\zeta(G(u_0))$ as many times as there are distinct routes in $G(u_0)$ between u_0 and u. If $m(u)$ is this number of times, it is easy to verify that: $m(v) = \Sigma m(u)$, on all the u such that the arc (u, v) is in $G(u_0)$; with $m(u_0) = 1$.

This gives $\zeta(G(u_0)) = \Sigma_{u \varepsilon G(u_0)} m(u), k(u, \hat{\imath})$; with the convention that $k(u, \hat{\imath}) = k(u)$ if u is terminal. For reasons of convenience, this definition will also be applied to partial solution, taking $k(v) = 0$ for a non-terminal state without successor in $G(u_0)$.

In the application to the plan generation, introduced above (sequential interpretation), the cost $k(v)$ will correspond to the application of the operator stage of the plan associated with the terminal state v; the decomposition rules for the problem may have a cost of nil, and the suggested criterion $\zeta(G(u_0))$ will be the sum of the cost of stages in the plan for the solution $G(u_0)$.

Note: In the generation of a plan with parallel interpretation, the sum of costs for the stages of the plan is $\Sigma k(u, \hat{\imath})$ for all the states of $G(u_0)$. This does not correspond to the criterion ζ except for any u: $m(u) = 1$, that is, if any solution in the AND/OR graph is a tree. Without this restrictive hypothesis, the search for an optimal solution for the criterion $\Sigma k(u, \hat{\imath})$ is an NP-hard problem (that is, with exponential combinatorial growth, see Sahni 1974).

Let h^*u_0 be the cost of a complete solution in H, optimal for the criterion ζ, and $h^*(u) = \min\{\zeta(G(u)) \mid G(u) \text{ the complete solution in H of root } u\}$. To guide the search for an optimal solution in H, the heuristic information will be used in the form of an application h: $u \rightarrow \mathbb{R}^+$ such that $h(u)$ is an estimate of $h^*(u)$. The definitions of the properties of this heuristic function can easily be generalized from those presented in the previous chapter, in particular, h is decreasing if $\forall u \varepsilon u : h(u) \leqslant h^*(u)$; h is monotonic if $\forall u \varepsilon u$, $i \varepsilon I(u) : h(u) \leqslant k(u, i) + \Sigma_{v \varepsilon s_i(u)} h(v)$; and h is coincident if $\forall_u \varepsilon T : h(u) = k(u)$.

A search in an AND/OR graph for an optimal solution is very different from a search aimed at attaining a particular solution (which was not the case for simple graphs). The introduction of costs brings about an important qualitative change in the search problem: it is very difficult, and algorithmically complex to calculate and maintain, for any state u generated, the cost of the best partial solution known at the current moment, and containing the state u (the equivalent of g(u) and of the route (u) from the previous chapter). This problem arises from the fact that any newly generated state v may appear in many sub-graphs and intervene in the cost of each of them with very different m(v) weightings.

The AO* algorithm, originally devised by Martelli (1973), solves this difficulty in the following way:

—for a developed state u, on each connector s(u) the cost estimate is maintained and updated: $f_i(u) = k(u, i) + \Sigma_{v\in s_i(u)}f(v)$, by noting the minimal estimate: $f(u) = \min\{f_i(u) \mid i \in I(u)\}$, and retaining a pointer $\hat{i}(u)$ to the minimal connector $f(u) = f_{\hat{i}}(u)$;

—for a generated, but not yet developed state, $f(u) = h(u)$ is adopted by definition (and $\hat{i}(u)$ is undefined).

It follows that, if $\hat{G}(u)$ is the current partial solution obtained by following the pointers $\hat{i}$ from u to the terminal or pending state, then $f(u) = \mathcal{f}(\hat{G}(u)) = \Sigma_{m(v)h(v)}$, for v pending. f(u) is therefore an estimate of the cost for minimal $\hat{G}(u)$, and $f_i(u)$ estimates the cost of the best current solution that uses the connector $s_i(u)$.

In addition to the data $f_i(u)$, f(u) and i(u), defined above, the algorithm AO* uses the following structures: Q, set of developed states; P, set of pending states (generated but not developed); $G(u_0)$, best partial solution known at the current moment; A, set of states of which the estimate f has been established; $I'(u)$, sub-set of connectors $s_i(u)$ of which the estimate f(u) is to be updated.

Algorithm AO*
Input data: u_0, T, $\{s_1, \ldots, s_M\}$, costs k, function h

1. Initialization: $P \leftarrow \{u_0\}; Q \leftarrow \phi; f(u_0) \leftarrow h(u_0); u \leftarrow u_0$
2. Iterate while [u $\neq$ nil and $f(u_0) \neq \infty$]
2.1 Delete u from P and place it in Q
2.2 Iterate on $\{i \in I(u)\}$
2.2.1 Iterate on $\{v \in s_i(u) \mid v \notin P \cup Q\}$
    $P \leftarrow P \cup \{u\}; f(v) \leftarrow h(v)$
2.2.2 $f_i(u) \leftarrow k(u, i) + \Sigma_{v\in s_i(u)}f(v)$
    End iteration 2.2
2.3 If $I(u) = \phi$ then $f(u) \leftarrow \infty$
2.4 If not do: $f(u) \leftarrow \min\{f_i(u) \mid it I(u)\}; \hat{i}(u) \leftarrow$ minimum index
2.5 $A \leftarrow s^{-1}(u)$
2.6 For $\{w \in s^{-1}(u)\}$ do: $I'(w) \leftarrow \{i \in I(w) \mid u \in s_i(w)\}$
2.7 Iterate while [A $\neq \phi$]
2.7.1 Take and delete from A a state v such that $A \cap \delta(v) = \phi$
2.7.2 For $\{i \in I'(v)\}$ do: $f_i(v) \leftarrow k(v, i) + \Sigma_{w \in s_i(v)}f(w)$
2.7.3 If $f_{\hat{i}}(v) \neq \min\{f_i(v) \mid i \in I(v)\}$ then $\hat{i}(v)$ new minimum index

If $f(v) \neq f_i(v)$ then do
$f(v) \leftarrow f_i(v)$
$A \leftarrow A \cup s^{-1}(v)$
For $\{w \in s^{-1}(v)\}$ do: $I'(w) \leftarrow I'(w) \cup \{i \in I(w)\} v \in s(w)$
2.7.4 $I'(v) \leftarrow \phi$
    End iteration 2.7
2.8 $G(u_0) \leftarrow$ Define–Solution (u_0)
2.9 $u \leftarrow$ Choose–Pending–State $(G(u_0))$
    End iteration 2
Output data: If $f(u_0) = \infty$ then there is no solution
               If not take solution $G(u_0)$ out of cost $f(u_0)$.

The algorithm AO^* functions with complete state developments, and controls a search ordered by the evaluation of cost f: each iteration examines the best partial solution $G(u_0)$ in relation to this evaluation (strategy 3a). The main iteration (2) of the algorithm can be decomposed into three states:

1. Development of a pending state in the partial solution $G(u_0)$ being explored (states 2.1, 2.2 and 2.3).

2. Ascendant update in H of the estimate f and the pointer i on the minimal connector for all the ascendants of the developed state u. For a father v of u, the indices $I'(v)$ of the connectors by which u is successor to v are noted, and $f_i(v)$ is recalculated for each one. If the min$\{f_i(v)\}$ has strictly dropped, the pointer $\hat{i}(v)$ is changed and the fathers of v are placed in A to be actualized in their turn. The ascending order of the update (a state is chosen in A without successor in A) and the absence of any circuit in H guarantee that each state concerned will be updated once, and once only.

3. Definition of the new best partial solution of H, $G(u_0)$, and choice of one of its pending states u on which the search will be continued (stages 2.7 and 2.8). The Define–Solution procedure generates $G(u_0)$ by moving down into H, from $G(u_0)$, and by following the connectors marked $\hat{i}$ (the formula from page 134 is used here, with deletion of lines 2.2 and 2.3 and transformation of 2.4), so that the pending and terminal states will not be disturbed, as follows:
2.4.1: If $[v \notin T \cup P]$ and $[v \in G(u_0)]$ then store v in B.

The Choice–Pending State then explores $G(u_0)$: it will return nil if this sub-graph has no pending state (complete solution), if not it will return one, chosen according to the adopted strategy, in depth or in breadth. This choice may be significant for the complexity of the algorithm, and will be made for each individual application.

The idea of developing a state does not have quite the same meaning in AO^* as in A^*. In the latter algorithm, a state u, the evaluation $f(u)$ of which has dropped, is re-established as pending, and will eventually be redeveloped to redirect the search from u to another of its successors. In the algorithm AO^*, the development of a state u is carried out once at the most, but the updating of its evaluation f(u) and of its pointer $\hat{i}(u)$ to the minimal connector $s_{\hat{i}}(u)$ will be carried out often as new descendants of u are developed. Note also another important difference: in A^*, all the partial routes of the graph G are directly accessible at any time from the algorithm, and the evaluations of their cost are known (that is, f(u) on the pending vertices); in AO^*, only one partial sub-graph $G(u_0)$ is known at one time, and each iteration redefines and recalculates its evaluation.

Example 7.2: let AO^* be applied to the AND/OR graph below, with the following cost distributions and heuristic: $K(u_0, 1) = 5$, $K(u_0, 2) = 19, \ldots,$ and $h(u_1) = 20$; $h(u_2) = 30$; $\ldots$; the terminal states $\{u_{16}, u_{17}, u_{21}, u_{22}, u_{23}, u_{20}, u_{15}\}$ have zero cost.

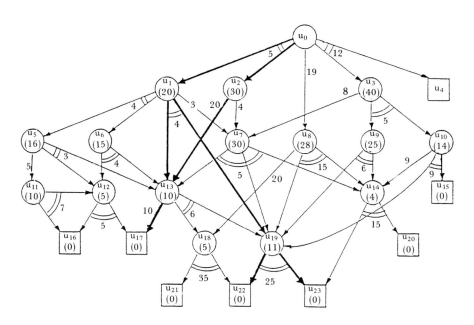

Figure 7.7 *Solution (bold lines) to Example 7.2*

The sequence of iterations (state development, actualization, definition of $G(u_0)$) carried out by AO^* on H is given by the following table. f(u) is found from the list (in left to right order) of the values $f_i(u)$, by underlining $f_{\hat{i}}(u)$. The solution obtained is shown in Figure 7.7, in bold lines, and its cost is $f(u_0) = 74 = \zeta(G(u_0))$.

Consider the properties of the algorithm AO^*.

u	h(u)	$f(u):(f_i(u), f_{i'}(u), \ldots)$	States actualized after development of u	States pending in $G(u_0)$
u_0		$(55, \underline{47}, 52)$	ϕ	u_8
u_8	28	$(\underline{25}, 30)$	$u_0 : (55, \underline{44}, 52)$	u_{18}
u_{18}	5	$(\underline{35})$	$u_8 : (55, \underline{30})$; $u_0 ; (55, \underline{49}, 52)$	u_{19}; u_{14}
u_{19}	11	$(\underline{25})$	$u_8 : (55, \underline{44}) : u_0 ; (55, 63, \underline{52})$	u_3
u_3	40	$(\underline{38}, 44)$	$u_0 : (55, 63, \underline{50})$	u_7
u_7	30	$(\underline{44})$	$u_3 : (52, \underline{44})$; $u_0 : (\underline{55}, 63, 56)$	u_1; u_2
u_1	20	$(35, 39, 47)$	$u_0 : (70, 63, \underline{56})$	u_9; u_{10}
u_9	25	$(\underline{35})$	$u_3 : (\underline{52}, 54) : u_0 : (70, \underline{63}, 64)$	u_{14}
u_{14}	4	$(\underline{15})$	$u_9 : (\underline{46})$; $u_8 : (55, \underline{55})$; $u_7(\underline{55})$ $u_1 : (\underline{35}, 39, 58)$; $u_3 : (\underline{63}, 65)$; $u_0 : (\underline{70}, 74, 75)$	u_5; u_2; u_8
u_5	16	$(\underline{15}, 18)$	$u_1 : (\underline{34}, 39, 58)$; $u_0 : (\underline{69}, 74, 75)$	u_2; u_6; u_{11}
u_2	30	$(\underline{30}, 59)$	ϕ	u_6; u_{13}; u_{11}
u_6	15	$(\underline{19})$	$u_1 : (\underline{38}, 39, 58)$; $u_0 : (\underline{73}, 74, 75)$	u_{13}; u_{11}; u_{12}
u_{13}	10	$(\underline{10}, 66)$	ϕ	u_{11}; u_{12}
u_{11}	10	$(\underline{12})$	$u_5 : (17, 18)$; $u_1 : (40, \underline{39}, 58)$ $u_0 : (\underline{74}, 74, 75)$	ϕ

7.3.1 CONVERGENCE

Assertion 7.1: for any AND/OR graph H, finite and without circuit, and for any application h of U in $\mathbb{R}^+$ such that: if $h(u) = \infty$ then there is no solution $G(u)$ for root u in H, and the algorithm AO^* converges: it stops and gives a sub-graph $G(u_0)$ of H if there is a solution, or else $f(u_0) = \infty$ in the absence of a solution.

Proof: AO^* will not develop a state u more than once. After a finite number of iterations, all the states of H are eventually developed. As a result of this, for any $u \in H$, if $f(u) = \infty$ then either u is non-terminal and without successor, or for any connector $s_i(u)$, $i \in I(u)$, $f_i(u) = \infty$: in either case, and given the hypothesis on **h**, there is no solution $G(u)$ with root u. The existence of a $G(u)$ implies that $f(u)$ is finite; after the development of all the descendants of u, the algorithm will generate a graph of this kind, by pursuing the minimal connectors. This is true for state u_0 in particular.

Assertion 7.2: If H and h verify the following hypotheses:

1. H is a finite or infinite AND/OR graph, without loop, with positive or nil costs, not including any partial or complete sub-graph that is infinite (in its number of states) and of limited cost, but containing at least one finite solution;

2. h is an application of U in $\mathbb{R}^+$ such that if $G^*(u_0)$ is an optimal solution in H, then there is an increasing η with $h(u) < \eta$ for any u in $G^*(u_0)$;

then the algorithm AO* converges, that is, it stops when it provides a solution.

Proof: (only the essential points of the argument are given here)

1. Let Hj be the sub-set of state of H known by AO^*, at the end of the jth main iteration. The hypothesis $|s(u)|$, which is finite for any u, implies that if j tends towards infinity and Hj includes an infinite number of states, then Hj must contain at least one infinite sub-graph $G(u_0)$ that is, there cannot be an infinite set of finite sub-graphs in Hj (perhaps established by recurrence on the maximum rank in states of Hj: if this rank is finite, then Hj has a finite number of states).

2. The hypothesis on H implies that there must exist an optimal solution. If K is the cost of the solution, assumed to be contained in H, and $\mathcal{G}$ is the set of solutions of cost less than or equal to K, then any element of $\mathcal{G}$ has a finite number of states: by a similar argument in 1, it is deduced that $\mathcal{G}$ is a finite set of solutions, and that it includes an element $G^*(u_0)$ which is the minimum cost.

3. The algorithm stopping with $f(u_0) = \infty$ and the absence of solution are impossible: by hypothesis on h, for any state u of $G^*(u_0) : h(u)\eta$ there is, therefore, an increasing M such that at any moment the estimate of the connector $s_i*(u)$, corresponding to u in $G^*(u_0)$, verifies $f_i*(u) \leqslant M$ (it is possible to take, for example $M = \Sigma_u \in G^*(u_0)m(u) \times \max \{h(u); k(u,i^*)\}$. This is true for all the state of $G^*(u_0)$, in particular for u_0, which gives $f(u_0) = \min_i\{f_i(u_0)\} \leqslant f_i^*(u_0) \leqslant M$.

4. The absence of any circuit in H and the fact that a state is developed once, at the most, mean that AO^* will not converge singly if it iterates to infinity by developing an infinite number of states. According to argument 1, however, the corresponding Hj contains an infinite sub-graph $G(u_0)$. Developing a state in $G(u_0)$ signifies that this partial graph is the one generated in the previous iteration, by Define–Solution, with $f(u_0) \geqslant s(G(u_0))$. By hypothesis on **h**, $s(G(u_0))$ cannot be finite and therefore $f(u_0) > M$, which contradicts argument 3.

7.3.2 ADMISSIBILITY

The proof of the admissibility of the algorithm is found with the establishment of the following lemma:

Assertion 7.3: If h is decreasing and coincident, then for any state u generated by the algorithm AO^*, the estimate f verifies, at the end of each of the iterations (2): $f(u) \leqslant h^*(u)$; and if $G(u)$ is complete: $f(u) = h^*(u) = s(G(u))$.

Proof: For a pending state, the proposition is simple:

$f(u) = h(u) \leqslant h^*(u)$ by hypothesis. For a developed state u, it should first be shown that if all the successors of u verify the proposition, then u also verifies it. By definition (in 2.3.2) or actualization (in 2.6.3), the following is found:

$$f(u) = \min_i \{k(u,i) + \sum_{v \in s_i(u)} f(v)\} \leqslant \min_i \{k(u,i) + \sum_{v \in s_i(u)} h^*(v)\} = h^*(u)$$

In addition, if $G(u)$ is complete (that is, the sub-graph of $G(u_0)$ generated by u and its descendants in $G(u_0)$ contains only developed or terminal states), then $\forall v \in G(u)$:

—either v is terminal and $f(u) = h(v)s(G(v))$, since h is coincident;
—or $G(v)$ is complete and by induction $f(v) = h^*(v) = s(G(v))$.
Hence:

$$f(u) = k(u, \hat{i}) + \sum_{v \in s_{\hat{i}}(u)} h^*(v) = \min_i \{k(u, i) + \sum_{v \in s_{\hat{i}}(u)} h^*(v)\} = h^*(u) = s(G(u))$$

The recurrence proposition can now be shown.

Basis: The first iteration (2) develops u_0:

$$f(u_0) = \min_i \{k(u_0, i) + \sum_{v \in s_i(u_0)} h(v)\} \leqslant \min_i \{k(u_0, i) + \sum_{v \in s_i(u_0)} h^*(v)\} = h^*(u_0)$$

Induction: If the proposition is true as far as the iteration preceding the one in which u is developed, then at the moment when u is developed, the following is found for all the successors already existing: $f(v) \leqslant h^*(v)$ by induction, and for all the successors newly placed in P: $f(v) = h(v) \leqslant h^*(v)$ by hypothesis on h. All the successors to u, therefore, verify the proposition, and u verifies it also, according to what precedes.

It remains to be established that the proposition is still true for all the other states developed previously, even after the actualization following the development of u. The procedure applied here is one of recurrence on the sequence of states actualized. Let v be the first state updated in the iteration (2.6): $f(v) = \min_i \{k(v, i) + \sum_{w \in s_i(v)} f(w)\}$ following this actualization. For each of the states w of this expression, either:

1. $f(w)$ has not yet been modified in the course of this actualization and, because of the absence of any circuit in H and the order of the actualizations in (2.6), $f(w)$ can no longer be modified: w verifies the proposition by induction; or

2. w is the state u, just developed, and in this situation the result is equally valid. All the successors to v verify the proposition, and therefore v verifies it too. An identical argument shows that for any successor w to an updated state, either w has not yet been modified and will be so no longer, or w has been actualized and verifies the proposition by induction, or else w is the state u, just developed.

Assertion 7.4: If h is reducing and coincident, and if H verifies the hypothesis of assertion 7.3, then AO* is admissible: it stops and provides an optimal solution.

Proof: A reducing and coincident heuristic verifies the hypothesis of assertion 7.4. So AO^* converges: it finds a complete solution $G(u_0)$. The previous proposition, applied to u_0, establishes the optimality of $G(u_0)$.

Naturally, if h is monotonic and coincident, h is also decreasing, and algorithm AO^* is equally admissible. The values of successive actualizations of $f(u)$, more than for a monotonic heuristic, can be established for a developed state u, and form a non-decreasing sequence. In principle, this allows phase 2 of the actualization to be simplified: only the fathers v of u to which (u) is successor on their minimal connector $s_î(v)$ are updated. Depending on the data structures used in an implementation of AO^*, however, this reduced actualization can be more costly to apply than a complete actualization.

7.3.3   EXAMPLE OF AN AND/OR GRAPH WITH CIRCUITS

In most applications, it is difficult to guarantee the absence of any circuit in the search graph. If this hypothesis is faulty, the preceding formulation of AO^* will not be convergent. For example, in a circuit, the Define–Solution procedure, or the ascending actualization will form an infinite loop.

A fairly substantial modification must be made to the algorithm. The basic idea is to detect a circuit as soon as it appears, then to break it by deleting one of its connectors. The problem lies in the choice of connector to delete: it is essential to avoid eliminating the only (or optimal) solution to the problem. The process adopted will, therefore, consist of a heuristic choice with questioning and backtracking if necessary.

The question of this possible return to the choice of connector deleted greatly complicates the application and implementation of the modification proposed. An intermediate solution (between not considering possible circuits and managing them completely) consists of making an irrevocable choice of the connector breaking the circuit, and is based on the following rules:

1. during development of a state u, a test is applied for each successor v of u (in iteration 2.3.1.1) if v appears among the known ascendants of u. If this is the case, then from the states of the circuit $(u, v, v', v'', \ldots, u)$ the sub-set $w, w', w'' \ldots$ is defined, in which each w admits at least one connector $s(w)$ which does not contain any state of the circuit. Two situations may arise:

2. either this sub-set is empty, and all the states of the circuit can be deleted definitively, without reducing the solution space. This will be done by scanning all the fathers of states in the circuit, and for each father x, $f_i(x) \leftarrow \infty$ is associated with each connector $s_i(x)$ containing a state of the circuit; or

3. the sub-set $(w, w', w'', \ldots)$ is not empty, in which case one of its elements must be chosen heuristically. The one with the most connectors,

other than those leading to the circuit, and in which the estimation of cost is better than that associated with the connectors in the circuit, will be chosen for preference (that is, the choice with the least chance, a priori, of being questioned). If w is the chosen state, then $f_i(w) \leftarrow \infty$ will be associated with the connectors $s_i(w)$ leading to states in the circuit, and for all successors $x \in s_i(w)$, w will be deleted from $s^{-1}(x)$.

By application of these rules, infinite loops in the circuits can be avoided, but the algorithm will not be convergent (or admissible) unless there is a solution (or optimal solution) that does not use any of the connectors deleted in order to break the circuits.

7.3.4 COMPLEXITY OF THE ALGORITHM

Very few results are available on the complexity of AO^*. Models and analyses carried out on A^* are unfortunately not transportable. It has been admitted, in particular, that the complexity of the algorithm A^* can be measured by the number of iterations on the principle loop, that is, the number of state developments, with all the other operations carried out by the algorithm intervening only as a constant factor on this number.

This hypothesis is not realistic in the case of AO^*: any state developed can lead to an actualization on all its ascendants in H, which would increase the complexity of the algorithm by a non-constant, but considerable factor. It can be admitted, however, that the development of a state and its actualization involve more or less the same operations (the calculation of the $f_i(u) \leftarrow k(u, i) + \Sigma f(v)$ and the search for min $\{f_i \mid i \leqslant I(u)\}$ being the most costly), and the complexity of the algorithm estimated from the total number of developments or state actualizations.

In this model, the algorithm AO^* will, at worst, carry out $\theta(N^2)$ operations, with N as the number of finite states H (or if H is infinite, N is the number of states to which the search is limited).

7.3.5 IMPLEMENTATION

As with A^*, the implementation can be achieved independent of any specific application. The program AO^* will call on two external procedures:

1. Successors (u): this provides the set s(u) of successor states to u in the form of a list $(\delta_i(u), \delta_{i'}, (u), \ldots)$ of connectors, with the costs k(u, i) that correspond to them.

2. Heuristic (u): this evaluates h(u). Two types of data structure are associated with each state u: (a) a coding of the data base characterizing u (returned by successors during the generation of u); and (b) an order number j associated with u by the program, allowing the following structures to be manipulated.

Fathers (j): list $\delta^{-1}(u)$ of numbers associated with fathers of u (actualized gradually as new fathers are encountered);

Sons (j): list of connectors $\delta_i(u)$, each one consisting of a list of numbers of the successor states (provided by Successors (u));

F(j): list $(f_i(u), f_{i'}(u), f_{i''}(u), \ldots)$;

I'(j): list of connectors to be actualized during the updating;

i(j): position in Sons(j) or F(j) lists of the minimal connector.

The sets P and Q will be made up of lists of state numbers. The Define–Solution and Choice–Pending–State procedures will be integrated into a single procedure, which stops the exploration of $G(u_0)$ as soon as a pending state is found, and if there are none, it returns 'nil' by defining $G(u_0)$ completely. The notation $f(u) \leftarrow \infty$ (stage 2.2) corresponds (in practice) to taking either a very large value (an increase of the cost) or any symbol which will be considered as an absorbant element for the addition during the actualization of costs (in 2.6.2).

Note that a correspondence between the two data structures associated with each stage should be allowed for, as well as an efficient means (appropriate to the application considered) of testing whether a state v has already been encountered.

The practical difficulties involved in carrying out this test will, however, make it necessary to resort to a redundant search in many applications.

7.3.6   REDUNDANT SEARCH—SEARCH IN AN AND/OR GRAPH

As for A^*, a redundant algorithm AO^* will be obtained by deleting set Q and the test $[v \in ?P \cup Q]$ in (2.3.1.1). All the successors of the developed state will be generated as new states, which will certainly be the case if the search is carried out in an AND/OR tree.

The hypothesis of an absence of any circuit in H guarantees that the number of developments of a state u will be, at the most, equal to the number of fathers in u. This number is finite, ensuring convergence, but not necessarily equal to 1, which can increase the complexity of the search. The loss of efficiency due to the redundancy can, in fact, be completely counter-balanced by the economy in state identification testing (and the simpler implementation resulting from it). In the presence of a circuit, the rules proposed above are not applicable in the redundant case. A hypothesis of non-zero cost on a circuit (transposition of the hypothesis on w-graphs), however, guarantees that the algorithm will stop if there is a solution of finite cost in H, but in the case of a finite H without solution, the search will not converge unless an increase of the cost Y is provided, with the addition of a stopping condition in iteration (2): $f(u_0) < Y$.

7.3.7 SEARCH WITH PRUNING

In cases where the available memory space is limited, two types of pruning can be applied:

1. during the creation of a state v, based on the heuristic h: if h(v) is greater than a threshold, $f(v) \leftarrow \infty$ is modified;
2. during actualization of the estimate f of a state: if f(v) is greater than a threshold, the same $f(v) \leftarrow \infty$ is modified.

For any state v such that $f(v) = \infty$, it is possible to delete the connectors $s_i(u)$ leading to $v(v \in s_i(u))$, once the actualization u is achieved.

7.3.8 SEARCH WITH PARTIAL DEVELOPMENT

The complete development of a state is a still more costly operation in the case of searching in an AND/OR graph than in that of a graph (note in AO* the two overlapping iterations 2.3.1 and 2.3.1.1 for each development). The comment in Section 6.3 on the interest of partial development is, therefore, even more pertinent here.

The BSH algorithm carries out partial development, but restricts itself to a blind search without cost. It is possible, however, in the interests both of admissibility and efficiency to take into account costs and heuristics with partial development. The corresponding algorithm AO*DP associated with each generated state u, the sub-set $I_d(u) \subset I(u)$ indexing the connectors of u that have already been explored: $\forall i \in I_d(u)$ all the successors in the set $s_i(u)$ have been generated. If $I_d(u) \neq I(u)$, u remains in P, and $f(u) = h(u)$ and $\hat{i}(u) = 0$ are maintained while $h(u) < \min\{f_i(u) \mid i \in I_d(u)\}$. If not, the same procedure is followed as for AO*. The algorithm is as follows:

Algorithm AO*DP
Input data: $u_0, T, \{s_1, \ldots, s_u\}$, cost k, function h
1. Initialization: $P \leftarrow \{u_0\} : Q \leftarrow \phi; f(u_0) \leftarrow h(u_0); u \leftarrow u_0$
2. Iterate while $[u \neq \text{nil and } f(u_0) \neq \infty]$
2.1. If $[I(u) = \phi]$ then do: $f(u) \leftarrow \infty]$;
   delete u from P and place it in Q
2.2 If not do:
2.2.1 $j \leftarrow$ Choose–Successor (u)
2.2.2 If $[j = \text{nil}]$ then do:
   $f(u) \leftarrow \min\{f_i(u) \mid i \in I\}; \hat{i}(u) \leftarrow$ minimum index
   Delete u from P and place it in Q
2.2.3 If not do:
2.2.3.1 $I_d(u) \cup I_d(u) \cup \{j\}$
2.2.3.2 Iterate on $\{v \in s_j(v) \mid v \notin P \cup Q\}$
   $P \leftarrow P \cup \{v\}; f(v) \leftarrow h(v); I_d(v) \leftarrow \phi$
   End iteration 2.2.3.2.

2.2.3.3 $f_j(u) \leftarrow k(u,j) + \Sigma_{v \in s_j(u)} f(v)$

2.2.3.4 If $h(u) < \min\{f_i(u) \mid i \in I_d(u)\}$ then do:
$f(u) \leftarrow h(u); \hat{i}(u) \leftarrow 0$

2.2.3.5 If not do: $f(u) \leftarrow \min\{f_i(u) \mid i \in I_d(u)\}$
$\hat{i}(u) \leftarrow$ minimum index
End if

2.3 $A \leftarrow s^{-1}(u)$

2.4 For $\{v \in s^{-1}(u)\}$ do: $I'(v) \leftarrow \{i \in I_d(u) \mid u \in s_i(v)\}$

2.5 Iterate while $[A \neq \phi]$

2.5.1 Take and delete from A a state v such that $A \cap s(v) = \phi$

2.5.2 For $\{i \in I'(v)\}$ do: $f_i(v) \leftarrow k(v,i) + \Sigma_{w \in s_i(v)} f(w)$

2.5.3 If $f(v) > \min\{f_i(v) \mid i \in I_d(v)\}$ then do:
$f(v) \leftarrow \min\{f_i(v) \mid i \in I_d(v)\}$
$i(v) \leftarrow$ new minimum index
$A \leftarrow A \cup s^{-1}(v)$
For $\{w \in s^{-1}(v)\}$ do: $I'(w) \leftarrow I'(w) \cup \{i \in I_d(w) \mid v \in s_i(w)\}$

2.5.4 $I'(v) \leftarrow \phi$
End iteration 2.5

2.6 $G(u_0) \leftarrow$ Define–Solution (u_0)
(* by stopping at states v such that $\hat{i}(v) = 0$ or $v \in T$ *)

2.7 $u \leftarrow$ Choose–Pending–State $(G(u_0))$
End iteration 2

Output data: if $f(u_0) = \infty$ then there is no solution, if not take solution $G(u_0)$ for cost $f(u_0)$

The Choose–Successor (u) procedure will return 'nil' if u is completely developed, that is, if all its successors $s_i(u)$ have been generated and the corresponding estimates $f_i(u)$ calculated, for any connector $i \in I(u)$. If not, it will choose and return one of the connectors not yet examined. The Define–Solution procedure will be modified so as to stop in $G(u_0)$ on the terminal and partly developed states, but on connectors among which none has an estimate $f_i(u)$ better than the heuristic $h(u)$. These will remain pending, and will eventually be redeveloped.

AO*DP converges: to establish this the assertion 7.2 must be established, noting that a single state u will not be partly developed more than $I(u)$ times. It is possible to show that 7.3 is equally valid for AO*DP: if u is completely developed $(I_d(u) = I(u))$, or if it is not $(I_d = \phi)$, and the same situation applies as for AO*; if u is partly developed, then either $f(u) = h(u) \leqslant h^*(u)$, or there exists $i \in I_d(u)$ such that $f(u) = f_i(u) \leqslant h(u) \leqslant h^*(u)$. It is impossible to be sure that the corresponding connector $s_i(u)$ is the best possible, except when the associated $G(u)$ is complete because then $f(u) = f_i(u) = \mathcal{G}(G(u)) \leqslant h(u) \leqslant h^*(u)\mathcal{G}(G^*(u))$ and therefore $G(u)$ is also an optimal solution. Consequently, the algorithm AO*DP is admissible.

The performance of this algorithm will depend strictly on the heuristic choices made by Choose–Successor. The comments made on A*DP remain valid here (including the fact that if h is monotonic, any state u will be completely developed before $\hat{i}(u) \neq 0$ can be taken).

7.4 ε-admissible searching: the AO algorithm

The basic idea here is the same as for A_ε, that is, to pursue the exploration and 'depth-first development' in H of a single partial solution for as long as it remains acceptable, that is, while $G(u_0)$ is the best partial solution known in H, or while the cost of $G(u_0)$ does not differ by more than $(1 + \varepsilon)$ times the estimate of cost from the optimal solution. The concept of acceptability, defined for the pending states in A_ε, is transposed here for the partial solution of the AND/OR graph.

There is, however, an important problem to be considered: in A^* there is a permanently available list of all the pending routes and an estimate of their costs (all vertices in P represent this type of route): in AO^*, only one partial solution, the one being developed, is known at any moment, and access to any other solution involves an ascending actualization of all H, followed by a descent.

Two conditions are necessary for an ε-admissible search to take place:

1. it must be possible, after the development of a state u, to update the overall cost of the partial solution $G(u_0)$ being explored, without ascending actualization of all H;

2. there must be permanently available an estimate of the cost of the second best partial solution, which will eventually become the best after the development of states on $G(u_0)$, and will be used to judge the acceptability of $G(u_0)$. Note that the development of a state of $G(u_0)$ may also arise in the second partial solution: it is therefore important that the estimate of its cost should also be updated if necessary (and without actualization of all H).

Let the following be adopted:

—F: cost $\mathcal{G}(G(u_0))$, updated during the development of the partial solution $G(u_0)$;

—F: estimate, also updated, of the cost $\mathcal{G}(G'(u_0), G'(u_0)$ being, after each actualization, the second best partial solution in H. To manage these two quantities, for each state u there must be available, not only the estimate $f(u) = f_{\hat{i}}(u) = \min\{f_i(u)\} f'(u) = \min\{f_i(u) \mid i \in I(u), i \neq \hat{i}(u)\}$, that is the estimate of the cost along the second best connector from u. If u has only one connector ($|I(u)| = 1$), then by definition $f'(u) = \infty$ is adopted (similar to $f(u) = \infty$ if $|I(u)| = 0$).

—$m(u)$ = number of distinct routes from u_0 to u in the current $G(u_0)$. In addition, $G(u)$ will be the sub-graph of $G(u_0)$ generated by u and its successors in G.

The algorithm AO_ε will use, in addition to this notation and that defined for AO $(P, Q, f_i, f, \hat{i})$, the following data structures:

—P' = set of pending states in the current $G(u_0)$;
—Solution = best complete solution known at the current instant;
—Y = cost $\mathcal{G}(G(u_0))$
—Threshold = threshold of acceptability of a solution, taken as equal to $(1 + \varepsilon)$ times the largest known reducing estimator of $h^*(u_0)$.

To simplify the presentation of the algorithm, the following procedures and functions will be used: INITIALIZE, DEVELOP, UPDATE, ACTUALIZE, DEFINE—SOLUTION, and CHOOSE-IN-P'; The algorithm is as follows:

Algorithm AO_ε
Input data: u_0, T, $\{s_1, \ldots s_m\}$, costs k, function h, parameter $\varepsilon \geqslant 0$

1. INITIALIZE
2. Iterate while $[Y > \text{Threshold and } P' = \phi \text{ and } f(u_0) \neq \infty]$
2.1 $u \leftarrow$ CHOOSE-IN-P'
2.2 DEVELOP (u)
2.3 If $[F \leqslant F' \text{ and } f(u) \geqslant h(u)]$ then do:
    $F' \leftarrow \min\{F'; F + \min\{m(v)(f'(v) - f(v)) \mid v \in G(u) \cap Q\}$
    Threshold $\leftarrow \max\{\text{Threshold}; (1 + \varepsilon)F\}$
2.4 If not do:
2.4.1 If $[f(u) \geqslant h(u)]$ then Threshold $\leftarrow \max\{\text{Threshold}; (1 + \varepsilon)f'\}$
2.4.2 Iterate while $[F \leqslant \text{Threshold and } P' \neq \phi]$
    $u \leftarrow$ CHOOSE-IN-P'
    DEVELOP (u)
    End iteration 2.4.2.
2.4.3 If $[F > \text{Threshold}]$ then do
2.4.3.1 If $[P' = \phi \text{ and } Y > F]$ then do:
    Solution $\leftarrow$ DEFINE-SOLUTION (u_0)
    $Y \leftarrow F$
2.4.3.2 ACTUALIZE
2.4.3.3 $G(u_0) \leftarrow$ DEFINE-SOLUTION (u_0)
2.4.3.4 $P' \leftarrow \{v \in G(u_0) \mid v \in P \text{ and } v \notin T\}$
2.4.3.5 $F \leftarrow f(u_0)$
2.4.3.6 $F' \leftarrow f(u_0) + \min\{m(v)(f'(v) - f'(v)) \mid v \in G(u_0) \cap Q\}$
2.4.3.7 Threshold $\leftarrow \max\{\text{Threshold}; (1 + \varepsilon)f(u_0)\}$
    End iteration 2
3. If $[P' = \phi \text{ and } Y > F]$ then do:
3.1 Solution $\leftarrow$ DEFINE-SOLUTION (u_0)
3.2 $Y \leftarrow F$
Output data: Si $[f(u_0) = \infty]$ then there is no solution
    If not take solution for cost Y and
    $\varepsilon' \leftarrow [(1 + \varepsilon)Y - \text{Threshold}]/\text{Threshold}$

The INITIALIZE procedure develops the root u_0 of H by creating all its successors, determines the estimates $f(u_0)$ and $f'(u_0)$, defines $m(v)$ for the successors of u_0 along the best connector, and initializes P, Q, P', A, as well as F, F', Y and Threshold.

INITIALIZE
1. $P \leftarrow \phi$; $Q \leftarrow \{u_0\}$; $A \leftarrow \phi$; $Y \leftarrow \infty$; $m(u_0) \leftarrow 1$
2. Iterate on $\{i \in I(u_0)\}$
2.1 Iterate on $\{u \in s_i(u_0)\}$
$\qquad\qquad f(v) \leftarrow h(v)$;
$\qquad\qquad m(v) \leftarrow 0$;
$\qquad\qquad I(v) \leftarrow \phi$
$\qquad\qquad P \leftarrow P \cup \{u\}$

$\qquad$ End iteration 2.1.
$\qquad f(u_0) \leftarrow k(u_0, i) + \Sigma v \in s_i(u_0) f(v)$
$\qquad$ End iteration 2
3. $F \leftarrow f(u_0) \leftarrow \min\{f_i(u_0); \hat{i}(u_0)\} \leftarrow$ minimum index
4. $F' \leftarrow f'(u_0) \leftarrow \min\{f_i(u_0) \mid i \neq \hat{i}(u_0)\}$
5. $P' \leftarrow \{v \in s_i(u_0) \mid v \notin T\}$
6. Threshold $\leftarrow \max\{h(u_0); F\}$
7. For $\{v \in P'\}$ do: $m(v) \leftarrow 1$
8. End

After the initialization, algorithm AO_ε consists of four phases:

1. Development of a pending state on $G(u_0)$, the best partial solution of H. The algorithm will iterate (iteration 2) by pursuing the development of other states of $G(u_0)$, for as long as $G(u_0)$ can be proved to be the best current solution. This phase also includes a surveillance and, eventually, a modification to the estimator F' of the cost of the second best solution in H, and to the threshold of admissibility. During these iterations, the actualization of the costs in H is not carried out: the states concerned are noted (during DEVELOP) and the actualization is carried forward.

2. Pursuit of pending state developments in $G(u_0)$, which is not necessarily the best current state, but which remains acceptable. Here, also, the actualization of H is carried forward. This phase takes place while $F \leqslant$ Threshold, and is located in the iteration (2.4.2). It represents a 'depth-first descent' in H, and may lead to a complete solution which, if acceptable, makes AO_ε stop ($F \leqslant$ Threshold and $P' = \phi$), and if not, may be stored as the best complete solution known up to that time (test 2.4.3.1).

3. Execution of all the updating carried forward to that point. This is carried out by the ACTUALIZER procedure which ascends through H, by actualizing the minimal connector $\hat{i}$ and the estimates f and f' of all the states, in which one successor has changed its estimator f.

Note that the minimal connector $\hat{i}(u)$ has changed, but the value of the minimum of $\{f_i(u)\}$ has stayed the same before and after the updating, then the actualization stops at u without modifying its ascendants.

4. Descent through H by the DEFINE–SOLUTION procedure, along the minimal connectors for the definition of the new $G(u_0)$, the set P' of its pending states, the estimates F, F' and Threshold, and the factors $m(v)$ on all the states of $G(u_0)$; those that do not appear in $G(u_0)$ are reset at zero (an implementation will, of course, reassemble the five instructions 2.4.3.3–2.4.3.7).

The choice in P', the set of pending states in $G(u_0)$, of the particular state u to be developed is carried out by the function CHOOSE-IN-P'. For the logic of the algorithm, this function can be arbitrary, but the performances of AO_ε will be sensitive (and to a larger extent than those of AO^*) to the pertinence of the choice.

The chosen state is then supplied as an argument to the DEVELOP procedure which generates its successors, determines $\hat{i}(u)$, $f(u)$ and $f'(u)$, then updates F, P' and if necessary, the set A and the factors $m(v)$ of the descendants of u along the connectors $\hat{i}(u)$:

DEVELOP (u)

1. Delete u from P and P' and place it in Q
2. Iterate on $\{i \in I(u)\}$
2.1 Iterate on $\{v \in s_i(u) \,|\, v \notin P \cup Q\}$
2.1.1 $P \leftarrow P \cup \{v\}$; $f(v) \leftarrow h(v)$
2.1.2 $m(v) \leftarrow 0$; $I'(v) \leftarrow \phi$
    End iteration 2.1
2.2 $f_i(u) \leftarrow k(u, i) + \Sigma_{v \in s_i(u)} f(v)$
    End iteration 2.
3. If $\{I(u) = \phi]$ then do: $f(u) \leftarrow \infty$; $f'(u) \leftarrow \infty$
4. If not do:
4.1 $f(u) \leftarrow \min\{f_i(u) \,|\, i \in I(u)\}$; $\hat{i}(u) \leftarrow$ minimum index
4.2 Iterate on $\{v \in \{s_{\hat{i}}(u)\}$
4.2.1 UPDATE $(v, m(u))$
4.2.2 If $[v \in P]$ then add v to P'
    End iteration 4.2
4.3 If $[\,|\,I(u)\,|\, = 1]$ then $f'(u) \leftarrow \infty$
4.4 If not $f'(u) \leftarrow \min\{f_i(u) \,|\, i \neq \hat{i}(u)\}$
    End if
5. $F \leftarrow F + m(u)(f(u) - h(u))$
6. If $[f(u) \neq h(u)]$ then do:
    $A \leftarrow A \cup s^{-1}(u)$
    For $\{w \in s^{-1}(u)\}$ do $I'(w) \leftarrow I'(w) \cup \{i \in I(w) \,|\, u \in s_i(w)\}$
    End

The updating of the factors $m(u)$ of the descendants of u along the connectors $\hat{i}$ is carried out very simply by the following recursive procedure:

UPDATE (v, y)

1. If $(v \notin T)$, then $m(v) \leftarrow m(v) + y$
2. If $(v \notin P')$ then for $\{w \in \hat{s_j}(v)\}$ do: UPDATE (w, y)
   End

The procedure that ensures the ascending actualization of H is the following:

ACTUALIZE

1. Iterate while $[A \neq \phi]$
1.1. Take and delete from A a state v such that $A \cap \hat{s}(v) = \phi$
1.2 For $\{i \in I'(v)\}$ do: $f_i(u) \leftarrow k(u, i) + \sum_{w \in s_i(v)} f(w)$
1.3 If $f_i(v) \neq \min\{f_i(v) \mid i \in I(v)\}$ then $\hat{i}(v) \leftarrow$ new minimum index
    If $f(v) \neq f_i(v)$ then do:
        $f(v) \leftarrow f_i(v)$
        $A \leftarrow A \cup s^{-1}(v)$
        For $\{w \in s^{-1}(v)\{$ do: $I'(w) \leftarrow I'(w) \cup \{i \in I(w) \mid v \in s_i(w)\}$
1.4 $I'(v) \leftarrow \phi$
1.5 $f'(v) \leftarrow \min\{f_i(v) \mid i \neq \hat{i}(v)\}$
    End iteration 1.

The actualization is similar to that of AO^*, except that to check for ascendency, it must be verified that $A \cap \hat{s}(v) = \phi$ (instead of $A \cap s(v)$ in AO^*), this being due to the fact that A receives states whenever the actualizations are carried forward (in an implementation, this test consists simply of storing the states in A by order of maximum rank and of taking them in that order). Note finally that after each actualization, the descent through H should correctly update the factors $m(v)$ on the set of states generated: if v does not feature in the new $G(u_0)$ then $m(v) \leftarrow 0$, if not, $m(v) \leftarrow \sum m(u)$ on all the arcs (u, v) of $G(u_0)$. This calculation will be integrated into the DEFINE–SOLUTION procedure:
   —initial setting at zero: $\forall v \in P \cup Q : m(v) \leftarrow 0$; and $m(u_0) \leftarrow 1$;
   —then: $m(v) \leftarrow m(v) + m(u)$ in the iteration (2.4) of DEFINE–SOLUTION.
   When the algorithm AO_ε stops, one of the four conditions is fulfilled:
   1. $[f(u_0) = \infty]$: this occurs following an actualization when $f_i(u_0) = \infty$ on all the connectors coming from u_0, in which case there is no solution in H.
   2. $[P' = \phi$ and $F \leqslant F']$: all through a sequence of state developments in $G(u_0)$, this remains the best partial solution in $H(F \leqslant F')$ until a complete solution $(P' = \phi)$ is obtained. In this situation, $F = \mathcal{G}(G(u_0)) =$ Threshold$/(1 + \varepsilon)$, and $\varepsilon' = 0$.
   3. $[P' = \phi$ and $F \leqslant$ Threshold$]$: following the acceptable development of states in $G(u_0)$, a complete solution $(P' = \phi)$ is obtained. In this case, $F = s(G(u_0)) =$ Threshold $x(1 + \varepsilon')/(1 + \varepsilon)$ and $\varepsilon' \leqslant \varepsilon$.

4. $[Y \leqslant \text{Threshold}]$: the best complete solution (Solution, of cost Y) known by the algorithm, which was not acceptable at the moment when it was attained, becomes acceptable. If the halting occurs at the same time as one of the two previous cases ($P' = \phi$), the algorithm will provide the better of the two solutions: $G(u_0)$ or Solution (test 3).

The preceding formulation of the algorithm is, in the interests of legibility, deliberately simplified; it does not profit from all the possibilities of the ε-admissible approach. It is possible to make use of the principle of acceptability (destined to reveal many alternatives, among which a judicious choice may be made for the reduction of complexity), not only to pursue the exploration for a solution $G(u_0)$ which is no longer strictly the best, but also to develop $G(u_0)$ along the connectors which are not the best, or in the case of backtracking, to return to another solution which is simply acceptable. So in the DEVELOP and ACTUALIZE procedures, it is not necessary to take systematically the $\min\{f_i(u)\}$ index for $\hat{\imath}(u)$: u can be pursued by any connector that retains the acceptability of $G(u_0)$. An equivalent procedure to selection, in A_ε could choose from the set:

$$\{i \in I(u) \mid f_i(u) \leqslant h(u) + (\text{Threshold} - F)/m(u)\}$$

+ either the index of the connector $s_i(u)$ corresponding to the most 'developed' sub-graph $G_i(u)$ (that is, the closest to being complete, by estimating this information on the basis of a heuristic h_c is available, or on the basis of the average or maximal rank of the pending states of $G_i(u)$) or the index corresponding to minimal $f_i(u)$, or a compromise.

It would be interesting to monitor and retain the connectors $s_i(u)$ of which all the states v are either terminal, or roots of a complete $G(v)$, but independent of the acceptability of the corresponding $f_i(u)$. This information could be managed by a specific pointer $i_T(u)$ towards the best current $s_i(u)$, and updated by ascending actualization (similar to the management of the SOLVED set in BSH). A complete sub-graph in H could be attached to Solution as soon as u_0 had a pointer $i_T(u_0)$. The translation of a given strategy by AO_ε, although possible in theory, would be very difficult to put into practice. A simplified version of this strategy can, however, be used in association with the previous extension: once a complete sub-graph is known in H, attempts can be made to render it acceptable by raising the value of Threshold. This can be achieved by: an ascending actualization of all H; a definition of the best partial solution $G(u_0)$ and the state $\hat{v}$ in $G(u_0)$ that corresponds to: $\min\{m(v)(f(v) - k(v) \mid v \in Q \cap G(u_0)\}$; the development of one or more descendant states from $\hat{v}$ in $G(u_0)$ and the corresponding update of F' and Threshold.

Example 7.3: AO_ε can be applied to the AND/OR graph from the previous example (Figure 7.8):

1. for $\varepsilon = 0.52$: the algorithm stops after developing three states (u_0, u_8 and u_{18}) and without any actualization, by providing the cost solution 74 (shown in bold lines in Figure 7.8);

2. for $\varepsilon = 0.43$: AOε results in the same solution by developing an additional state (u_{19}) and by carrying out a single actualization (after u_{18});

3. for $\varepsilon = 0.06$: after developing nine states (u_0, u_8, u_{18}, u_{19}, u_3, u_7, u_1, u_9 and u_{14}) continuing with five actualizations (after u_{18}, u_{19}, u_7, u_1, and u_{14}), the algorithm stops with the same solution as before and $\varepsilon' = 0$. Note that in the same example, AO* carries out 14 state developments and 11 actualizations.

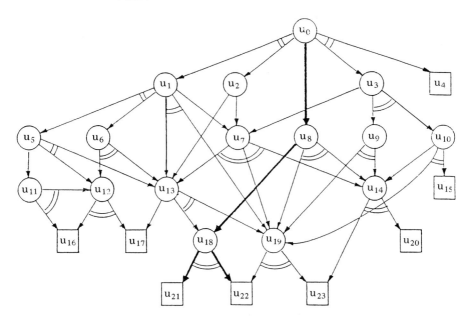

Figure 7.8 *AO$_\epsilon$ applied to the AND/OR graph of Example 7.2*

7.4.1 CONVERGENCE, ε-ADMISSIBILITY AND COMPLEXITY OF AO$_\varepsilon$

For any finite $\varepsilon \geqslant 0$, the algorithm AO$_\varepsilon$ is convergent and admissible. The proof of the convergence is obtained by a generalization of the one for AO*. In fact the two assertions 4 (with finite H) and 4 (with infinite H, adding the hypothesis for finite ε) remain valid for AO$_\varepsilon$. Their demonstrations are transposed without difficulty (noting for assertion 7.3 that in this case $F \leqslant (1 + \varepsilon)f_i^*(u_0) \leqslant (1 + \varepsilon)M$ instead of $f(u_0) \leqslant f_{ix}(u_0) \leqslant M$).

The property of ε-admissibility, valid for a reducing and coincident heuristic, is more difficult to establish (see Ghallab 1982). Note that if H verifies these hypotheses, then the value ε' returned by the algorithm is the best known improvement in the relative shortfall from the optimum cost in the solution (this is especially true when $\varepsilon' = 0$: AO_ε finds an optimal solution and provides a guarantee of its exact optimality).

In the case of a monotonic heuristic, the inequality $[f(u) \geqslant h(u)]$ is always verified. This allows the corresponding tests in (2.3) and (2.4.1) to be deleted from AO_ε, and above all the actualization of H to be carried even further forward by pursuing the development of state on $G(u_0)$ while $[F \leqslant F']$. Once this inequality is no longer verified, Threshold is updated by Threshold $\leftarrow$ max{Threshold; $(1 + \varepsilon)F'$}. The algorithm naturally remains ε-admissible.

Concerning the complexity of AO_ε, the remarks made in relation to AO^* (in the absence, so far, of any theoretical characterization for the complexity of search in an AND/OR graph) can also be applied. Because of the single development (at maximum) per state, in the worst instance AO_ε, like AO^*, is in $\theta(N^2)$. In the case of infinite H, however, the subgraph to which the search is limited is larger (in its number of states) for AO_ε than for AO^* (see parallel discussion in A_ε and A^*).

In practice, the average behaviour of the algorithm, as compared with that of AO^*, depends on a large number of factors, such as the value of the parameter ε, the heuristic $\mathbf{h}$, or the procedure CHOOSE-IN-P'. It might appear, a priori, that AO_ε is penalized relative to AO^*, by the management of a larger number of data structures, necessary to the ε-admissible search ($f', F, F', m, \ldots$). Nevertheless, it is important to avoid seeing the conceptual complexity of the algorithm AO_ε (which certainly makes its implementation more difficult than that of AO^*) as being equivalent to a necessarily higher level of algorithmic complexity. The ε-admissible approach offers a number of advantages. It avoids the actualization of all of H and the redefinition of $G(u_0)$ systematically with each iteration (as is the case with AO^*); by concentrating the search on an acceptable solution, it carries this actualization as far forward as possible (or may not even carry it out at all, if the solution becomes complete). It also allows the terminal states to be checked so that every complete solution encountered, even if not acceptable, is retained, and so leads the search towards an improvement of the threshold of acceptability, or even to envisage stopping the search according to a compromise between this solution and the calculation resources still available.

It is likely, then, that for many applications, the benefits of the ε-admissible approach will compensate very largely for the additional cost of data management required for its application. This is particularly the case for the following type of problem, often encountered in practice, where these additional calculations can be simplified to a large degree.

7.4.2 SEARCH IN A SPACE H, FOR WHICH ALL THE SOLUTION
SUB-GRAPH IS A TREE STRUCTURE

This concerns exploring an AND/OR graph in which no state v has an ascendant u with several routes from u to v using a single connector $s_i(u)$ (see counter-example in Figure 7.2, where there are two routes from d to c by the connector R2; the choice of this connector in state d leads to the sub-graph solution in Figure 7.3, which is not a tree structure). A specific example of space H, in which the previous property is always verified is when every state of H has only one predecessor: H is then an AND/OR graph.

A general characterization of an AND/OR graph H, in which every solution is tree-structured could be formed as follows: the successors to a state u along the same connector have disjunct sets of descendants:

1. $\forall u$, $\forall i \in I(u)$, and $\forall v \in s_i(u)$, $\forall w \in s_i(u)$: $\hat{s}(v) \cap \hat{s}(w) = \phi$. It can easily be verified in advance that any sub-graph $G(u_0)$ generated by Define–Solution in such a space H has no circuit: $G(u_0)$ is a tree-structure (with root u_0).

Problems that can be formulated by searching in a space H, verifying the property 1 above are often encountered. In plan generation by problem breakdown, a frequent situation is that in which the AND/OR graphs are explored. Another specific case involves the breakdown of two distinct problems u and v, providing all distinct sub-problems (although this does not necessarily result in an AND/OR graph, see node 'a' in Figure 7.2). Another application in robotics concerns the generation of classifiers in the form of decision trees. For a space H verifying 1), it is easy to see that whatever the sub-graph $G(u_0)$ of H, and for any $u \in G(u_0)$, $m(u) = 1$. It is also clear that even during the development of a state u such that $f(u) < h(u)$, it is possible to follow the application of F and F′, and therefore to carry forward the actualization by pursuing the same acceptable partial solution.

The simplifications of algorithm AO_ε that result are as follows: $m(u)$ is deleted wherever it appears and is replaced by the unitary coefficient; in the same way, the UPDATE procedure is also deleted along with the instruction (4.2.1) to DEVELOP; the instructions (2.3), (2.3.1) and (2.4.1) are replaced in AO_ε respectively by:

2.3 If $[F \leqslant F']$ then do
2.3.1 'f' $\leftarrow \min\{F'; F' + f(u) - h(u); F + \min\{f'(v) - f(v) \mid v \in G(u) \cap Q$
2.4.1 'Threshold $\leftarrow \max\{$Threshold$; (1 + \varepsilon)F'\}$

It can then be established that for H verifying 1 and for h reducing and coincident, the AO_ε algorithm thus modified is ε-admissible.

An empirical model of the average behaviour of AO for a space H verifying 1 has been developed (Ghallab 1982). The experimentation

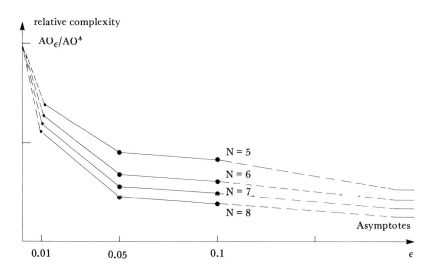

Figure 7.9 *Complexity of AO_ϵ relative to that of AO^*, as a function of ϵ*

applied to a problem of optimization of decision trees (NP-complete problem) and the results obtained go the same way as the previous intuitive considerations. The following curves (Figure 7.9) give, as a function of ϵ, the complexity of AO_ϵ relative to that of AO^*, and with various values for the size of N (the instance of the problem considered). In the worst case, AO^* and AO_ϵ are both at $O(5^N)$ on this problem. The experimentally measured indicator of complexity takes into account the number of developments and actualizations. The model developed for this problem shows an average complexity of between $\theta(2^N)$ for $\epsilon = 0$ (that is, for AO^*) and $\theta(1.3^N)$ for $\epsilon = \infty$.

Chapter 8

First order predicate logic

In this section a formal language, 'first order predicate language', will be discussed. This language allows complex knowledge to be expressed concisely, along with the methods by which this knowledge can be combined to give new forms. This language and its methods have been used and developed with the aim of equipping robotic systems with advanced capabilities for making decisions.

Some of the more important ways in which first order predicate logic can be used will be discussed. For additional information, the reader may refer to Nilsson (1971, 1980). A more complete study can be found in Chang (1973), Wos (1984) and Siekmann (1983).

The 'syntax' presented below, in Section 8.1 specifies the way in which expressions of the language which are, by definition, correct, can be constructed. The inference rules, considered in Section 8.2 are a means of establishing correspondence between correct expressions. 'Semantics', introduced in Section 8.3, concerns the meaning attributed to these expressions according to what will be referred to as specific 'interpretations': semantics govern the way in which expressions of the language are understood in view of specific applications. In Section 8.4, the relationships that can be established between syntax and semantics via the inference rules will be examined. Later sections will make use of these relationships to form methods of 'automatic demonstration'.

8.1 The syntax of first order predicate language

The correct expressions of the language, known as 'terms', 'atoms', 'literals' and 'well formed formulae', are constructed using a 'symbol alphabet'.

8.1.1 ALPHABET

This comprises:

1. A set of symbols known as 'separators', in this case the set of three symbols ',' '(' and ')'.

2. A set of symbols known as 'constants', in this case the lower case

letters of the roman alphabet and concatenations of these letters. For example: 'a', 'block'.

3. A set of symbols known as 'variables', in this case upper case letters of the roman alphabet and concatenations of these letters. For example: 'X', 'NAME'.

4. A set of symbols known as 'predicates', in this case, similar to variables, they will be chains of upper case letters of the roman alphabet such as 'P', 'Q', 'ON' or 'BETWEEN. When a particular predicate is to be manipulated, its 'order' or 'number of arguments' must be acknowledged. The order is a positive whole number; for example, it would be possible, for a particular application of the language, to acknowledge that the orders of P, Q, ON and BETWEEN were 2, 0, 1 and 2 respectively. When the order is fixed at 0, the predicate is also known as a 'proposition'.

5. A set of symbols known as 'functions' formed, in this case, in a way similar to constants, of lower case chains such as: 'f', 'g', 'successor' and 'weight'. In the same way as for predicates, each function symbol will have a fixed order (or number of arguments). The order will be a strict positive whole number (it is generally accepted that the constants are functions of nil order).

6. A set of symbols known as 'connectors', in this case , $\neg, \wedge, \vee, \rightarrow$ and $\leftrightarrow$ which are read respectively as: 'negation' (or 'no'), 'conjunction' (or 'and'), 'disjunction' (or 'or'), 'implication' and 'mutual implication'.

7. Two symbols known as 'quantifiers': $\exists$ and $\forall$ which are read respectively as: 'there exists' ('existential quantifier') and 'for all' ('universal quantifier').

8.1.2 TERMS

By definition, any term is formed by the application of the two following laws:

1. The constants and the variables are terms.
2. If f is a symbol of order function $n(n \geq 1)$ and if $t_1, \ldots, t_n$ represent terms then $f(t_1, \ldots, t_n)$ is a term, (where $t_1, \ldots, t_n$ are replaced by their values).

For example: successor(X, Y), or weight(b), or successor$(b, weight(Z))$ are terms, but $P(X, blue)$ or weight$(P(b))$ are not.

8.1.3 ATOMS (OR ATOMIC FORMULAE)

By definition, any atom is formed by application of the two following laws:

1. The propositions (predicates of order 0) are atoms.
2. If P is a predicate of order n $(n \geq 1)$ and if $t_1, \ldots, t_n$ represent terms, then $P(t_1, \ldots, t_n)$ is an atom (where $t_1, \ldots, t_n$ are replaced by their values).

For example: P(X, blue), EMPTY and BETWEEN(table, X, support(window)) are atoms, but successor(X, Y) or support(window) are not.

8.1.4 WELL-FORMED FORMULAE (OR FORMULAE, ABBREVIATED AS WFFS).

By definition, any well-formed formula (wff) is formed by the application of the three following laws:

1. Atoms are wffs.

2. If G and H represent wffs, then ($\neg$G), (G$\wedge$H), (G$\vee$H), (G $\rightarrow$ H) and (G $\leftrightarrow$ H) are wffs (where G and H are replaced by their values; henceforth this type of replacement will not be underlined in the text).

3. If G is a wff and X is a variable, then ($\exists$X)G and ($\forall$X)G are wffs.

For example, ($\exists$X)($\forall$Y)((P(X, Y)$\vee$Q(X, Y)$\rightarrow$R(X)) and (($\neg$(P(a) $\rightarrow$ P(b))) $\rightarrow$ P(b) are wffs, whereas ($\neg$f(a)) and f(P(a)) are not.

Notes:

—A wff which is an atom or in the form ($\neg$G), with G an atom, is called a 'literal'.

—In a wff, as many 'blanks' or 'spaces' as required can be placed before or after the separator, connector, constant, variable, function and predicate symbols: it will still be considered as the same wff.

—In the rest of the text it will be assumed that any variable appearing in a formula is 'quantified'. This means that the occurrence of the symbol representing this variable follows immediately on from a symbol $\exists$ or $\forall$, before any other occurrence of the same variable. Generally speaking, depending on the previous definition, a wff may include unquantified variables (known as 'free variables'). For example, P(X) and ($\exists$Y)Q(X, Y) are wffs including free variables.

—The expression 'first order' in 'first order predicate logic' is associated with the preceding definition of the wffs which forbids the quantification of predicate or function symbols. For example, ($\forall$P)P(a) and ($\forall$f)($\forall$X)P(f(X), b) are not first order predicate logic wffs.

8.2 Inference rules

An inference rule is the representation of a process for exhibiting (or deriving), from one or more wffs, other wffs. For example:

—the inference rule known as the 'modus ponens', based on two wffs of the form G and (G $\rightarrow$H) respectively, exhibits the wff H (note the convention applied here: identifiers such as G or H must be replaced by the wffs they represent);

—the 'universal specialization' inference rule based on a wff in the form ($\forall$X)G(X) and any constant, for example 'a', exhibits the wff G(a): all occurrences of 'X' in G are replaced by 'a';

—the inference rule known as the 'modus tollens', based on two wffs in the form ($\daleth$ H) and (G $\rightarrow$ H), respectively, exhibits the wff ($\daleth$ G).

Given a fixed set of inference rules, the following type of problem can be considered: is it possible to obtain a predetermined wff from a chosen set of wffs, by applying the inference rules an arbitrary (but finite) number of times? The wffs chosen initially are called 'axioms'. The wffs obtained by application of the inference rules are called 'theorems'. A series of applications of inference rules leading from the axioms to a theorem constitutes a 'proof' of the theorem.

Certain techniques for problem solving introduced in other chapters, such as that of searching in state spaces, can be considered with a view to finding a proof for a given theorem; thus, in terms of state spaces, the set of axioms can constitute an initial state, and the inference rules can act as state transformation operators, the state-goals will therefore be wff sets including the proposed theorem.

8.3   Semantics of first order predicate language

The bases that allow the wffs to be used for the representation of (and reasoning on) the truth values attributed to the knowledge already possessed will now be examined, with a view to establishing the truth value of other knowledge.

8.3.1   INTERPRETATIONS

An interpretation of a wff G is defined by the five following stages:

1. The choice of a non-empty 'interpretation domain' D, that is, of a non-empty set of elements.
2. The attribution of an element of D to each constant of G.
3. The attribution of an element from the particular set: (true, false) to each proposition (predicate of order 0).
4. The attribution of an application of D in the set (true, false) to each predicate of order n ($n > = 1$).
5. The attribution of an application of D in D to each function of arite n ($n > = 1$). There can then be said to be an interpretation of G on D.
Examples:
Consider the wffs:

$$G_1(\forall X)P(X)$$

$$G_2(\forall X)(\exists Y)Q(X, Y)$$

$$G_3(\forall X)(R(X) \rightarrow T(f(X), a))$$

Hereafter, the interpretations I_1, I_2, I_3 will be defined as G_1, G_2, G_3 on

D_1, D_2, D_3 respectively. F will stand for the 'false' element of {true, false}, and T will stand for 'true'.

I_1: $D_1 = \{1, 2\}$

P(1)	P(2)
F	T

I_2: $D_2 = \{1, 3\}$

Q(1, 1)	Q(1, 3)	Q(3, 1)	Q(3, 3)
F	T	F	F

I_3: $D_3 = \{4, 5\{$

a	f(4)	f(5)
4	5	4

R(4)	R(5)
T	F

T(4, 4)	T(4, 5)	T(5, 4)	T(5, 5)
T	F	T	T

Note: It may sometimes occur that interpretations referred to as being incomplete are considered, in which the necessary attributions are only partly specified.

8.3.2 FORMULA VALUE ACCORDING TO AN INTERPRETATION

Consider an interpretation I, in area D, of a formula G.

—If G is a proposition: the value attributed to it by the definition of I is called the 'value of G according to I'.

—If G is a non-propositional literal: then for each choice $\mathcal{C}$ of values in D for the variables of G (if there are any), a 'true' or 'false' value will be obtained by following the definition of I. This value is known as the 'value of G according to I for the choice $\mathcal{C}$ of values of the variables'. For example, in G_3 (see below), interpreted according to I_3, the atom T(f(X), a) takes the value T if element 4 of D_3 is attributed to X, and also the value T if X receives the other value (in this case: 5) of D_3.

—If G is in the form: $(\forall X)G'$, the value of G will be defined according to I as T ('true') if the value of G' according to I for all values of the variable X (in D) is T, and if not, as F ('false'). For example: the value of G_1 (see below), interpreted according to I_1 is F.

—If G is in the form $(\exists X)G'$, the value of G will be defined according to I as T, if the value of G' according to I for at least one value of X (in D) is T, and if not, as F. For example, the value of Q(X, Y) interpreted according to I_2 is T when 1 is attributed to X and 3 to Y. The result is that the value of $(\exists Y)Q(X, Y)$ according to I_2, when X is given 1, is T. The value of G_2 according to I_2, however, is F.

—If G is in the form: $(\neg G')$, the value of G will be defined according to I, when that of G according to I is defined, by using the table:

value of G' according to I	value of (.G') according to I
	(or G)
T	F
F	T

—If G is in the form (G'∨G") or (G'∧G") or (G' → G") or (G' ↔ G"), the value of G will be defined according to I, when the values of G' and G" according to I are certain, by using the following tables respectively:

G'	G"	(G'∧G")
F	F	F
F	T	T
T	F	T
T	T	T

G'	G"	(G'∧G")
F	F	F
F	T	F
T	F	F
T	T	T

G'	G"	(G' → G")
F	F	T
F	T	T
T	F	F
T	T	T

G'	G"	(G' ↔ G")
F	F	T
F	T	F
T	F	F
T	T	T

For example, the value of G_3 according to I_3 (see above) is T. The tables shown above are called 'truth tables' for the connectors ⌐, ∨, ∃, → and ↔ respectively.

When a formula G is T according to an interpretation I, I is said to be a 'model' of G. Note that the value of a formula according to a given interpretation is defined in an entirely univocal way once all the variables have been quantified. It is important to remember (see Section 8.1.4 that only formulae with quantified variables will be considered from now on.

8.3.3   VALIDITY (AND INVALIDITY), INCONSISTENCY (AND CONSISTENCY) OF A FORMULA

A formula is valid if, and only if, its value is T according to any interpretation. If not, it is invalid. A formula is inconsistent if, and only if, its value is F according to any interpretation. If not, it is consistent. Examples:

$$G_1: (∀X)(P(X)∨(⌐Q(X)))$$
$$G_2: (∀X)(P(X)∨(⌐P(X)))$$
$$G_3: ((∀X)P(X)∧(∃Y)(⌐P(Y)))$$

The formula G_1 is consistent because the following interpretation I_1' gives it the value T:

$$I_1': 0 = \{1\}P(1)\,|\,V\ Q(1)\,|\,V$$

but it is invalid because the following interpretation I'' gives it the value T:

$$I_1'': 0 = \{1\}P(1)\,|\,FQ(1)\,|\,V$$

The formula G_2 is valid unless I is an interpretation of area D that falsifies G_2; there is, therefore, a value 'a' of X, taken in D, such that $(P(a)\lor(\urcorner P(a)))$ is F, which is impossible by the definition of the connectors $\lor$ and $\urcorner$; thus G_2 is valid.

The formula G_3 is inconsistent, unless I is a model of G, of area D; I must satisfy $(\exists Y)(\urcorner P(Y))$, therefore 'a' exists in D with F applying to $P(a)$; but then $(\forall X)P(X)$ cannot be satisfied in D. G is therefore inconsistent.

Note: some writers refer to valid formulae as 'tautologies' and to inconsistent formulae as 'contradictions'. These expressions will be introduced later, but with a more restricted meaning.

8.3.4 INDECIDABILITY AND SEMI-DECIDABILITY OF FIRST ORDER PREDICATE LOGIC

When a formula does not contain any variables, it is possible by using the truth tables, to determine whether the formula is valid or not, or inconsistent or not in a fixed number of operations. The situation is far more complex when there are variables (and therefore quantifiers).

It can be shown that it is impossible to propose a general algorithm capable of deciding, in a finite number of operations, the validity or non-validity of any first order predicate logic formula. This is why first order predicate logic is said to be 'indecidable'. It is possible, however, to propose general algorithms to decide the validity of certain families of wff. In particular, there are algorithms designed so that if they are applied to a valid wff, they will stop after a finite number of operations, concluding that the wff is valid. This type of algorithm, applied to a non-valid wff, will not stop. This is why first order predicate logic is said to be 'semi-decidable'.

8.3.5 EQUIVALENT FORMULAE

Two wffs G and H are equivalent if, and only if, they take the same values (T and F) for any interpretation (notation: for any interpretation I, $I(G) = I(H)$). For example, $(P(a) \rightarrow Q(b))$ and $((\urcorner P(a)\lor Q(b)))$ are equivalent (this can be verified with the truth tables).

There follows, without justification, a list of equivalence in common usage. G, H and K represent any wffs; G(X) or H(X) represent wffs where X is free; $\boxplus$ represents any valid wff, and $\square$ represents any inconsistent wff.

	Equivalent formulae	Names (possible)
$(G \rightarrow H)$	$((\neg G) \vee H)$	
$(G \leftrightarrow H)$	$((G \rightarrow H) \wedge (H \rightarrow G))$	
$(\neg(\neg G))$	G	
$(\neg(G \vee H))$	$((\neg G) \wedge (\neg H))$	De Morgan laws
$(\neg(G \wedge H))$	$((\neg G) \vee (\neg H))$	
$(G \wedge (H \vee K))$	$((G \wedge H) \vee (G \wedge K))$	distributive laws
$(G \vee (H \wedge K))$	$((G \vee H) \wedge (G \vee K))$	
$(G \vee H)$	$(H \vee G)$	commutative laws
$(G \wedge H)$	$(H \wedge G)$	
$((G \vee H) \vee K)$	$(G \vee (H \vee K))$	associative laws (authorizes cancellation
$((G \wedge H) \wedge K)$	$(G \wedge (H \wedge K))$	of following parentheses)
$(G \rightarrow H)$	$((\neg H) \rightarrow (\neg G))$	contraposition law
$(G \vee \square)$	G	
$(G \vee \boxplus)$	$\boxplus$	
$(G \wedge \square)$	$\square$	
$(G \wedge \boxplus)$	G	
$(G \vee (\neg G))$	$\boxplus$	
$(G \wedge (\neg G))$	$\square$	
$\forall X G(X)$	$(\forall Y)G(Y)$	silent variable laws
$(\exists X)G(X)$	$(\exists Y)G(Y)$	
$(\neg(\exists X)G(X))$	$(\forall X)(\neg G(X))$	
$(\neg(\forall X)G(X))$	$(\exists X)(\neg G(X))$	
$(\forall X)(G(X) \wedge H(X))$	$((\forall X)G(X) \wedge (\forall Y)H(Y)$	
$(\exists X)(G(X) \vee H(X))$	$((\exists X)G(X) \vee (\exists Y)H(Y))$	

8.3.6 LOGICAL CONSEQUENCE FORMULAE

The formula G is the logical consequence of the formulae $H_1, \ldots, H_n$ if, and only if, any model of $H_1 \wedge, \ldots, \wedge H_n$ is a model of G. For example, P(a) is the logical consequence of $(\forall X)P(X)$, whereas $(\forall X)Q(X)$ is the logical consequence of $(\forall X)((\neg P(X)) \vee Q(X)$ and $(\forall X)P(X)$. It is easy to show that G is the logical consequence of $H_1, \ldots, H_n$ if, and only if, $((H_1 \wedge, \ldots, \wedge H_n) \rightarrow G)$ is valid, or else, if, and only if, $H_1 \wedge, \ldots, \wedge H_n \wedge (\neg G))$ is inconsistent.

8.4 Relationship between the idea of theorems and of logical consequences

The definition of rules of inference and the production of theorems and proofs are independent, a priori, of the concepts of interpretation (and of the afferent introduction of 'true' and 'false' values), equivalence and logical consequence.

8.4.1 SOUND GROUPS OF INFERENCE RULES

When the theorems obtained by application of a given group of inference rules are systematically logical consequences of the set of axioms, no matter what this set is, the set of rules is said to be 'sound'. For example, it is easy to show that the modus ponens, introduced in Section 8.2, is sound, and the same is true for the rule of universal specialization.

8.4.2 COMPLETE GROUPS OF INFERENCE RULES

A given group of inference rules is referred to as 'deduction complete' if, no matter what the set of wffs, all the logical consequences can be derived from them as theorems (that is, by application of group rules, a finite number of times). For example, the group of rules reduced to the single modus ponens is not 'deduction complete'.

8.4.3 SOUND OR COMPLETE: RATIONALE FOR APPLICATION

In problem solving systems, first order predicate logic is used to represent true or false assertions in specific areas of application; particularly of interest are the interpretations of the wffs. If inference rules are used in these systems, they will be expected to form a sound group.

It is clearly desirable that the groups of rules should be complete (that is, that any logical consequence of the axioms should be a theorem, and could therefore be discovered by chaining the inference rules), but in practice this is not always the case.

In Section 8.5 (see below), an inference rule, known as 'the resolution principle', or more simply 'the resolution' is discussed. It is important because of its role in the solution of problems based on first order predicate logic. The resolution principle, on its own, constitutes a group of sound inference rules. In addition, it satisfies a property similar (and equivalent on a practical level) to completeness for deduction: 'completeness for refutation'. This will be discussed further on.

8.5 The resolution principle

This is an inference rule that is applied to a particular family of wffs, known as 'clauses'.

8.5.1 CLAUSES

This term is given to all wffs in the form of a disjunction of literals (particularly isolated literals). For example, $(R(Z, a, g(X)) \lor (\lnot T(U)) \lor (\lnot V(b, K(C))))$.

8.5.2   NORMAL PREFIX FORM OF A WFF

This is a formula derived from a wff by applying the following sequence
of transformations.

8.5.2.1   *Elimination of the connectors ↔ and →*

To achieve this, the laws of equivalence are used between: $(G \leftrightarrow H)$ and
$((G \rightarrow H) \land (H \rightarrow G))$ on the one hand and $(G \rightarrow H)$ and $((\neg G) \lor H)$ on
the other.

8.5.2.2   *Linking the connectors ¬ with the atoms concerned*

For this, the laws of equivalence are used between: $(\neg(\neg G))$ and G,
$(\neg(G \lor H))$ and $((\neg G) \land (\neg H))$, $(\neg(G \land H))$ and $((\neg G \lor (\neg H))$ (De
Morgan laws), $(\neg(\exists X)P(X))$ and $(\forall X)(\neg P(X))$, $(\neg(\forall X)P(X))$ and
$(\exists X)(\neg P(X))$.

8.5.2.3   *Distinguishing the variables*

This is done in such a way as to make each quantifier govern an original
variable. To achieve this, the laws of equivalence are used between:
$(\forall X)P(X)$ and $(\forall Y)P(Y)$, $(\exists X)P(X)$ and $(\exists Y)P(Y)$ (silent variable laws).
    NB: The transformations a, b and c lead to a wff which is equivalent
(in the sense explained in Section 8.3.5) to the initial wff, since it uses
laws of equivalence.

8.5.2.4   *Displacement of all the quantifiers to the left of the formula*
           (without changing their relative order)

This displacement leads to the formation of a new wff equivalent to the
preceding one because, after Stage c, there is no conflict possible between
the labels of quantified variables.
    NB: At the end of these four stages, the normal prefix form (by
definition) of the initial wff, which is also equivalent to it, is formed. The
sequence of quantifiers itself is referred to as 'prefix', and the rest as
'matrix'.
    Note: There may be a variety of normal prefix forms for a single wff,
formed by using laws of equivalence that respect the effects of stages
8.5.2.1–8.5.2.4

Examples.
For wff G:

$$((\forall X)((P(X) \land Q(X, a)) \rightarrow (R(X, b) \land (\forall Y)((\forall Z)R(Y, Z)$$

$$\rightarrow T(X, Y)))) \lor (\forall X)S(X))$$

After stage a, the following is obtained:

$$((\forall X)((\lnot (P(X) \land Q(X, a))) \lor (R(X, b) \land (\forall Y)((\lnot (\forall Z)R(Y, Z))$$
$$\lor T(X, Y)))) \lor (\forall X)S(X))$$

After stages b and c (assuming, for simplicity of notation, that the connector $\lnot$ is applied to the following atom), the following is obtained:

$$((\forall X)((\lnot P(X) \lor \lnot Q(X, a)) \lor (R(X, b) \land (\forall Y)((\exists Z)(\lnot R(Y, Z))$$
$$\lor T(X, Y)))) \lor (\forall U)S(U))$$

After stage d, a normal prefix form of G is obtained:

$$(\forall X)(\forall Y)(\exists Z)(\forall U)((\lnot P(X) \lor \lnot Q(X, a)) \lor (R(X, b) \land (\lnot R(Y, Z)$$
$$\lor T(X, Y)))) \lor S(U))$$

or else, by associativity of the connector:

$$(\forall X)(\forall Y)(\exists Z)(\forall U)(\lnot P(X) \lor \lnot Q(X, a) \lor (R(X, b)$$
$$\land (\lnot R(Y, Z) \lor T(X, Y))) \lor S(U))$$

8.5.3 TRANSFORMATION IN CLAUSE FORM OR CLAUSAL FORM

On the basis of a normal prefix form G' or a wff G, a 'clausal form' G'' of G can be formed by the transformations 8.5.3.1–8.5.3.5 described below. It should be stressed that although the formulae G and G' are still equivalent, the same is not so of G and G''. It can only be established that inconsistent G is equivalent to inconsistent G''; this point will be more extensively considered further on. It will be shown next that this simple relationship is sufficient to establish automatic demonstration methods.

8.5.3.1 *Elimination of existential quantifiers*

Consider a formula of the type $(\exists Z)G(X)$, which is a sub-formula for one or more formulae, universally quantified relative to $Y_1, \ldots, Y_r$. $(\exists X)$ is removed and each occurrence of X in $G(X)$ is replaced by a function such as: $f(Y_1, \ldots, Y_r)$; note that this function will include as many arguments as there are universal quantifiers on the left of the formula $G(X)$. This function expresses simply the existence of a correspondence, a priori, between any group of values for $Y_1, \ldots, Y_r$ and the values of X, the existence of which is confirmed by the symbol $\exists$. These functions are known as 'Skolem functions'. Since nothing is known in advance about these functions (apart from the argument variables), an original symbol must be used to represent them each time one is introduced, that is, at each elimination of an existential quantifier. When there is no '$\forall$' on the

left of the '∃' under consideration, the Skolem function introduced will
not have any argument: it will therefore be a new constant, known as the
Skolem constant.

Examples:
(∃X)P(X) becomes P(a); (∀X)(∃Y)FOLLOWS(Y, X); becomes (∀X)
FOLLOWS(f(X), X). The normal prefix form obtained at the end of
Section 8.5.2 becomes:

(∀X)(∀Y)(∀U)(¬P(X)∨¬Q(X, a)∨(R(X, b)

$$\land(\lnot R(Y, g(X, Y))\lor T(X, Y)))\lor S(U))$$

8.5.3.2 Elimination of all the quantifiers

At the end of the preceding stage there remained only universal
quantifiers. The notation is simplified by removing them: it is thereafter
assumed that all the variables are universally quantified. The formula for
the last example thus becomes:

¬P(X)∨¬Q(X, a)∨(R(X, b)∧(¬R(Y, g(X, Y))∨T(X, Y)))∨S(U)

8.5.3.3 Moving into normal conjunctive form

This refers to a conjunction of literal disjunctions, that is a conjunction
of clauses. To this effect, the laws of associativity and distributivity for the
connectors ∨ and ∧ are used. For example: ¬P(X)∨Q(X, a)∧¬
R(Y, f(X), b)) becomes (¬P(X)∨Q(X, a))∧(¬P(X)∨¬R(Y, f(X), b))
and the formula from the previous paragraph becomes (¬P(X)∨¬
Q(X, a)∨R(X, b)∨S(U))∧(¬P(X)∨¬Q(X, a)∨¬R(Y, g(X, Y))∨T(X, Y)
∨S(U))

8.5.3.4 Elimination of the connectors ∧

The conjunction of clauses obtained at the end of the previous stage is
traditionally considered to be a set of clauses. For example, a set of two
clauses from the last expression in the previous paragraph.

8.5.3.5 Distinguishing between the variables of distinct clauses

For example, for the previous expression:

{¬P(X)∨¬Q(x, a)∨R(x, b)∨S(u), ¬P(y)∨¬Q(y, a)

$$\lor \lnot R(z, g(y, z))\lor T(y, z)\lor S(v)\}$$

This transformation is based on the general law of equivalence between $(\forall x)(G(x) \wedge H(x))$ and $((\forall x)G(x) \wedge (\forall y)H(y))$

8.5.4 RELATIONSHIP BETWEEN A SET OF WFFS AND A SET OF CLAUSE FORMS OF THESE WFFS

Consider the wffs $G_1, \ldots, G_r$. Let $G_1'', \ldots G_r''$ be clause forms of $G_1, \ldots, G_r$ respectively, obtained by applying the stages 8.5.3.1–8.5.3.5 and preceded, if necessary, by the stages 8.5.2.1–8.5.2.4, producing the normal prefix forms $G_1', \ldots, G_r'$. Each G'' is in the form: $G_i'' = \{C_i', \ldots, C_i^{ki}\}$.

$\{G_1, \ldots, G_r\}$ can be shown to be inconsistent if, and only if, $U_{i=1,r}G_i''$ is inconsistent.

A variant of this result consists of stating that any formula that is the logical consequence of $\{G_1, \ldots, G_r\}$ is also the logical consequence of $U_{i=1,r}G_i''$.

Notes:

—It is generally possible to produce several clause forms for a single initial wff. In this way, it is possible to eliminate the existential quantifiers (stage 8.5.3.1) before (rather than after) movement to the left of all the quantifiers (stage 8.5.2.4). This can reduce the number of arguments of the Skolem functions introduced. For example, if, at the end of stage 8.5.2.3, the following wff is found, $((\forall X)P(X) \wedge (\exists Y)Q(Y))$, stage 8.5.2.4 leads to $(\forall X)(\exists Y)(P(X) \wedge Q(Y))$; then stage 8.5.3.1 will give $(\forall X)(P(X) \wedge Q(f(X)))$, and thus finally the clause form $\{P(X), Q(f(Z))\}$ whereas by carrying out 8.5.3.1 then 8.5.2.4 the following is obtained: $(\forall X)(P(X) \wedge Q(a))$ which leads to $\{P(X), Q(a)\}$ The above results apply whatever the clause form obtained.

—In the application of first order predicate logic, one of the common aims is to show that a wff H is the logical consequence of wffs $G_1, \ldots, G_n$. Section 8.3.6 indicated that this is equivalent to indicating the inconsistency of the wff $K = G_1 \wedge \ldots \wedge G_n \wedge \neg H$. Taking into account the previous results it is preferable, a priori, to find separately and then reunite the clause forms of $G_1, \ldots, G_n$ and $\neg H$ rather than look for a clause for K directly, according to stages 8.5.2.1–8.5.2.4 and then 8.5.3.1–8.5.3.5.

—If G'' is a clause form of G, the equivalence between G and G'' is only certain if G and G'' are inconsistent. If G is consistent, then it is generally not equivalent to G''. For example, G is the wff $(\exists X)P(X)$ and G'' is the clause $P(a)$; if the interpretation of area $D = \{1, 2\}$, specified by $a \mid 1$ and

P(1)	P(2)
F	T

is considered, it is clear that it leads to G being true and G'' being false.

This shows that a great deal of care must be taken, if it is to be proved that H is the logical consequence of G, to put G and $\neg$ H into clause form, and not G and H.

8.5.5 THE RESOLUTION PRINCIPLE APPLIED TO CONCRETE CLAUSES

A literal is said to be 'concrete', or 'concretely instanted' if it has no variables. For example, $\neg P(a)Q(a, f(b))$ are concrete literals, but $\neg (P(X)$ or $Q(a, f(Y))$ are not.

A concrete clause is a disjunction of concrete literals. Consider two concrete clauses $G = G_1 V \ldots V G_n$ and $H = \neg G_1 V H_2 V \ldots V H_m$ where G_i and H_j are concrete literals. The literals G_1 and $\neg G_1$, in G and H respectively are said to be 'complementary literals'. The inference rule known as the 'resolution principle' produces from G and H, which are called 'parent clauses', the clause $K = G_2 V \ldots V G_n V H_2 V \ldots V H_m$, known as the 'resolvant clause' or the 'resolvant' of G and H. It can also be said that G and H are resolved in K. A resolvant is defined by elimination of complementary literals and disjunction of all the other literals of the parent clauses.

Specific examples:

—A resolvant of the concrete clauses G and $\neg GVQ$ (or else G and $G \rightarrow Q$ is Q. The resolution principle therefore covers the inference rule known as the 'modus ponens' (when restricted to concrete clauses).

—A resolvant of the concrete clauses $\neg GVH$ and $\neg HVK$ (or else: $G \rightarrow H$ and $H \rightarrow K$ is $\neg GVK$ (thus $G \rightarrow K$). This inference rule which appears as a specific case in the resolution principle is known as 'chaining' (here restricted to concrete clauses).

—The concrete clauses G and $\neg G$ are resolved in 'the empty clause' (that is, the set of empty clauses).

Notes:

—Two concrete clauses may not have the same resolvant; for example G and $\neg H$, or G and H are different literals.

—Two concrete clauses may have several resolvants; for example GVHVK and $\neg GV \neg HVL$ are resolved into $HV \neg HVKVL$ or $GV \neg GVKVL$ (which are, in fact, equivalent clauses).

Before introducing a general definition of the resolution principle (that is, as applied to clauses which are not necessarily concrete), part of the mechanism (of clause production) that it brings into play must be defined. More specifically, the general application of the resolution principle to any type of clause leads to 'complementary literals', in a more extended meaning of the phrase, being found in the 'parent clauses'. This search uses an operation known as 'unification', which is discussed below.

8.5.6 UNIFICATION

Consider, for example, the clauses $\neg G(X)VH(X)$ and $G(f(Y))$. If the first clause was replaced by $\neg G(f(Y)) \lor H(f(Y))$, the resolution principle for concrete clauses would be easily extended: after elimination of the ('complementary') literals $\neg G(f(Y))$ and $G(f(Y))$, the clause $H(f(Y))$ would be obtained. In fact, the operation of unification allows clauses to be transformed with a view to making complementary literals appear, by application of 'substitutions'.

8.5.6.1 Substitutions

A substitution is a finite set of pairs, denoted $t_i \,|\, V_i$ where the values t_i are terms and V_i are distinct variables which do not feature in t_i. If $i = 0$, the substitution is 'empty'. The application of a substitution $s = \{t_i \,|\, V_i\}$ to any expression E ('expression' is taken to mean a term or a wff) is noted as Es, and is called an instantiation (or E according to s). It consists of replacing all the occurrences of each variable V_i in E by t_i. For example, consider:

$$E = G(f(X), a, Y)$$

$$s_1 = \{Z \,|\, X, U \,|\, Y\} \qquad\qquad s_2 = \{b \,|\, X\}$$
$$s_2 = \{Y \,|\, X, g(X) \,|\, Y\} \qquad\qquad s_4 = \{a \,|\, X, K(c) \,|\, Y\}$$
$$Es_1 = G(f(Z), a, U) \qquad\qquad Es_2 = G(f(b), a, Y)$$

which becomes;

$$Es_3 = G(f(Y), a, g(X)) \qquad\qquad Es_4 = G(f(a), a, k(c))$$

Notes:

—To progress from E to Es_3, it is only the occurrences of X and Y in E that are the object of substitution (and not the occurrences that appear during the application of s_3; because of this, the result is independent of the order of application of the substitution elements.

—Es_4 is a 'concrete instance' of E by s_4.

—The values t_i and V_i are called respectively 'terms' and 'variables' of the substitution.

The composition of two substitutions s_1, s_2, noted $s_1 o s_2$, is the substitution obtained by applying s_2 to the terms of s_1 and by reuniting the new pairs obtained in this way with those of s_2, the variables of which were not variables of s_1.

For example, $\{a \,|\, X, g(Y, Z, U) \,|\, V\} o \{b, \,|\, X, c \,|\, Y, f(X) \,|\, Z, K(d) \,|\, V,$ $f(X) \,|\, W\} = \{a \,|\, X, g(c, f(X), U) \,|\, V, c \,|\, Y, f(X) \,|\, Z, f(X) \,|\, W\}$ It can be shown that $(Es_1)s_2 = E(s_1 o s_2)$. It is also clear that the composition of substitutions is associated, such that $(s_1 o s_2) o s_3 = s_1 o (s_2 o s_3)$. Clearly, it is generally the case that $s_1 o s_2 \neq s_2 o s_1$.

8.5.6.2 Unifiers

A set $\{E_i\}_i$ of expressions (in this case, terms or formulae) is said to be 'unifiable' by s, or that s is a 'unifier' of $\{E_i\}$ if, and only if, all the E_is are identical. The single expression produced by a unifier s will be noted: $\{E_i\}$s.

For example, s = $\{a \mid x, c \mid y, c \mid v, b \mid z, b \mid u, g(b) \mid w\}$ is a unifier of $\{E_i\}_i$ = $\{G(X), f(Y), g(b)) \vee G(X, f(c), g(Z)), G(X, f(c), g(U)), G(X, f(V), W)\}$ since all the expressions are instantiated in $G(a, f(c), g(b))$.

There may be several unifiers for a given set of expressions. The term 'most general unifier' (mgu) of a set $\{E_i\}_i$ of expressions is applied to a unifier r of $\{E_i\}$ such that for any other unifier s of $\{E_i\}_i$, there is a substitution s' with s = ros'. It is easy to show that for any unifiable set E, there is an mgu and that, if r_1 and r_2 are mgus of $\{E_i\}$, then $\{E_i\}r_1$ and $\{E_i\}r_2$ are identical to the names of the close variables.

For the previous example, an mgu of $\{E_1, E_2, E_3\}$ is: r = $\{c \mid Y, c \mid V, b \mid Z, b \mid U, g(b) \mid W\}$ (note: s = ro$\{a \mid X\}$.

8.5.6.3 *A unification algorithm*

The recursive algorithm introduced informally below produces an mgu for a finite set E of unifiable expressions. If E is not unifiable, the algorithm stops and declares it. The algorithm is called by: UNIFY(E, $\mathcal{E}$), where $\mathcal{E}$ denotes the empty substitution.

The algorithm uses the concept of a 'discordance set' (noted as $\mathfrak{D}$) of a set $\mathcal{E}$ of expressions (terms or formulae). This set is constructed by simultaneously shifting from left to right all the elements of $\mathcal{E}$ up to the first character position that shows a difference between these elements, and then extracting from each element of $\mathcal{E}$ the expression (term of formula) that starts in this discordant character position. The set of these expressions makes up $\mathfrak{D}$. For example, for

$$\mathcal{E} = \{G(X, f(a, Y)), G(X, b), G(X, f(a, g(Z)))\}$$

a discordance appears in the fifth character position, so:

$$\mathfrak{D} = \{f(a, Y), b, f(a, g(Z))\}$$

UNIFY $(\mathcal{E}, \sigma)$

1. if: $\mathcal{E}$ is a singleton then: stop by editing σ as mgu
2. form the discordance set $\mathfrak{D}$ of $\mathcal{E}$
3. if: there are two elements V and t of $\mathfrak{D}$ such that V is a variable, t is a term and V does not appear in t then: start $\sigma \leftarrow \sigma o\{t \mid V\}$ $\mathcal{E} \leftarrow \mathcal{E}o\{t \mid V\}$
UNIFY $(\mathcal{E}, \sigma)$
end
4. halt: the starting set is not unifiable.

Note: It is natural to demand, at stage 3, that V should not appear in t: the substitution of t with V would complicate greatly, and with no result, the expressions still to be unified. For example, $\{X \mid f(X)\}$ applied to G(X, a) and G(f(X), a) transforms them into G(f(X), a) and G(f(f(X)), a) . . .

Examples.
Let E = {P(a, X, f(g(Y))), P(Z, f(Z), f(X))}
Start: UNIFY(E, $\mathcal{E}$) so: $\mathcal{E} \leftarrow$ E, $\sigma \leftarrow \varepsilon$

Stages 1 and 2:
$\qquad \mathcal{D} \leftarrow \{a, Z\}$
Stage 3: with
$\qquad V \leftarrow Z, t \leftarrow a$
$\qquad \sigma \leftarrow \varepsilon_0 \{a \,|\, Z\} = \{a \,|\, Z\}$
$\qquad \mathcal{E} \leftarrow \mathcal{E}\{a \,|\, Z\} = \{P(a, X, f(g(Y))), P(a, f(a), f(u))\}$

$\qquad$ call: UNIFY $(\mathcal{E}, \sigma)$

Stages 1 and 2:
$\qquad \mathcal{D} \leftarrow \{X, f(a)\}$

Stage 3: with
$\qquad V \leftarrow X, t \leftarrow f(a)$
$\qquad \sigma \leftarrow \{a \,|\, Z\} o \{f(a) \,|\, X\} = \{a \,|\, Z, f(a) \,|\, X\}$
$\qquad \mathcal{E} \leftarrow \mathcal{E}\{f(a) \,|\, X\} = \{P(a, f(a), f(g(Y))), P(a, f(a), f(U))\}$

$\qquad$ call: UNIFY $(\mathcal{E}, \sigma)$

Stages 1 and 2:
$\qquad \mathcal{D} \leftarrow \{U, g(Y)\}$

Stage 3: with
$\qquad V \leftarrow U, t \leftarrow g(Y)$
$\qquad \sigma \leftarrow \{a \,|\, Z, f(a) \,|\, X\} o \{g(Y) \,|\, U\} = \{a \,|\, Z, f(a) \,|\, X, g(Y) \,|\, U\}$
$\qquad \mathcal{E} \leftarrow \{P(a, f(a), f(g(Y)))\}$

$\qquad$ call: UNIFY $(\mathcal{E}, \sigma)$

Stage 1: an mgu is found, so $\sigma = \{a \,|\, Z, f(a) \,|\, X, g(Y) \,|\, U\}$
Let E = {Q(f(a), g(X)), Q(Y, Y)}

Start UNIFY(E, ε) so: $\mathcal{E} \leftarrow$ E, $\sigma \leftarrow \varepsilon$

Stages 1 and 2:
$\qquad \mathcal{D} \leftarrow \{f(a), Y\}$

Stage 3: with
$\qquad V \leftarrow Y, t \leftarrow f(a)$

$\sigma \leftarrow \varepsilon_0 \{f(a) \mid Y\} = \{f(a) \mid Y\}$

$\mathcal{E} \leftarrow \mathcal{E} \{f(a) \mid Y\} = \{Q(f(a), g(X)), Q(f(a), f(a))\}$

call: UNIFY $(\mathcal{E}, \sigma)$

Stages 1 and 2:
$$\mathfrak{D} \leftarrow \{g(X), f(a)\}$$

Stage 4: set E is not unifiable.

8.5.7 THE RESOLUTION PRINCIPLE APPLIED TO ARBITRARY CLAUSES

Consider two clauses G and H, assumed to have been prepared in such a way as to have no variables in common (Section 8.5.3.5), to which the resolution principle is to be applied. If this inference rule is applicable, the clause derived from G and H will be called a 'resolvant' of G and H (known as parent 'clauses'). G and H (and the possible resolvants) are noted here as sets of literals: $\{G_i\}$ and $\{H_j\}$.

Let it be supposed that there is a sub-set, noted $\{G_{i'}\}$, of $\{G_i\}$ (i' assumes certain values of i) and a sub-set, noted $\{H_{j'}\}$, of $\{H_j\}$ such that the set of literals

$$\mathcal{L} = \{G_{i'}\} \cup \{\neg H_{j'}\}$$

is unifiable.

If r is an mgu of $\mathcal{L}$, a resolvant of G and H will be defined (as a set of literals) by:

$$(\{G_i\} - \{G_{i'}\}) \cup (\{H_j\} - \{H_{j'}\})r$$

For example:

$G = P(X, f(a)) \vee P(X, f(Y)) \vee Q(Y)$ and $H = \neg P(Z, f(a)) \vee \neg Q(Z)$

—An mgu of $G_1 = P(X, f(a))$ and $\neg H_1 = P(Z, f(a))$ is $r_1 = \{X \mid Z\}$ which gives the resolvant: $P(X, f(Y)) \vee Q(Y) \vee \neg Q(X)$

—An mgu of $G_2 = P(X, f(Y))$ and $\neg H_1$ is $r_2 = \{X \mid Z, a \mid Y\}$ which gives the resolvant: $P(X, f(a)) \vee Q(a) \vee \neg Q(X)$.

—An mgu of $G_3 = Q(Y)$ and $\neg H_2 = Q(Z)$ is $r_3 = \{Y \mid Z\}$ which gives the resolvant: $P(X, f(a)) \vee P(X, f(Y)) \vee P(Y, f(a))$.

—An mgu of G_1, G_2 and $\neg H_1$ is $r_4 = \{X \mid Z, a \mid y\}$ (which is r_2) which gives the resolvant: $Q(a) \vee \neg Q(X)$.

In this way, four distinct resolvants have been found. In other cases there may be no resolvant.

Before finally accepting the non-existence of resolvants in a particular case, it is important to distinguish the variables of the initial clauses. For example:

$$G(X, a) \text{ and } \neg G(f(X), X)$$

do not, as such, have a resolvant (see note in Section 8.5.6, but by rewriting the second of these $\neg G(f(Y), Y)$ an mgu $\{f(Y) \mid X, a \mid Y\}$ can be made to appear, giving rise to a resolvant equal to the empty clause.

The distinction between variables is, of course, only legitimate at the time of launching of the unification algorithm. Thus, in looking for a resolvant between $G(X, X)$ and $\neg G(f(X), X)$, the last clause is rewritten: $\neg G(f(Y), Y)$; the substitution $\{f(Y) \mid X\}$ gives rise to $G(f(Y), f(Y))$ and to $\neg G(f(Y), Y)$ which are not unifiable (independently of '$\neg$').

8.5.8 A VARIANT IN THE PRESENTATION OF THE RESOLUTION PRINCIPLE

Some authors (Chang 1973) present the resolution principle in a different way. This method of presentation is explained below, and it is interesting to note the emphasis placed on the inference rule, known as factorization.

The 'principle of binary resolution' is first introduced. Let G and H be two clauses, the variables of which are distinct, noted as sets of literals $\{G_i\}$ and $\{H_j\}$; let G_r and H_g be two literals of $\{G_i\}$ and $\{H_j\}$ respectively, such that G_r and $\neg H_g$ are unifiables; if r is an mgu of G_r and $\neg H_g$, a 'binary resolvant' of $\{G_i\}$ and $\{H_j\}$ can be defined, as a set of literals, by $(\{G_i\} - G_r)^n \cup (\{H_j\} - H_g)^n$. It is clear that 'binary resolution' is a specific case of the 'resolution' introduced in Section 8.5.7. Next a second inference rule, called 'factorization' is introduced. Let G be an inference clause expressed as a set of literals: $\{L_i\}_{i=1,r}$ represents two or more literals of G, unifiable by an mgu r. Starting from G, and using 'factorization', the following clause (called a 'factor' of G) can be found: $(G - \{L_i\}_{i=2,r})^n$ that is, Gr is derived, but by fusing all the literals $L_i r$ into one. For example, starting from $G = P(X) \vee P(Y) \vee Q(b)$, the factor $P(X) \vee Q(b)$ can be found.

Finally, the (non-binary) resolution principle is introduced as a new inference rule combining the operations applied in the binary resolution rule and the factorization rule; starting with two clauses G and H, the resolution principle allows either a binary resolvant of G and H, a binary resolvant of H and of a factor of G, or a binary resolvant of a factor of G and of a factor of H to be derived. The resolvants that can be obtained according to this second definition are the same as those that can be obtained by the first, and vice-versa.

8.5.9 GENERAL PROPERTIES OF THE RESOLUTION PRINCIPLE

8.5.9.1 *A sound rule*

It is easily proved that the resolution principle is a sound inference rule, that is (see Section 8.4), any resolvant is the logical consequence of the two parent clauses. The result is that, if a series of resolutions results in an empty clause being produced, this is because the initial set G is inconsistent. If not, there would be an interpretation I satisfying G and therefore, in terms of logical consequences, the parent clauses H_1 and H_2 of the empty clause; if r is the mgu used to resolve H_1 and H_2, it is natural that I should satisfy H_1r and H_2r, while H_1r is the complement of H_2r, so I cannot exist: G is certainly inconsistent.

Note: Consider a set G of clauses, and a series $G'_1 \ldots G'_2$ of distinct clauses, such that: G'_r is the empty clause, $\forall_i$ of 1 to r, or G'_i belongs to G, or G'_i is a resolvant of two anterior clauses of the series.

Such a series $\{G'_i\}$, which demonstrates the inconsistence of G, is called a 'refutation by resolution' of G.

8.5.9.2 *Completeness of the resolution principle for refutation*

It has been shown (Siekmann 1983; Chang 1973; Nilsson 1971), that if a set of clauses is inconsistent, there is a finite series of applications of the resolution principle to these clauses and to the resolvants that come to light, which produces the empty clause. When, however, a wff H is the logical consequence of a set G of wffs, this is equivalent to the inconsistence of any clause form of $G \vee \neg H$. If, then, a wff H is the logical consequence of a set G of wffs, there is a refutation of any clause form of $G \vee \neg H$. This property is called 'completeness for refutation': the group of inference rules reduced to the single 'resolution principle' is thus 'complete for refutation'.

The completeness of the resolution principle for refutation can also be expressed in the following way. $\mathcal{R}(G)$ designates the reunion of a set G of clauses with all the resolvants of all the pairs of clauses. $\mathcal{R}^{r+1}(G)$ is the expression used for the set of clauses $\mathcal{R}(\mathcal{R} + (G))$. The completeness of the resolution principle for refutation means that: $\forall G$ is an inconsistent set of clauses, $\exists n$ is a positive integer such that the empty clause belongs to $R^n(G)$.

Notes.

1. It is common, colloquially, to use the abbreviation 'the completeness' of the solution principle. This does not mean 'completeness for deduction', as defined in Section 8.4.2. (If H is a logical consequence of a group G of wffs, the property satisfied by the solution principle is not: there exists a finite sequence of applications of the inference rule which, starting from G, produced H; firstly, the rule applies only to clauses, and not to any wffs, and above all, it must be applied to a clause form of $G \wedge \neg H$, and not of G, to derive the empty clause, and not H.)

2. Binary solution (inference rule introduced in Section 8.2) is not complete for refutation. This can be seen in the inconsistent set of clauses:

$$E = \{P(X) \lor P(Y), \lnot P(W) \lor \lnot P(Z)\}$$

However the binary solution is applied, binary resolvants are always obtained with two literals: for this reason, the empty clause will never be obtained.

3. The set of two rules 'binary resolution' and 'factorization' forms a complete system for refutation. In the previous example, the inconsistency of E can be proved by applying one rule, then the other (for example: two factorizations and a resolution). Note that the inconsistency of E can also be proved by applying the principle of (non-binary) resolution on its own.

4. An example showing that binary resolution, the system of two rules for binary resolution and factorization, and non-binary resolution are not complete for deduction. Consider the set E of clauses containing only one element $P(a)$. The clause $G = Q(Z) \lor \lnot Q(Z)$ is a logical consequence of E, since it takes the value V for any interpretation. But G cannot be derived from E by any of the three rules systems considered.

8.6   Systems for refutation by resolution

If G is a set of clauses, since the principle of resolution is a sound and complete inference rule, it can be affirmed that G is inconsistent and equivalent to a: there is a refutation of G by resolution. In the same way, if G is a set of wffs, the wff H is the logical consequence of G equivalent to a: there is a refutation for any form of clauses of $G \lor \lnot H$. For example, consider the following axioms: $(\forall x)(\exists y)(\lnot P(x) \to Q(y))$ and $(\forall z)(P(b) \to R(a, z))$ if it is to be proved that: $\lnot R(a, b) \to (\exists u)Q(u)$ a refutation can be sought in the set of clauses: $\{P(x) \lor Q(f(x)), \lnot P(b) \lor R(a,z), \lnot R(a, b), \lnot Q(u)\}$.

Some methodological aspects will now be studied, relative to the application of the principle of resolution in the search for refutations.

8.6.1   GENERAL (NON-DETERMINIST) PROCEDURE FOR REFUTATION BY RESOLUTION

If it is to be proved that the wff H is the logical consequence of the set of wffs: $G = \{Gi\}$, the general procedure for this task is given below:
PROOF-BY-RESOLUTION (G, H)

1. constitute C, the set of clause forms, for the wffs of G,
2. add a clause form of $\lnot H$ to set C,
3. while: the empty clause is not in C, do:
   3.1 start: choose two distinct clauses in C
   3.2 if: they have a resolvant then: add it to C
      end

Notes:

—By virtue of the property of 'completeness for refutation', if H is really the logical consequence of G, there is at least one choice sequence (state 3.1) that leads to the empty clause being introduced, and therefore to the procedure being halted.

—Nevertheless, in the previous procedure, there is no way of guaranteeing that such a sequence, when it exists, will be found: state 3.1 is non-deterministic and rudimentary (so this procedure does not prevent the same pair of clauses from being solved several times from the same literals).

8.6.2 COMPLETE RESOLUTION STRATEGIES FOR REFUTATION

The general procedure PROOF-BY-SOLUTION can be refined at stages 3.1 and 3.2. Depending on the way in which the clauses (and the literals of these clauses) are chosen, various 'strategies for refutation by resolution' can be defined. A strategy of this type restricts or orders the choice of clauses and literals on which the resolution will be attempted, according to its own criteria.

A resolution strategy will be qualified as 'complete for refutation' if it guarantees that when there is a refutation by resolution of the initial set G (that is, a sequence of resolutions leading to the empty clause), there will also be one that satisfies the criteria of choice or order specific to that strategy.

It is also possible to express the 'completeness for refutation' of a resolution strategy S, in the following way. The expression $\Re_c(G)$ denotes the reunion of a set G of clauses with all the resolvants of all the pairs of clauses of G that can be obtained by respecting the criteria, represented by C, attached to the strategy S. $\Re_c^{r+1}(G) = \Re_c(\Re_c^r(G))$ is the expression for this. The resolution strategy S is complete if, and only if, for any inconsistent set of clauses, there is a positive integer $\exists n$ such that the empty clause belongs to $\Re_c^n(G)$.

Notes:

—The completeness of a resolution strategy (for refutation) must not be confused with the completeness of the principle of resolution (for refutation).

—Non-complete strategies can be of practical importance.

—The fact that a strategy is complete does not mean that by satisfying its criteria of choice or order, it is invariably possible to find, in a finite number of resolutions, the empty clause from any inconsistent set G of clauses. Henceforth, when a strategy presents this property it will be said to be 'directly complete'.

8.6.3 DERIVATION, SEARCH AND REFUTATION GRAPHS

For any system of inference rules, given a set of axioms, the set of
theorems that can be produced (and the method of producing them) can
be represented in the form of a graph called the 'derivation graph'. In the
case of the principle of resolution, the vertices are clauses and the arcs link
the parent clauses to the resolvents. For example, for the set of clauses:
$\{P(X) \lor Q(f(X)), \neg P(b) \lor R(a, Y), \neg R(a, b), \neg Q(Z)\}$ the derivation graph
can be represented as follows:

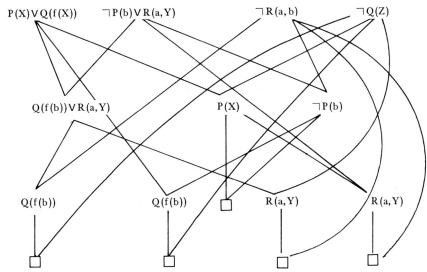

The symbol $\square$ appears in the empty clause; in the interest of clarity, the
resolvants that can derive from different couples of parent clauses have
been duplicated, and the arrows have been left off the arcs.

From this derivation graph, various 'refutation graphs' can be derived,
such as:

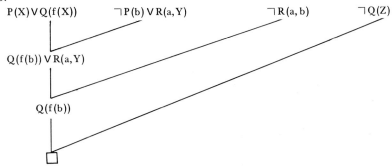

A number of strategies corresponding to various methods of finding
refutation graphs in a derivation graph are briefly explained below. The
part of the derivation graph made explicit to allow a refutation graph to
be found in it is called a 'search graph'.

8.6.4 STRATEGY FOR BREADTH-FIRST RESOLUTION

A depth is associated with each clause: 0 for the initial clauses, 1 for their resolvants, ..., n for the resolvants of two clauses, the deepest of which is at depth n − 1. A constraint is imposed to the effect that a clause of depth P will not be produced while it is possible to produce one of depth p − 1 (this obviously means that when a resolvant appears for the first time, it has the lowest depth obtainable from two parent clauses). In cases where two depths are equal, the order of resolution is not important.

The example presented at the start of Section 8.6, when treated with this strategy, leads, at the moment of halting, to the following search graph (with more or less the same equality of depth).

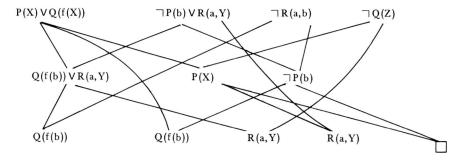

from which the refutation graph below is taken:

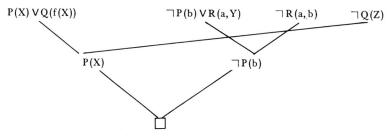

Notes:

1. This strategy does not rule out the production of any elements from the derivation graph of a set G of clauses; it does, however, govern the progressive explanation (search graph) of the derivation graph, by dictating that $\mathcal{R}^r(G)$ should appear before $R^{r+1}(G)$ (see the notation for '$\mathcal{R}$' in 8.5.9.2). This strategy is therefore complete.

2. In addition, from finite G it is deduced that $\mathcal{R}^r(G)$ is finite, $\forall_{p=1,2,...,n}$. The structure is 'directly complete': if G is inconsistent, it inevitably leads to the empty clause appearing.

3. Finally, a refutation is obtained in which the empty clause is at the least possible depth.

8.6.5 STRATEGIES FOR RESOLUTION BY REFUTATION, OR SET OF SUPPORT RESOLUTION

Let G be an unsatisfiable set of clauses and T a sub-set of G such that the set of clauses G−T is consistent. By definition, the set of support for G relative to T (assumed satisfactory for the previous property), assembles the clauses of the derivation graph which either belong to T, or are descendants of T.

A resolution strategy (for a given set of clauses G) using the support set relative to T (G−T assumed to be consistent) imposes that for each resolution, a parent clause is taken from the support set relative to T. This type of strategy is not limited to ordering, like the breadth first strategy, that the derivation graph should be made explicit: it tends to restrict the research graph that can be produced. These strategies are shown to be complete.

It is also possible to order, without further restriction, the production of the resolvants by controlling their depth in the same way as for the breadth first strategy. Under these conditions, the support set strategies are directly complete.

A search graph obtained in this way is shown below, based on the example at the beginning of Section 8.6. Initially, only clauses ⌐R(a, b) and ⌐Q(Z) make up the support set. The clauses of the search graph that belong to the support set are underlined.

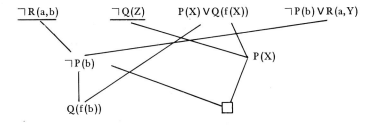

from which the refutation graph may be extracted

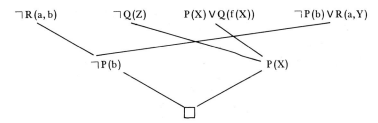

Note that in this example, the search graph is smaller than (that is, contained in) the one obtained by the breadth first strategy, but the refutation graph is the same.

To apply a set support strategy, T must be chosen such that G–T is consistent. Three simple methods for this are given below.

a. Define T as the set of clauses that do not contain negative literals (a negative literal is an atom preceded by a negation). G–T cannot be empty, otherwise an interpretation that gives all the literals T the value V would be a model of G, which is, in fact, inconsistent. Each clause of G–T contains a negative literal; G–T is consistent because an interpretation that gives the value V to all the negative literals of G–T is a model of G–T.

b. Define T as the set of clauses not containing positive literals. It will be seen that G–T is consistent by similar reasoning to that applied above.

c. Define T as the set of clauses resulting from the negation of the wff to be proved. In this case, G–T is the set of axioms which are naturally assumed to be a consistent set. It is possible to verify, in the previous example, that the set T chosen satisfies the proposition c (see Section 8.6 for the original problem), and also proposition b.

8.6.6 STRATEGIES FOR RESOLUTION BY REFUTATION (LOCK RESOLUTION)

All the literals of the initial clauses are numbered in an arbitrary way. The resolution of two clauses can only involve the literals of the smallest number in each. The literals of the resolvants inherit the numbers of the parent clauses (in cases of double possibility, the lower number is retained). These strategies are complete.

It is also possible to order, without applying further restrictions, the production of the resolvants by controlling their depth in the same way as for the breadth first strategy. Under these conditions, the lock strategies are directly complete.

The example at the start of Section 8.6, treated in this way, can give, with the arbitrary numbering mentioned above, the following search graph:

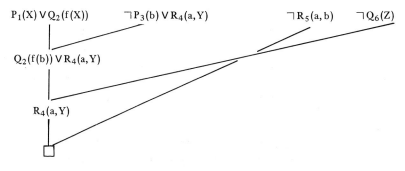

$P_1(X) \vee Q_2(f(X))$ $\neg P_3(b) \vee R_4(a,Y)$ $\neg R_5(a,b)$ $\neg Q_6(Z)$

$Q_2(f(b)) \vee R_4(a,Y)$

$R_4(a,Y)$

Here the refutation graph entirely covers the search graph.

8.6.7 STRATEGIES FOR RESOLUTION BY REFUTATION (LINEAR RESOLUTION)

Let G be an inconsistent set of clauses C_0, such that $G - \{C_0\}$ forms a consistent set of clauses, called the central starting clause. All the resolvants authorized will have C_0 as their ancestor, and will be called 'central clauses'. Linear strategies only authorize resolutions between a central clause CC (at the outset only C is central), and a clause (called the 'side clause') CB that must be chosen either from the clauses of G ('input clauses'), or from the resolvants (and therefore central clauses) that are ancestors for CC.

Note: A central clause cannot be resolved with another central clause unless one is the ancestor of the other. A refutation can be schematized as follows:

central starting clause

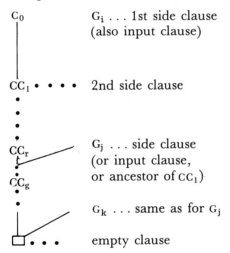

C_0 G_i ... 1st side clause
(also input clause)

CC_1 • • • • 2nd side clause

CC_r G_j ... side clause
(or input clause,
or ancestor of CC_1)

CC_g

G_k ... same as for G_j

empty clause

or, by placing the names of the side clauses on the arcs joining the central clauses.

It is because of the appearance of the second type of graph that the expression 'linear strategies' is used. The 'linearity' arises from the fact that two central clauses cannot be resolved together unless one is the ancestor of the other.

Examples.

1. The search graph produced in Section 8.6.4 by the application of the breadth-first strategy cannot be produced by linear strategy, whatever the choice of C_0 from the input clauses. The refutation graph presented is also non-linear.

2. The same remarks apply as for the search and refutation graphs produced in Section 8.6.5, by application of a set support system.

3. The search graph produced in Section 8.6.6, by application of a lock strategy can also be seen as the result of application of a linear strategy from the clause:

$$C_0 = P(X) \lor Q(f(X)) \text{ or else } C_0 = \lnot P(b) \lor R(a, Y)$$

It can happen that the refutation graph obtained is mistaken for the search graph.

4. A search graph is shown below, obtained according to a linear strategy from $C_0 = P(X) \lor Q(f(X))$ again, but it does not exhibit the peculiarity mentioned above:

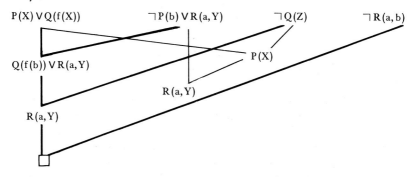

The refutation graph is shown in bold type. This search graph was obtained by 'breadth first' governing of the application of linear strategy from $P(X) \lor Q(f(X))$. The linear strategies are complete.

If the production of the central clauses is governed as in breadth-first strategy, they are directly complete. Note that the completeness relies on the hypothesis that the starting central clause C_0 is such that $G - \{C_0\}$ is consistent. Usually one of the clauses resulting from the negation of the wff to be proved (that is, the conjecture) is taken for C_0.

It can be assumed that $G - \{C_0\}$ is a set consisting of clauses: it includes only the clause forms of the axioms and possibly only part of those arising from the conjecture; if the negation of the conjecture has given rise to only one clause, $G - \{C_0\}$ must be consistent, because it is the set of axioms; let it be assumed that the negation of the conjecture has given rise, for example, to two clauses C_1 and C_2. The conjecture was therefore in the form $\lnot C_1 \lor \lnot C_2$. If $G - \{C_1\}$, for example, is inconsistent, it is because $\lnot C_2$ is the logical consequence of the axioms, which signifies that the conjecture $\lnot C_1 \lor \lnot C_2$ was too imprecise: the more suitable conjecture $\lnot C_2$ could be proposed in its place. If the suitability of the conjecture is in any doubt, there may be reason to apply the linear strategy, starting from each clause arising from the conjecture, in turn.

8.6.8 'LUSH RESOLUTION' STRATEGIES

These are strategies from the linear and by input family, but with more restrictions on the resolutions authorized. In the current central clause, a literal can be chosen arbitrarily, with consideration only for the resolutions that apply to this fixed literal. These strategies are complete for Horn clauses.

Note:

1. The name 'LUSH' comes from 'Linear resolution with Unrestricted Selection for Horn clauses'. The qualifier 'Unrestricted' underlines the fact that the choice of literal, in each of the central clauses, is arbitrary (a relaxation of the method would consist of guiding the choice of the literal, so as to avoid any disastrous arbitrary choices).

2. The PROLOG language manipulates directly only Horn clauses. It uses a LUSH resolution strategy, with two distinguishing characteristics:

—the resolution must apply to the first negative literal (in order, from left to right) in the central clause;

—the resolutions are carried out 'depth first', that is, only one resolution is carried out with the current central clause: the resolvant obtained is used immediately as a central clause (the other resolutions by input, that could have been produced with the same current central clause, are not considered); in addition, the input clauses are considered as ordered once and for all, and the first resolvable (because of its single positive literal) input clause must be used with the central clause (because of its first negative literal, as explained above).

As a result of this second characteristic, the strategy used by PROLOG is not directly complete.

Chapter 9

Future prospects for knowledge-based robots

9.1 Introduction

So far, this book has been about historical research and the algorithmic principles of knowledge-based systems. It has been argued that the principles of AI have led to useful techniques for searching knowledge bases, new logical methods of programming and, ultimately, expert systems that enable the translation of human knowledge into the knowledge base in the computer. In this final part of the book we devote attention to current research and draw conclusions about the impact that this might have on robotics.

There is no doubt that the future will be defined by the national and international programmes discussed in Chapter 1. Here we shall take a closer look at the Alvey programme as an example of the way that such endeavour aims to direct and control the future. Although this programme is based in the UK, it reflects, in a well documented way, similar operations in the USA (DARPA) and Japan (ICOT). This chapter should therefore not be seen as being 'about' the Alvey programme, but about the way such programmes in general affect the future of high technology.

In this case it is the future of decision making and control in robots that gives a focus to the discussion. Although the Alvey programme is not specifically directed at robots, it supports the only research in knowledge engineering in the UK with long-term horizons. The other programme of relevance to robots in the UK is ACME (Advanced Computer Manufacturing and Engineering). However this is directed towards more immediate rewards and is not currently contributing to the future of knowledge-based approaches. Therefore this chapter has only one major reference: the mid-term Alvey report (Alvey, 1985). A complete reference to all the projects named in this chapter may be found in this report.

9.2 Structure of the Alvey Programme

The broad structure of the Alvey programme was raised in Chapter 1. Here we describe this in greater detail so that the reader can judge what sort of impact such programmes are likely to have. In addition to the four major areas originally described *(very-large-scale integration, software engineering, intelligent knowledge-based systems and man-machine interfaces)* two other areas of endeavour have been added since the start of the programme. These are, *computer architectures and large-scale demonstrators*. It is to the latter that we shall devote some attention, since it is in this area that work on automated production has been specifically directed.

Right from the start of the programme it was decided that approximately £35 million (ie 10% of the total funds) would be devoted to cross-boundary projects which aimed at demonstrating that research in this area could be profitably applied to the creation of products. The critical objective of the demonstrators is to 'pull-through' technologies such as man-machine interfaces and knowledge-based systems from being objects of attention in research laboratories to being central factors that determine the usability and marketability of real products. Of specific interest in the context of automated production is a demonstrator which we shall discuss in some detail below.

9.3 The design-to-product demonstrator

This project, priced at £8.9 million is intended to provide design support using knowledge-based systems in such a way that production constraints (including robot control limitations) may be taken into account to optimize the design across the production process. The target has been selected as the components of a fuel pump; the knowledge base contains standards and procedures relevant to design, manufacture, assembly and maintenance, as well as data on costs, tolerances, standard parts and so on. There are two parts to the project: the first is the design support environment and the second is a factory system.

Through the design system, the user will be able to express his ideas at different levels of detail. This will rely heavily on a stored taxonomy of available modular parts. At suitable points in the design process the user will be able to expose his design to computations related to downstream processes, that is, machining, assembly and so on.

With the creation of this project researchers have entered the area which is likely to be the most difficult for knowledge-based systems. The first complication arises from the fact that design is the bringing together of knowledge from different areas of expertise. As an example, consider the design of a new model of a ball-point pen that is going to be assembled by a robot. (This may be a more familiar starting point than a fuel pump, for the sake of illustration).

The highest level of design concerns aesthetics and market information. The designer needs to address the knowledge base in order to discover what designs exist already and at what prices they are being sold on the market. So far this would largely involve a conventional data base and a graphics output. But at this high level the designer, needs to ask questions such as 'what mix of metal and plastic leads to what cost?'. Or he may require information on the relative cost of metal part manufacture to plastic processing. Much of this information may be cast in the form of logical rules elicited from human experts, and is therefore a candidate for an expert system data structure. We note that this is a second base that needs to be incorporated and possibly linked to the first.

Then comes the design of the retraction mechanism which involves a knowledge of springs, mechanical latches and advance mechanisms: a third knowledge base which again needs to be linked to the two. Although at this point the design seems complete it lacks the most important consideration: can it be manufactured using selected processes? In this case we have expressed the need to assemble the pen with robots. At this point the designer requires a knowledge of the processes that are required to manufacture the individual parts, or, whether it is merely a question of getting them out of stores and turning them out on conveyor belts. This may therefore be the fourth knowledge base that needs to be searched and integrated with the others. There may be many others, including the planning type of module that we normally associate with the blocks-world operations described in Section 2.7.

9.3.1 THE DESIGN SYSTEM

The demonstrator project has been partitioned along similar lines. There are two major sections: The DESIGN system and the FACTORY system. The first of these is further partitioned into the headings: 'the geometry engine', 'the machining engine' and 'the assembly engine'. The geometry engine is a development of an existing computer-aided design package that allows the user to create solid objects and observe them through a graphics display. This will be augmented by a shell which provides links to other sectors of the system.

The machining engine turns the design emerging from the geometry engine into data for numerically controlled tools. This includes knowledge-based assessments of whether all the machining rules have been observed. For example, it checks that wall thicknesses of, say, a hollow cylinder are not below a level where they might be distorted by the cutting tool. It is here that much of the reward of such systems is found. Classically the design fault may only be discovered once the metal is being cut, leading to waste. With conventional CAD some of this waste may be avoided, since the design may be tested against numerical limits stored in a data base. The subtle promise of knowledge-based systems is that a much more complex structure of logical rules elicited from a human production engineer may be used and thus a larger number of errors may be avoided. Clearly, the best way of using this program is to allow a great deal of interaction between the user and the machine. Response times must be high so as to allow design cycles to be used freely in order to achieve an optimum.

In addition to the above rule checker, other interesting features are being planned. A central part of the system is a process planning program that operates on the basis of the geometrical features of the part, the raw material and the machines available for manufacture. To see how this may be solved by logic programming, consider that rules may be expressed as:

. . .

If plastic/metal mix of part x is $>$ 30% then a lathe and an extrusion machine are required

If part x has edging $<$ 30 degrees plastic cannot be extruded

. . .

It is clear that this is precisely the type of information that can be handled by PROLOG programs as mentioned in Chapters 3 and 8 (provided that it is recast into first order predicate form, of course). This planner operates at several/ levels. What has been described in the example is knowledge at a macro-scale. However, it is planned to expand sections of this to the detail that is required to generate code for numerically controlled machines.

9.3.2 THE FACTORY SYSTEM

The FACTORY system is being designed around two salient flexible cells: a machining cell and an assembly cell. The machining cell contains a lathe, a machining centre and an inspection machine. The loading will be controlled by a single robot. All the elements of the cells will be in full communication with one another and with control computers through an Ethernet scheme. The assembly cell is being developed on the basis of a parallel process control architecture designed to control a 'Gadfly' robot. The main features of such a system are the use of real-time sensory feedback and a reconfigurable gripper. A knowledge base will have to be developed to plan the actions of this cell so that it allows for appropriate branching according to information gathered from the sensors. This will test the ability of logical programs to enter the real-time domain. Also, interesting advances will be required in the links between the design system and the factory system. For example, within the design system one might find rules of the type:

If extruded plastic has edges $<$ 30 degrees and has hardness factor $<$ H then it may be damaged by the reconfigurable gripper

It is clear that projects of this kind will not only provide a testing ground for existing research ideas, but may also be instrumental in determining the performance weaknesses of knowledge-based implementations and so provide targets for future research.

9.4 Other demonstrator projects

It would be wrong to base a discussion of the future of robot decision and control by restricting this to future-looking work which only contains robots. The whole field of logic programming and knowledge engineering in general needs research both at fundamental and practical levels. Therefore any advances made in this area, whatever the application, will provide roboticists with techniques they can use in decision making and control. Within the Alvey programme, four other demonstrator projects have been agreed, and there may be room for others.

The first of these is the demonstrator for the Department of Health and Social Security. Outside of the fact that this civil service department is one of the partners in the consortium, the work is distinguished by being directed towards intractable problems within that department that cannot be tackled using conventional data processing techniques. It seeks to channel knowledge-based methods and novel software engineering ideas towards these problems with considerable regard for the man-machine interface as well. The systems that are under development are assistance for adjudication officers and claimants in the context of claims and benefits; training systems for assessment officers and assistance for policy makers. In the context of automation, this type of work will directly help in areas where regulatory issues need to be included in product design. Even fuel pumps may be the subject of regulations that could considerably affect their design.

The second of this group of projects is focused on systems linked by communication media. Under the title of 'mobile information systems' it concentrates on non-voice services that may be required by those on the move. For example, a lorry driver may wish to interrogate a knowledge base that informs him of optimized routes, or which may warn him of approaching danger. In the context of production this type of work may improve stock controlin multi-site organizations. Again, man-machine aspects will be important; it would be dangerous to ask a lorry driver to use a keyboard while he was travelling at 70 mph.

It is precisely in the context of no-hands input that the third of these projects is being developed. It is called a 'speech input word processor and work station'. The objective is simple: to display spoken words on a screen as part of continuous text. This is well-known to be a very difficult problem, one that has, to date, not been blessed with many successes. However, a new knowledge-based strategy is being developed: one that involves the most advance data set on the English language ever used to. The principles are those discussed in Chapter 2, but central to the strategy is a study of specially developed parallel architectures that can do the task in real time. The benefits that success in this area may bring to robot control have been extolled elsewhere in this book.

9.5 Support from chips and software

One of the noticeable characteristics of technology's advance towards intelligence is the degree of support this requires from basic techniques. In particular, hardware has to perform to ever increasing speed demands and software becomes ever more voluminous. It is for this reason that a large proportion of the funds of the Alvey programme has been directed towards these two basic needs. In the context of the development of intelligent robot support systems, cost-effectiveness of the equipment is a crucial issue. If the performance of the chips is poor or the design of software assumes too prominent a role in the cost of an intelligent product, the reward one can obtain from the robot is reduced.

A great deal of research funding has gone into supporting new, specialized architectures within single chips. For example, Grimsdale at the University of Sussex is developing chips that can rapidly feed graphics data to the user, while Lea at Brunel University is designing chips that can handle vision signals.

On the software side, designers are in need of computing systems that make the design and generation of voluminous quantities of software feasible without a great deal of human intervention. In other words software designers are in need of computer-aided schemes to do their own work in the same way as an engineer does when he is designing a machine. Under the Alvey programme a great deal of effort is being funded to provide such 'software development support environments'. An ingenious thought is that expert systems could, in themselves, be helpful towards this aim. Rattray at Stirling University together with ICL is investigating precisely this possibility.

Another area of much activity in software engineering is the use of formal specification methods. This is a mathematical endeavour which provides a rigorous framework within which the specifications and aims of a complex system may be stated. The use of such methods introduces clarity from the start of a design process. This not only makes necessary modifications to the specification obvious at the outset, but also is amenable to automatic design. Software Sciences is responsible for a major investigation in this area in an industrial context.

9.6 Knowledge system development

Knowledge-based systems are relatively young. Although the performance of some expert systems and logical programs has been impressive in terms of logical power, there is still much work to be done on large, realistic data bases and on the speed with which these would need to be accessed in a real-time application such as robot control. Therefore much of the effort is being directed at designing machines that are particularly aimed at knowledge systems, whose hardware is made fast (through parallelism, mainly). Over £15 million is being devoted to a project known as the FLAGSHIP within which a parallel architecture is being developed that is optimized for declarative programming (see Chapter 3). This is rightly named, as out of all the Alvey projects, it is likely to define a standard for a fifth generation general-purpose computer (in the UK, anyway). Central to this effort is a computer chip known as a Trasputer, developed by INMOS in the UK specifically for the implementation of parallel systems.

Interesting also is a brief feasibility study carried out by McCabe on the creation of a PROLOG machine, which is merely awaiting commercial exploitation.

This part of the programme also addresses the application of knowledge engineering in specific areas of industry. In the mechanical industry, a consortium consisting of Solartron Instruments, Ricardo Consulting Engineers and Westland is developing expert systems that aid the interrogation of vast amounts of machine health monitoring data. This is being applied to the gearboxes of helicopter lifting gear and internal combustion engines. The possibility of applying the same techniques to the health monitoring of robots may be of considerable importance.

9.7 Pattern analysis

In the Alvey programme the words pattern analysis are used to cover work on speech processing and image processing. The work comes under the heading of both man-machine interfaces and intelligent knowledge-based systems. In both speech and vision, the use of knowledge-based methodology is seen as being most important.

Much of the Marr philosophy mentioned in Chapter 2 is being developed in some of the projects in the knowledge-based manner. Optical flow techniques (the Marr two and a half dimensional sketch) are being used to analyse motion from image pairs and three dimensional information is being extracted from stored models of objects and stereoscopic cues. Although much of this work is concerned with the design and testing of algorithms based on a sound computational theory of vision, this work does not tackle the problem of real-time performance directly. Under the man-machine interface label, funding has been provided for fast processor arrays that could resolve the problem of real-time implementation. Notable is the work of Duff at University College, London where progressive generations of the CLIP array of processors are being developed.

9.8 Conclusions

In this volume of the *Robot Technology* series on intelligent decision making and control, it has become evident that the subject is supported by the most advanced work currently in progress in computer science in general. It has been argued that the advancement of robots is dependent on the development not only of intelligent programs but also on their real-time performance. It has also been argued that this is a strategic advance which, initiated in Japan with the fifthgeneration programme, has been adopted as a matter for national concern by most industrial nations of the world through other nationally and internationally promoted programmes. This is bound to accelerate progress in a field which in the early 1970s seemed not to have practical outlets. It is hoped that the examples given in this last chapter have provided a flavour of the intensity of directed research and the level of investment devoted to this field.

The prospect for rapid practical advancement is therefore better than it ever has been. The likelihood of knowledge-based robot decision making and control becoming a part of the standard armoury of automated manufacturing techniques is rapidly becoming a certainty.

Bibliography

Chapter 1

Burks, A.W.; Goldstine, H.M.; Von Neumann, J. *A Preliminary Discussion of the Logical Design of an Electronic Computing Instrument* Princeton Institute of Advanced Study, 1946.

Coiffet, P. *Interaction with the Environment: Robot Sensors and Sensing* Robot Technology, Volume 2, Kogan Page, London, 1983.

Engelberger, J. *Robotics in Practice* Kogan Page, London, 1980.

Feigenbaum, E.A.; McCorduck, P. *The Fifth Generation* Addison Wesley, New York, 1983.

Parent, P.; Laurgeau, C. *Logic and Programming* Robot Technology, Volume 5, Kogan Page, London, 1983.

Chapter 2

Addis, T.R. *Designing Knowledge-Based Systems* Kogan Page, London, 1985.

Aleksander, I. (Ed) *Artificial Vision for Robots* Kogan Page, London, 1983.

Ambler, A.P. *et al.* A versatile system for computer-controlled assembly. *Artificial Intelligence* 6, 129–156, 1975.

Barlow, H. Understanding Natural Vision. In Sleigh, A.C.; Braddick, O. (Eds) *The Physical and Natural Processing of Visual Signals* Springer Verlag, Heidelberg, 1982.

Boden, M. *Artificial Intelligence and Natural Man* Harvester Press, Hassocks, 1977.

Fikes, R.E.; Nilsson, N.J. STRIPS: a new approach to the application of theorem proving to problem solving. *Artificial Intelligence* 2 (3/4), 189–208, 1971.

Guzman, A. Decomposition of a visual field into 3-D objects. In Grasselli, A. (Ed) *Automatic Interpretation and Classification of Images* Academic Press, London, 1969, pp. 243–276.

Hinton, G. Learning in parallel networks. *Byte* 10/4, 265–273, April 1985.

Holte, R.C. Artificial intelligence approaches to concept learning. In Aleksander, I. (Ed) *Advanced Digital Information Systems* Prentice Hall International Inc., London, 1985.

Newell, J.; Shaw, J.; Simon, H. *Report on a General Problem Solving Program for a Computer* Proc. Int. Conf. on Information Processing, UNESCO, Paris, 256–264, 1960.

Kowalski, R.A. *Logic for Problem Solving* North-Holland, London, 1979.

Lighthill, J. *A Report on Artificial Intelligence* UK Science Research Council, London, 1973.

Marr, D. *Vision* Freeman, New York, 1982.

McCarthy, J. *Programs with Common Sense* Symp. Proc., National Physical Lab., HMSO London, 1958.

McCarthy, J. *et al. Lisp 1.5 programming manual* MIT Press, Cambridge, Mass., 1965.

Michie, D. Computers that Play Games *Science Journal* 6, 74–78, 1968.

Minsky, M.; Papert, S. *Perceptions: an Introduction to Computational Geometry* MIT Press, Cambridge, Mass., 1969.

Minsky, M. A framework for representing knowledge. In Winston, P.H. (Ed) *The Psychology of Computer Vision* McGraw-Hill, New York, 1975, pp. 211–277.

Nilsson, N.J. *Principles of Artificial Intelligence* Tioga Press, Palo Alto, 1980.

Roberts, L.G. Machine perception of 3-D Solids. In Tippett, *et al. Optical and Electro-Optical Information Processing* MIT Press, Cambridge, Mass., 1965, pp. 159–198.

Rosenblatt, F. *Principles of Neurodynamics* Spartan, Washington, 1962.

Samuel, A.L. Some studies in machine learning using the game of checkers. *IBM Journal of Research and Development* 3, 211–229, 1959.

Shannon, C.E. Programming a computer for playing chess *Phil. Mag. (Series 7)* 41, 256–275, 1950.

Winograd, T. *Understanding Natural Language* Edinburgh University Press, Edinburgh, 1972.

Chapter 3

Aikins, J.S.; Kunz, J.C.; Shortliffe, E.H.; Fallat, R.J. PUFF: an expert system for interpretation of pulmonary function data. *Computers and Biomedical Research* 16, 199–208, 1983.

Auvert, B.; Van Look, F.; Le Thi Huong Du; Aegerter, P.; Gilbos, V.; Emmanuelli, X.; Bosseau, J.F.; Boutin, P.; Landre, M.F.; Philippe, A.M. Conception d'un système général d'aide à la décision médicale pour les infirmiers des pays en voie de développement. *Journée Inf. et Médecine* Marseille, 30th November–1st December 1984.

Bennett, J.S.; Hollander, C.R. DART: an expert system for computer fault diagnosis. *VIIth IJCAI* Vancouver, 843–845, August 1981.

Billmers, M.A.; Swartwout, M.W. AI-SPEAR: computer system failure analysis tool. *ECAI 84*, pp. 65–73, Pisa, September 1984.

Bobrow, D.; Winograd, T. KRL: another perspective. *Cognitive Science* 3, pp. 29–42, 1977.

Bonnet, A.; Harry, J.; Ganascia, J.G. LITHO: un système expert inférant la géologie du sous-sol. *TSI* 1(5), 393–402, 1982.

Buchanan, B.G.; Shortliffe, E.H. *Rule-Based Expert Systems: The MYCIN Experiments of the Stanford Heuristic Programming Project* Addison-Wesley, Reading, 1984.

Buisson, J.C.; Farreny, H.; Prade, H.; Un système-expert en diabétologie accessible par minitel. *5émes Journees ADI-AFCET Systèmes-Experts* Avignon, May 1985.

Sté Cognitech, Démonstration d'un système-expert en diagnostic et traitement des maladies et accidents culturaux de la tomate. *4èmes Journées ADI-AFCET Systèmes-Experts* Avignon, May 1984.

Colmerauer, A. *PROLOG II, Manuel de Référence et Modèle Théorique* GIA, Faculté des Sciences de Luminy, Marseille, 1982.

Courteille, J.M.; Fabre, M.; Hollander, C.R. An advanced solution: The drilling advisor SECOFOR. *58th Annual Technical Conf. and Exhibition* San Francisco, October 1983.

Demonchaux, E.; Quinqueton, J. OURCIN: un langage interactif en logique propositionnelle. *Bull. de l'INRIA* 94, 1984.

Descottes, Y. *Représentation et Exploitation de Connaissances "Expertes" en Génération de Plans d'Actions* Thèse de 3e cycle, INP de Grenoble, December 1981.

Duda, R.; Gaschnig, J.; Hart, P. Model design in the PROSPECTOR consultant system for mineral exploration. In *Expert Systems in the Micro-electronic Age* (D. Michie Ed), Edinburgh University Press, 1979.

Ernst, C. *Un Métalangage de Programmation Logique Orienté Vers le Contrôle Sémantique de Systèmes-experts de Gestion* Thèse d'Etat, Univ. P. Sabatier, Toulouse, January 1985.

Farreny, H. *Un Système Pour l'Expression et la Résolution de Problèmes Orienté Vers le Contrôle de Robots* Thèse d'Etat, Université Toulouse III, September 1980.

Farreny, H. *Systèmes-experts: Principles et Exemples* CEPADUES-Editions, June 1985.

Feigenbaum, E.A.; McCorduck, M. *The Fifth Generation* Addison-Wesley, 1983.

Feigenbaum, E.A. Knowledge engineering: the applied side. In, *Intelligent Systems, the Unprecedented Opportunity* Hayes, J.E.; Michie, D. (Eds), pp. 37–55, 1984.

Fieschi, M. *Intelligence Artificielle en Médecine* Masson, Coll. Méthodes et Programmes, 1984.

Forgy, C.L.; *The OPS5 User's Manual* Carnegie Mellon Univ., 1980.

Fox, M.S.; Lowenfeld, S.; Kleinosky, P. Techniques for sensor-based diagnosis, *VIIIth IJCAI*, Karlsruhe, pp. 158–163, August 1983.

Friedland, P. Knowledge-based experiment design in molecular genetics. *VIth IJCAI* Tokyo, pp. 285–287, August 1979.

Gascuel, O. *SAM: Un Système Expert dans le Domaine Médical* Thèse de 3e cycle, Université Paris VI, November 1981.

Griesmer, J.H.; Hong, S.J.; Karnaugh, M.; Kastner, J.K.; Schor, M.I.; Ennis, R.L.; Klein, D.A.; Milliken, K.R.; Van Woerkom, H.M. YES/VMS: a continuous real time expert system, *AAAI 84* pp. 130–136, August 1984.

Helser, J.F.; Brooks, R.E.; Ballard, J.P. Progress report: Computerized psychopharmacology Advisor, *11th Collegium Int. Neuropsychopharmacologicum* Vienna, 1978.

Lagrange, M.S.; Renaud, M. *SUPERIKON: Un Essai de Cumul de Six Expertises en Iconographie: Érudition ou Trivialité* Report No. 6, Lab. CRA et LISH, CNRS, Paris, November 1984.

Lauriere, J.L.; *Un langage déclaratif: SNARK*. Univ. Paris-VI, December 1984.

Lefevre, J.M. Systèmes-experts: l'avalanche. *Micro et Robots* 13, pp. 11–16, 1984.

McDermott, J. R1: a rule-based configurer of computer systems. *Art. Int.* 19(1), pp. 39–88, September 1982a.

McDermott, J. XSEL: a computer sales person's assistant. *Machine Intelligence* 10, Hayes, J.E.; Michie, D.; Pao, Y.H. (eds), Ellis Horwood, 1982b.

Martin-Clouaire, R. *Une Approche Système-expert et Théorie des Possibilités Appliquée en Géologie Pétrolière* Thèse de 3e cycle, Univ. P. Sabatier, Toulouse, October 1984.

Martin-Clouaire, R.; Prade, H. SPII-1, un moteur d'inférences simple capable de traiter des informations imprécises ou incertaines. *Actes Cognitiva 85*, Paris, June 1985.

Masui, S.; McDermott, J.; Sobel, A. Decision-making in time-critical situations. *VIIIth IJCAI* Karlsruhe, pp. 233–235, August 1983.

Michalski, R.S.; Davis, J.H.; Bisht, V.S.; Sinclair, J.B. PLANT/ds: an expert consulting system for the diagnosis of soybean diseases, *ECAI 82* Orsay, pp. 133–138, July 1982.

Michalski, R.S.; Baskin, A.B. Integrating multiple knowledge representations and learning capabilities in an expert system: the ADVISE system. *VIIIth IJCAI* Karlsruhe, pp. 256–258, August 1983.

Minsky, M. A framework for representing knowledge. In, *The Psychology of Computer Vision* Winston, P.H. (ed), McGraw-Hill, 1975.

Mulet-Marquis, D.; Gondran, M. *Un Langage Pour les Systèmes-experts: ALOUETTE* HI/4773-02, EDF, Clamart, May 1984.

Nilsson, N. *Principles of Artificial Intelligence* Tioga, 1980.

Picardat, J.F. *Manuel ARGOS-II* Report LSI, Univ. P. Sabatier, Toulouse, February 1985.

Rousset, M.C. *TANGO, Moteur d'Inférences pour une Classe de Systèmes-experts avec Variables* Thèse de 3e cycle, Univ. de Paris-Sud, Orsay, October 1983.

Schank, R.; Abelson, R. *Scripts, Plans, Goals and Understanding* Lawrence Erlbaum, 1977.

Shortliffe, E.H. *Computer-based Medical Consultations: MYCIN* Elsevier, New York, 1976.

Soula, G.; Vialettes, B.; San Marco, J.L. PROTIS: a fuzzy deduction-rule system-application to the treatment of diabetes. *Proc. MEDINFO 83* Amsterdam, 1983.

Van Melle, W. *A Domain-independent System that Aids in Constructing Knowledge-based Consultation Programs.* PhD dissertation, Stanford University, 1980.

Vialatte, M. *SNARK 2*, Thesis, Univ. Paris VI, May 1985.

Waterman, D.A. Adaptative production systems. *IVth IJCAI* Tbilissi, pp. 296–303, September 1975.

Waterman, D.A.; Hayes-Roth, F. (Eds), *Pattern-Directed Inference Systems* Academic Press, 1978.

Weiss, S.M.; Kulikovski, C.A.; Amarel, S.; Safir, A. A model-based method for computer-aided medical decision-making. *Art. Int.* 11(1-2), pp. 145–172, August 1978.

Vesonder, G.T.; Stolfo, S.J.; Zielinski, J.E.; Miller, F.D.; Copp, D.H. ACE: an expert system for telephone cable maintenance. *VIIIth IJCAI*, Karlsruhe, pp. 116–121, August 1983.

Vignard, P. CRIQUET: un logiciel de base pour élaborer des systèmes-experts, *Coll. Inter. d'Int. Art.*, Marseille, pp. 81–88, October 1984.

Chapter 4

Anzai, Y.; Ishibashi, N.; Mitsuya, Y.; Ura, S. Knowledge-based problem solving by a labelled production system. *Proc. VIth IJCAI* Tokyo, pp. 22–24, August 1979.

Barr, A.; Feigenbaum, E.A. (Eds), *The Handbook of Artificial Intelligence* Vols. I, II, III, Heuristic Press, 1982.

Bennett, J.S.; Engelmore, R.S. SACON: A Knowledge-Based Consultant for Structural Analysis. *Proc. VIth IJCAI* Tokyo, pp. 47–49, August 1979.

Bennett, J.S.; Hollander, C.R. DART: An Expert System for Computer Fault Diagnosis. *Proc. VIIth IJCAI*, Vancouver, pp. 843–845, August 1981.

Bocquet, J.C.; Tichkiewitch, S. An "expert system" for identification of mechanical drawings. *Proc. PROLAMAT-82 (IFIP-IFAC)* Leningrad, May 1982.

Bonissone, P.P. Outline of the design and implementation of a diesel electric engine troubleshooting aid. *Proc. Expert Systems 82* Brunel University, September 1982.

Bonnet, A.; Harry, J.; Ganascia, J.G. LITHO: un système expert inférant la géologie du sous-sol. *Technique et Science Informatique* 1(5), pp. 393–402, 1982.

Brown, J.; Burton, R.; Bell, A. SOPHIE: a step towards creating a reactive learning environment. *Int. Journal of Man-Machine Studies* 7, pp. 675–716, 1975.

Buchanan, B.G.; Sutherland, G.; Feigenbaum, E.A. Heuristic DENDRAL: a program for generating explanatory hypotheses in organic chemistry. *Machine Intelligence* 4, pp. 209–254, 1969.

Buchanan, B.G. Issues on representation in conveying the scope and limitations of intelligent assistant programs. *Machine Intelligence* 9, pp. 407–425, 1979.

Buisson, J.C.; Farreny, H.; Prade, H. Report on DIABETO, May 1985.

Cordier, M.O.; Rousset, M.C. TANGO: moteur d'inférences pour un système-expert avec variables. *LRI* 123, Faculté d'Orsay, January 1982.

Courteille, J.M.; Fabre, M.; Hollander, C.R. An advanced solution: The drilling advisor SECOFOR, *58th Annual Technical Conf. and Exhibition* San Francisco, October 1983.

Dalle, P.; Debord, P.; Castan, S. Présentation générale du système SACSO. *Actes 3e Cong. AFCET Rec. des formes et Int. Artif.* Nancy, pp. 297–308, September 1981.

Davis, R.; Lenat, D.B. *Knowledge-Based Systems in Artificial Intelligence* McGraw-Hill, 1982.

Descottes, Y. *GARI: Un Système-expert Pour la Conception de Gammes d'Usinage* Thèse de 3e cycle, Université de Grenoble (IMAG), 1981.

Dincbas, M. *Contribution à l'Étude des Systémes-experts* Thèse de docteur-ingénieur, ENSAE, Toulouse, 1983.

Duda, R.O.; Gaschnig, J.G. Knowledge based expert systems come of age. *Byte* pp. 238–283, September 1981.

Engelmore, R.; Terry, A. Structure and function of the CRYSALIS system. *Proc. VIth IJCAI* Tokyo, pp. 250–256, August 1979.

Ernst, C. Thèse, MANAGER, January 1985.

Fargues, J. *Contribution à l'Étude du Raisonnement: Application à la Médecine d'Urgence* Thèse d'Etat, Université Paris VI, May 1983.

Farreny, H. *Un Système pour l'expression et la Résolution de Problèmes Orienté vers le Contrôle de Robots* Thèse d'Etat, Université Toulouse III, September 1980.

Fieschi, M. *SPHINX: Un Système-expert d'Aide à la Décision en Médecine* Thèse d'Etat, Université d'Aix-Marseille-II, March 1983.

Forgy, C.L. *The OPS5 User's Manual* Technical Report, University of Carnegie Mellon, 1980.

Friedland, P. Knowledge-based experiment design in molecular genetics. *Proc. VIth IJCAI* Tokyo, pp. 285–287, August 1979.

Gascuel, O. *SAM: Un Système Expert dans le Domaine Médical* Thèse de 3e cycle, Université Paris VI, November 1981.

Gini, G.; Gini, M.; Morpurgo, R. A knowledge-based consultation system for automatic maintenance and repair. *Proc. PROLAMAT-82 (IFIP-IFAC)* Leningrad, May 1982.

Hayes-Roth, F.; Waterman, D.A.; Lenat, D.B. (Eds), *Building Expert Systems* Addison-Wesley, 1983.

Helser, J.F.; Brooks, R.E.; Ballard, J.P. Progress report: Computerized psychopharmacology Advisor. *Proc. 11th Collegium Int. Neuropsychopharmacologicum* Vienna, 1978.

Konologe, K. An inference net compiler for the PROSPECTOR rule-based consultation system. *Proc. VIth IJCAI* Tokyo, pp. 487–489, August 1979.

Kunz, J.C.; Fallat, R.J.; McClung, D.H.; Osborn, J.J.; Votteri, B.A.; Nii, H.P.; Aikins, J.S.; Fagan, L.M.; Feigenbaum, E.A. *A Physiological Rule Based System for Interpreting Pulmonary Function Test Results* Memo HPP-78-20, Stanford University, December 1978.

Latombe, J.C. *Une Application de l'Intelligence Artificielle à la Conception Assistée par Ordinateur* Thèse d'Etat, Université de Grenoble, November 1977.

Lauriere, J.L.; Perrot, A. Représentation et utilisation des connaissances dans l'industrie pétrolière. *Journées AFCET-ADI Systèmes-Experts* Avignon, May 1981.

Lauriere, J.L. Représentation et utilisation des connaissance. *Technique et Science Informatiques* 1, 2, pp. 25–42, 109–133, 1982.

Lindsay, R.K.; Buchanan, B.G.; Feigenbaum, E.A.; Lederberg, J. *Applications of Artificial Intelligence for Organic Chemistry: the DENDRAL project* McGraw-Hill, 1980.

McDermott, J. R1: a rule-based configurer of computer systems. *Artificial Intelligence* 19(1), pp. 39—88, September 1982.

Martin-Clouaire, R. *Une Approche Système-Expert et Théorie des Possibilités Appliquée en Géologie Pétrolière* Thèse de 3e cycle, Université P. Sabatier, Toulouse, October 1984.

Melle, W. Van, A domain-independent production-rule system for consultation programs. *Proc. VIth IJCAI*, Tokyo, pp. 923—925, August 1979.

Michalski, R.S.; Davis, J.H.; Bisht, V.S.; Sinclair, J.B. PLANT/ds: an expert consulting system for the diagnosis of soybean diseases. *Proc. ECAI 82* Orsay, pp. 133-138, July 1982.

Michie, D. (Ed), *Expert Systems in the Microelectronic Age* Edinburgh University Press, 1979.

Moore, R.C. The role of logic in knowledge representation and common reasoning. *Proc. AAAI 82*, Pittsburgh, pp. 428—433, August 1982.

Newell, A. The knowledge level. *AI Magazine* 2(2) pp. 1—20, Summer 1981.

Perrot, A.; Lebailly, J.; Courteille, J.M. The ELFIA project at ELF Aquitaine. *Symposium CNRS/NSF*, Washington, August 1983.

Recoque, A. Le groupe BULL et la recherche. *Bulletin de l'INRA*, 96, 1984.

Roussel, P. PROLOG: Manuel de référence et d'utilisation. *Groupe Int. Art.*, Université d'Aix-Marseille, September 1975.

Rousset, M.C. *TANGO, Moteur d'Inférences Pour une Classe de Systèmes-experts avec Variables* Thèse de 3e cycle, Université de Paris-Sud, Orsay, October 1983.

Rychener, M.D.; Newell, A. An instructable production system: basic design issues, in [Waterman 1978], pp. 135—153, 1978.

Sacerdoti, E.D. *A Structure for Plans and Behavior*. Elsevier, New York, 1977.

Shortliffe, E.H. *Computer-based Medical Consultations: MYCIN* Elsevier, New York, 1976.

Soula, G.; Vialettes, B.; San Marco, J.L. PROTIS: a fuzzy deduction-rule system-application to the treatment of diabetes. *Proc. MEDINFO 83*, Amsterdam, 1983.

Stallman, R.M.; Sussman, G.J. Problem-solving about electrical circuits. In, *Artificial Intelligence, an MIT Perspective* Winston, P.H.; Brown, R.H. (Eds), MIT Press, 1979.

Todd Wipke, W.; Ouchi, G.I.; Krishnan, S. Simulation and Evaluation of Chemical Synthesis — SECS: an application of artificial intelligence techniques. *Artificial Intelligence* 11(1-2), pp. 173—193, August 1978.

Waterman, D.A. Adaptative production systems. *Proc. IVth IJCAI* Tbilissi, pp. 296—303, September 1975.

Waterman, D.A.; Hayes-Roth, F. (Eds), *Pattern-Directed Inference Systems* Academic Press, 1978.

Weiss, S.M.; Kulikovski, C.A.; Amarel, S.; Safir, A. A model-based method for computer-aided medical decision-making. *Artificial Intelligence*, 11(1-2), pp. 145—172, August 1978.

Wesson, R.B. Planning in the world of the air traffic controller. *Proc. Vth IJCAI* Cambridge, pp. 473-479, August 1977.

Chapter 8

Chang, C.L.; Lee, R.C.T. *Symbolic Logic and Mechanical Theorem Proving* Academic Press, 1973.

Nilsson, N. *Problem-solving Methods in Artificial Intelligence* McGraw-Hill, 1971.

Addendum

Chapter 5

Gaschnig, J. *Performance Measurement and Analysis of Certain Search Algorithms* Thesis, Carnegie-Mellon Univ., Pittsburgh, 1979.

Ghallab, M. *Optimisation de Processus Decisionnels pour la Robotique* Thesis, Univ. Paul Sabatier, Toulouse, 1982.

Ghallab, M.; Allard, D.G. A_ϵ: an efficient near admissible heuristic search algorithm. *Proc. 8th IJCAI* Karlsruhe, August 1983.

Kumar, U.; Kanal, L. A general branch and bound formulation for understanding and synthesizing And/Or tree search procedures. *Artificial Intelligence* 21, 179–198, 1983.

Pearl, J.; Kim, J.H. Studies in semi-admissible heuristics. *IEEE Trans. PAMI* 4(4), 392–400, 1982.

Chapter 6

Chatila, R. Path planning and environment learning in a mobile robot system. *Proc. 2nd ECAI* Orsay, July 1982.

Gaschnig, J. *Performance Measurement and Analysis of Certain Search Algorithms* Thesis, Carnegie-Mellon Univ., Pittsburgh, 1979.

Gelperin, D. On the optimality of A^*. *Artificial Intelligence* 8, 69–76, 1977.

Ghallab, M.; Allard, D.G. A_ϵ: an efficient near admissible heuristic search algorithm. *Proc. 8th IJCAI* Karlsruhe, August 1983.

Gouzènes, L. Strategies for solving collision-free trajectory problems for mobile and manipulator robots. *Robotics Research* 3(4), 51–65, 1984.

Harris, L.R. The heuristic search under conditions of error. *Artificial Intelligence* 5, 217–234, 1974.

Hart, P.E.; Nilsson, N.J.; Raphael, B. A formal basis for the heuristic determination of minimal cost paths. *IEEE Trans. SSC* 4, 100–107, 1968.

Hart, P.E.; Nilsson, N.J.; Raphael, B. Correction to: a formal basis for the heuristic determination of minimal cost paths. *SIGART Newsletter* 3, 28–29, 1972.

Huyn, N.; Dechter, R.; Pearl, J. Probalistic analysis of the complexity of A^*. *Artificial Intelligence* 15(3), 241–253, 1980.

Ibaraki, T. Theoretical comparison of search strategies in branch-and-bound algorithms. *Int. J. Computer and Information Sciences* 5(4), 315–344, 1976.

Lozano-Pérez, T. Automatic planning of manipulator transfer movements. *IEEE Trans. SMC* 11(10), 681–689, 1981.

Martelli, A. On the complexity of admissible search algorithms. *Artificial Intelligence* 8, 1–13, 1977.

Nilsson, N.J. *Problem-Solving Methods in Artificial Intelligence* McGraw-Hill, 1971.

Pearl, J.; Kim, J.H. Studies in semi-admissible heuristics. *IEEE Trans. PAMI* 4(4), 392–400, 1982.

Pearl, J. Knowledge versus search: a quantitative analysis using A*. *Artificial Intelligence* 20, 1–13, 1983.

Pohl, I. First results on the effect of error in heuristic search. In *Machine Intelligence 5* Meltzer and Michie (eds), Edinburgh University Press, 1970, pp. 219–236.

Pohl, I. Bi-directional search. In *Machine Intelligence 6* Meltzer and Michie (eds), Elsevier, 1971, pp. 127–140.

Pohl, I. Practical and theoretical considerations in heuristic search algorithms. In *Machine Intelligence 8* Elcock and Michie (eds), Ellis Horwood, 1977, pp. 55–71.

Vanderburg, G.J. Problem representations and formal properties of heuristic search. *Information Sciences* 11, 279–307, 1976.

Chapter 7

Ghallab, M. *Optimisation de Processus Decisionnels pour la Robotique* Thesis, Univ. Paul Sabatier, Toulouse, 1982.

Kumar, U.; Kanal, L. A general branch and bound formulation for understanding and synthesizing And/Or procedures. *Artificial Intelligence* 21, 179–198, 1983.

Martelli, A.; Montanau, U. Additive and/or graphs. *Proc. 3rd IJCAI*, Stanford, 1973, pp. 1–11.

Vanderburg, G.J. Problem representations and formal properties of heuristic search. *Information Sciences* 11, 279–307, 1976.

Nilsson, N. *Principles of Artificial Intelligence* Tioga, 1980.
Siekmann, J.; Wrightson, G. (Eds) *Automation of Reasoning* Springer-Verlag, 1983.
Wos, L.; Overbeek, R.; Lusk, E.; Boyle, J. *Automated Reasoning* Prentice Hall, 1984.

Chapter 9

The Alvey Directorate: Annual Report, 1985 IEE Publishing, Stevenage, UK, 1985.

Index